ROMANTICISM
AND CONTEMPORARY
CRITICISM

Romanticism

AND CONTEMPORARY

Criticism

*The Gauss Seminar
and Other Papers*

PAUL DE MAN

edited by
E. S. Burt, Kevin Newmark, Andrzej Warminski

THE JOHNS HOPKINS UNIVERSITY PRESS

BALTIMORE AND LONDON

© 1993 The Johns Hopkins University Press
All rights reserved
Printed in the United States of America on acid-free paper

The Johns Hopkins University Press
2715 North Charles Street
Baltimore, Maryland 21218-4319
The Johns Hopkins Press Ltd., London

Library of Congress Cataloging-in-Publication Data

De Man, Paul.
  Romanticism and contemporary criticism : the Gauss Seminar
and other papers / Paul de Man ; edited by E. S. Burt, Kevin
Newmark, Andrzej Warminski.
    p.   cm.
  Includes bibliographical references.
  ISBN 0-8018-4460-6. — ISBN 0-8018-4461-4 (pbk.)
  1. Romanticism.   2. Criticism.   I. Burt, E. S.   II. Newmark,
Kevin, 1951-   .   III. Warminski, Andrzej.   IV. Title.
PN603.D39   1993
809'.9145—dc20   92-23340

A catalog record for this book is available from the British Library.

Contents

Editors' Preface

*T*HIS VOLUME contains material written by Paul de Man over nearly thirty years, between 1954 and 1981, but never published by him. Found among his papers in the spring of 1987, the material includes five of the six lectures de Man delivered as the Gauss seminar at Princeton in the spring of 1967 under the general title "Romanticism and Contemporary Criticism"; three papers on romantic and postromantic topics written in the 1950s and 1960s, probably for various lecture occasions; an essay on Roland Barthes commissioned in the 1970s by the *New York Review of Books* but rejected for publication; and responses to papers by Frank Kermode and Murray Krieger delivered in the early 1980s.

The Gauss lectures and the papers on romanticism have a determinable place in the context of de Man's work and its development. In general terms, they are quite clearly part of his long-term reflection on some of the major texts of English, German, and French romanticism and on their reception in twentieth-century literary criticism and theory. But for de Man romantic literature and its aftermath is not just one academic topic among others. As is explicit in these lectures and papers—and from various indications elsewhere in de Man's work—the interest of romanticism goes beyond the merely antiquarian or philological because in the case of the romantics we are dealing with "a truly historical consciousness," as the opening of the fifth Gauss lecture puts it. And since this romantic historical consciousness is, according to de Man, a powerful "source" for our own consciousness, a historical study of romanticism would also necessarily be a reflection on our own historical predicament, our history. De Man had in fact projected such a historical study of romanticism and, around 1968, had collected the Gauss lectures and his other essays on romantic texts in a manuscript volume entitled *The Unimaginable Touch of Time*.[1] But he never published this volume and abandoned the project for reasons spelled out in the preface to *Allegories of Reading* (1979): "*Allegories of Reading* started out as a historical study and ended up as a theory of reading. I began to read Rousseau seriously in preparation for a historical reflection on Romanticism and found myself unable to progress beyond local difficulties of interpretation. In trying to cope with this, I had to shift from historical definition to the problematics of reading."[2] That these "local difficulties of interpretation" included a sense in which the "truly historical consciousness" of the romantics resists the categories and methods of traditional literary history is already legible in the Gauss lectures and in de Man's work of the 1970s and 1980s. In any case, although a number of the essays included in *The Unimaginable Touch of Time* ultimately found their way into the posthumously published *Rhetoric of Romanticism* (New York: Columbia University Press, 1984), the Gauss lectures themselves remained unrevised and unedited (with the exception of the fifth and sixth lectures, which, after extensive rewriting, became the two halves of "The Rhetoric of Temporality" [1969]).

In addition to their place in de Man's reflection on the question of romanticism—and in addition to their intrinsic merit and interest—the Gauss lectures also begin to mark a certain moment of transition or articulation in de Man's development: in short, between the thematics and vocabulary of "consciousness" and "temporality" characteristic of his work in the 1960s and the language-oriented concerns and rhetorical terminology of the 1970s and 1980s. This is particularly legible in the case of "Time and History in Wordsworth," which has several interpolated passages that de Man wrote for a later lecture occasion (around 1972) and that recontextualize the interpretation of Wordsworth within the question of reading as such and recast the essay's terminology of authentic temporality and finitude in explicitly rhetorical terms. It should also be noted that the contemporary critics of romanticism studied in the

Gauss lectures provide additional instances, if not the prototype, of the pattern de Man uncovers on the example of other critics in *Blindness and Insight* (New York: Oxford University Press, 1971). Finally, we should also mention that "Roland Barthes and the Limits of Structuralism" (1972)—despite its apparently "journalistic" tone and occasion—offers one of de Man's most explicit and suggestive discussions of the question of ideology, which increasingly occupied his thinking in later years.

A truly collective effort, this volume could not have appeared without the important contributions of the following individuals and institutions: Patricia de Man, who generously made the material available in the first place and who assisted the editors at every stage; Kathryn Aschheim, Thomas Keenan, Thomas Pepper, and Deborah White, who provided the initial labor of transcribing and editing the mostly handwritten material comprising the volume; Janie Vanpée and Barbara Spackman, who were instrumental in the final editing and preparation of several of the chapters; Peter Brooks, who assisted in finding financial support for the project at an early stage; the President's Fund and the Griswold Fund at Yale University, and the Research and Travel Grant Fund at the University of California, Irvine.

The following chapters have previously appeared in print—"The Double Aspect of Symbolism," *Yale French Studies* 74 (1988); "Time and History in Wordsworth," *Diacritics* (Winter 1987); and "Roland Barthes and the Limits of Structuralism," *Yale French Studies* 77 (1990). The editors express their gratitude for permission to reprint them here.

In conclusion, it should be noted that the editors made only minimal interventions in the extensive preparation of the volume for publication. Their intention was to avoid giving a misleading impression about the status of this material, most of which de Man never intended for publication. The editors have limited themselves to supplying footnotes and missing bibliographical references, correcting grammatical inconsistencies, and translating citations into English where necessary. Unless otherwise noted, square brackets are the editors'.

Part I

THE GAUSS SEMINAR OF 1967

1

The Contemporary Criticism of Romanticism

I T WOULD BE impossible to prove, by presumably objective criteria, that romanticism is a privileged topic for contemporary criticism. Much work is being done on romanticism, both here and abroad, and some of it is of the highest quality. But the same is true of other periods as well, and some critics have been able to state, with some semblance of truth, that romanticism is no longer a particularly relevant topic for us. Baroque, renaissance, or medieval topics may seem of greater urgency than romanticism, and even the problems of modernism can be approached, as is often the case in France and Germany, with scant reference to romantic antecedents.

Still, it could be shown that whenever romantic attitudes are implicitly or explicitly under discussion, a certain heightening of tone takes place, an increase of polemical tension develops, as if something of immediate concern to all were at stake. Few of the contemporary writings on romanticism are free of polemical overtones, to the point that it remains exceedingly difficult to consider the topic with the historical detachment that applies to the study not only of earlier but also of some later topics in literary history. This is not just because of the relative proximity of the period, for it will be found that trends that actually lie closer to us in time, such as Parnassian or Pre-Raphaelite poetry, fin-de-siècle decadence, or even surrealism, seem much more suitable to "objective" historical treatment than romanticism. In France, for instance, where the belief in an objective historiography of literature is probably still more alive than elsewhere, no comprehensive historical description of the romantic movement is in existence, whereas numerous works deal with genuine historical insight into the period that stretches "from Baudelaire to surrealism."[1] And in the other countries, writings about romanticism are often more controversial than historical; even intellectual historians who had been writing about the period with a certain degree of objectivity have had a tendency to become more polemically "engaged" as time goes on. In some of the larger works that attempt syntheses and take panoramic views upon Western literature while inaugurating novel categories of historical classification (such as in Auerbach, Curtius, Lukács, etc.) romanticism is often avoided not because it is considered unimportant but because it seems to be too embattled a topic for systematic treatment.

Embattled it indeed remains, even in the rather sedate world of American and English criticism, where it continues to be a bone of contention around which methodological battles are being fought. All the more so in countries where polemics about criticism are traditionally more vigorous and articulate, such as France. From its inception, the history of romanticism has been one of battles, polemics, and misunderstandings: personal misunderstandings between the poets themselves; between the poets, the critics, and the public; between the successive generations. This is still the case. Recent polemics on the problem of modernism in Germany echo some of the differences between Weimar and Jena in the days of Goethe and Friedrich Schlegel. Irving Babbitt's cantankerous treatment of Rousseau and romanticism[2] bears some likeness to the attacks of the Tory press on Keats and Hazlitt. And in the lively methodological debates that have been in progress in France during the last two or three years, romanticism is still, though in an almost entirely negative way, the point at issue.

To further our understanding of the persistently polemical nature of romanticism, we can take as our point of departure the antiromantic overtones that are always implied in certain recent developments in French criticism. In so doing, I am not implying that these developments have an inherent importance that makes it imperative to concern ourselves with them at the exclusion of all others. Far from it; I am merely using them as a starting point because they come accompanied by a theoretical apparatus that allows for a faster and more direct exposition than would be the case with less theoretically self-conscious forms of criticism. As will, hopefully, become clear from subsequent lectures, similar problems can be reached by different paths, with starting points that are located elsewhere, in American or in German critical practice.

What is nowadays being referred to, in a somewhat modish term, as French "structuralism" does not primarily represent itself as a historically oriented trend that defines itself in opposition to a previous movement, be it romanticism or another form of thought. Since structuralism is methodologically rather than ideologically oriented, concerned with synchronic relationships of similarity rather than diachronic relationships of difference, it does not openly engage in historical self-definition. Nor is it, as is well known, primarily concerned with literature, since it deals most of all with the methodology of the social sciences, especially linguistics and anthropology. Nevertheless, the potential importance of structuralist approaches for literary criticism has been so strongly felt that the theoretical discussion of structuralist criticism has in fact preceded the existence of such a criticism; in typical French fashion, the recent heated debates have mostly been about a still nonexistent entity. This may suffice to indicate that a highly sensitive relationship potentially exists between structuralism and literary criticism. And by the same token, an equally sensitive relationship exists between the historically determined aspects of literature and a timeless method such as structuralism. A very definite preconception of literary history underlies the work of critics such as Roland Barthes and René Girard who have been most strongly attracted toward structuralism. And this preconception can only be defined as being overwhelmingly antiromantic. René Girard, the author of one of the most interesting critical essays to have been published in France during the last years, is probably the clearest example of this trend, since in him the antiromanticism receives explicit thematic expression. His book *Mensonge romantique et vérité romanesque*[3] preceded the actual advent of institutionalized

structuralism and was the result of his own private meditations carried out at some remove from the intellectual fashions
of Paris. But his genuine affinity with structuralism has since
been confirmed by his overt alignment with structuralist
groups and his acceptance in their midst.

René Girard uses the word *romantic* in a more than historical sense, not just to designate one particular period at the
beginning of the nineteenth century but what he considers to
be a recurrent aberration that plagues the mind of Western
man at least since the Renaissance. This aberration is the illusory autonomy of the self, and the subsequent priority of the
problem of the subject considered in and by itself over the
problems of the self considered in relation to other entities—
other subjects as well as things. But the term *romanticism* as he
uses it also has a certain historical relevance, for the delusion is
particularly strong at the so-called romantic period: romantic
individualism, the cult of the self as the independent and gen-
erative center of the work, the Promethean claim to confer
upon the human will absolute attributes reserved to divine
categories of Being—all these affirmations of the autonomous
self are, for Girard, forms of romantic deceit, "mensonges ro-
mantiques." The deceit operates on two levels, the first one
general, the second more specifically aesthetic. Self-autonomy
is asserted as a philosophical truth about the nature of human
existence, a descriptive statement about our way of being in
the world. This assertion is based, however, on the constitutive nature of the work of art as a self-engendered world of the
subject's own making. Such a world would radiate from a place
of origin or constitutive focus that is ontologically prior to it,
that is, revealed as having a relationship to all parts of this
world that differs from the relationships existing between
these parts by being the necessary precondition to the existence of all relationships. A Girard-oriented study of the postromantic novel reveals, however, an altogether different structure. These novels still revolve around the apparent center of a
main character, but serve to reveal not the strength but the
ontological weakness of this center. The central subject is
shown to be entirely dependent on another subject, who acts
as a mediator and governs in fact all the decisions it proudly

claims as its own. Therefore, the relationship between the main character and the mediator takes precedence over the relationships the character initiates in the body of the fictional narrative. Don Quixote's relationship to Amadis de Gaula, Julien Sorel's relationship to Napoleon, Mme Bovary's relationship to the heroines of bad fiction, Marcel's relationships to the Guermantes, possess an ontological priority over all other dimensions in the book since the latter could never be what they are in the absence of the initial involvement with the mediator.

The relationship between the character (which is itself presumably an extension of the author's own subjectivity) and the mediator is not just one of formal imitation or identification: it is instead one of warped desire. The objects that the main figure seems to pursue with such relentless energy, whether they be wealth, social prestige, or women, are in fact not desired for their own sake but receive their attractiveness from being accessible to the other person he would want to be. The desire is never for the object but for the mediator: it is the desire of the self not to be what it is but to be another, not to assert but to flee from its autonomy. More important still, like the proverbial husband, the hero of the novel is the last to find out about how he is being deceived, mystified by his own weakness. He may be a perfectly sensible and rational person, but in anything involving the mediator he is totally lacking in self-insight, radically blind to the actual state of his consciousness. This self-delusion is what leads him to call himself autonomous at the moment when he is in fact the unconscious slave of another's decisions. This mystified claim at autonomy characterizes for Girard the romantic false consciousness. "The prestige of the mediator," he writes, "passes into the object of desire and confers upon it an illusory value. The triangular desire," that is, the desire involving the mystified self, an indifferent object, and the all-powerful mediator,

> is the kind of desire that transfigures its subject. Romantic literature is by no means ignorant of this transformation; to the contrary, it feeds upon it and glories in it, but it never reveals its true mechanism. . . . Only the novelist is capable of describing the

true genesis of an illusion which the romantic always locates in a solitary subject. The romantic defends a "parthenogenesis" of the imagination. Committed as he is to the notion of autonomy, he refuses to bow down before his own gods. The solipsistic poetics that succeed each other for more than one hundred fifty years are expressions of this refusal. (25–26)

The historical scheme thus becomes quite clear. The development of the nineteenth-century novel is the salutary reaction against the self-mystification of romanticism. The subject matter of these novels is this deluded consciousness of the solipsistic romantic: Julien Sorel, Emma Bovary, the Marcel of Proust's novel, are all of them the deluded romantic heroes that the authors have exorcized *by means of* their novels. The nineteenth-century novel is the demystification of romanticism. "We believe," writes Girard, "that the *novelistic* genius (*génie romanesque*) is a painful conquest over the attitudes that we have generally called romantic, and all of which seem to us devised to maintain the illusion of a spontaneous desire and of a subjectivity that would be quasi-divine in its autonomy. It is only slowly and painfully that the novelist overcomes in himself the romantic he used to be and who refuses to die. This overcoming takes place in the novelistic work and in this work only" (35–36).

Similar antiromantic formulations occur frequently in contemporary criticism. They are perhaps best classified under the general heading of demythification, a process that is explicitly operative over a wide spectrum of intellectual concerns since the late nineteenth century, in the Hegel-oriented early Marx as well as in Nietzsche and in the "realistic" novelists referred to by Girard. Demythification is perhaps the best common denominator under which to group such diverse aspects of contemporary thought as neo-Marxism, neo-Freudianism, phenomenological and existential analysis[4] both theological and secular, and even certain forms of linguistic analysis. The openly antiromantic slant of this tendency is most apparent in the field of literary criticism, where it takes a variety of forms. In a formalist tradition, it is often the formal incoherence, the apparent inconclusiveness of certain romantic texts that be-

comes a target of criticism (Bostetter).[5] In a more ethically oriented context, the attack on romanticism takes on ideological
forms, some of the left, as in Lukács's later books on realism
and on irrationalism, some of the right, as in the Babbitt–
Hulme–Eliot–New Criticism line. But the attack of Girard,
seen in the structuralist framework, reaches further. It transcends categories such as form and morality toward their common ground in the self. By stating the problem in terms of a
dialectical relationship between an authentic and a false consciousness, it is the degree of transparence of a consciousness
to its own light that comes under investigation. The myth is
that of the possibility of consciousness; hence the shift from
the general understanding of a mythical theme (or demythification) to that of the particular myths by which the self deliberately conceals its own being (or de*myst*ification). By calling
this movement of self-concealment (Husserl speaks of it as
Selbstverhülltheit) a myth, we imply by the same token that the
main entity by means of which and within which this dialectic
of concealment and revelation takes place is language. The
particular myth under scrutiny then becomes that of a privileged language that would belong to a truly autonomous subject, a myth that is historically defined as the central myth of
romantic literature.

   This emphasis would suffice by itself to explain René
Girard's alignment (at least for the time being) with the structuralist group in France.[6] For the main, social language is an
intricate system of rhetorical devices to escape from the direct
expression of desires that are, in the fullest sense of the term,
unnameable—not because they are ethically shameful (for this
would make the problem a very simple one) but because unmediated expression is a philosophical impossibility. And we
know that the individual who would choose to ignore this
fundamental convention would be slated either for crucifixion,
if he were conscious, or, if he were naive, destined to the total
ridicule of such heroes as Candide and all other fools that
appear, fortunately, more often in fiction than in life. The particular structuralist contribution to this age-old problem comes
by way of an astute rephrasing of the problem that develops
when a consciousness gets involved in interpreting another

consciousness, the basic pattern from which there can be no escape in the social sciences if there is to be such a thing. Lévi-Strauss, for instance, started out years ago from the need to protect anthropologists engaged in the study of a so-called primitive society from the error made by earlier positivistic anthropologists when they projected upon this society certain preconceived assumptions that remained non-consciously (*impensé, ungedacht*—not "subconsciously") determined by the inhibitions and shortcomings of their own social situation. Prior to making any valid statement about a distant society, the observing subject must be as clear as possible about his attitude toward his own; he will soon discover, however, that the only way in which he can accomplish this self-demystification is by a (comparative) study of his own social self as it engages in the observation of others, and by becoming aware of the pattern of distortions that this situation necessarily implies. The observation and interpretation of others is always also a means that leads to the observation of the self; true anthropological knowledge (in the ethnological as well as in the philosophical, Kantian sense of the term) can only become worthy of being called knowledge when this alternating process of mutual interpretation between the two subjects has run its course. Numerous complications arise, because the observing as well as the observed subject are by no means constant, and each time the observer actually succeeds in interpreting his subject he changes it, and changes it all the more as his interpretation comes closer to the truth. But every change of the observed subject requires a subsequent change in the observer, and the oscillating process seems to be endless. Worse, as the oscillation gains in intensity and in truth, it becomes increasingly less clear who is in fact doing the observing and who is being observed. Both parties tend to fuse into a single subject as the original distance between them disappears. The gravity of this development will at once be clear if I allow myself to shift, for a brief moment, from the anthropological to the psychoanalytical or political model. In the case of a genuine analysis of the psyche, it means that it would no longer be clear who is analyzing and who is being analyzed; consequently the highly embarrassing question arises who should be paying whom. And on a political level, the equally distressing question as to who should be exploiting whom is bound to arise.

The need to safeguard reason from what might become a dangerous *vertige*, a dizziness of the mind caught in an infinite regression, prompts the methodological rationalism of such theoreticians of structuralism as Lévi-Strauss. The fallacy of a finite and single interpretation derives, as we saw, from the postulate of a privileged observer; this leads, in turn, to the endless oscillation of an intersubjective demystification. As an escape from this predicament, one can propose, with Lévi-Strauss, a radical relativism that operates from the most empirically specific to the most loftily general level of human behavior. There are no longer any standpoints that can a priori be considered privileged, no structure that functions validly as a model for other structures, no postulate of ontological hierarchy that can serve as an organizing principle from which particular structures are derived. All structures are, in a sense, equally fallacious and are therefore called myths or "mythemes." But no myth ever has sufficient coherence not to flow back into neighboring myths or ever has an identity strong enough to stand out by itself, independently of an arbitrary act of interpretation that defines it. The relative unity of traditional myths always depends on the existence of a privileged point of view to which the method itself denies any status of authenticity. "Contrary to philosophical reflection," writes Claude Lévi-Strauss in *Le Cru et le cuit*, "which claims to return to the source, the reflective activities (involved in the structural study of myths) deal with light rays that issue from a virtual focal point."[7] Lévi-Strauss's method aims at preventing this *virtual* focus from being made into an *actual* source of light. The analogy with optics is perhaps misleading, for in literature everything hinges on the existential status of the focal point. It is one thing to say that the focal point is privileged but virtual, another to subscribe to Lévi-Strauss's further statement that "the determination of the real center of a work is impossible," that, therefore, "myths have no authors" (25–26), and that, in the terms of Jacques Derrida, the absence of the center is equivalent to the disappearance of the self as constitutive subject.

These remarks have made the transition from anthropology to the field of language and, finally, of literature. In the act of anthropological intersubjective interpretation, a fundamental discrepancy always prevents the observer from coinciding fully with the consciousness he is observing. The same discrepancy exists in everyday language, in the impossibility of making the actual expression coincide with what has to be expressed, of making the actual sign coincide with what it signifies. It is the distinctive privilege of language to be able to conceal meaning behind a misleading sign, as when we hide rage or hatred behind a smile. But it is the distinctive curse of all language, as soon as any kind of interpersonal relation is involved, that it is forced to act this way. The simplest of wishes cannot express itself without hiding behind a screen of language that constitutes a world of intricate intersubjective relationships, all of them potentially inauthentic. In the everyday language of communication, there is no a priori privileged position of sign over meaning or of meaning over sign; the act of interpretation will always again have to establish this relation for the particular case at hand. The interpretation of everyday language is a Sisyphean task, a task without end and without progress, for the other is always free to make what he wants differ from what he says he wants. The methodology of structural anthropology and that of post-Saussurian linguistics thus share a common problem: that of a built-in discrepancy within the intersubjective relationship. As Lévi-Strauss, in order to protect the rationality of his science, had to come to the conclusion of a myth without an author, so the linguists have to conceive of a metalanguage without speaker in order to remain rational.

Literature, presumably, is a form of language, and one can argue that all other art forms, including music, are in fact protoliterary languages. This was, in fact, Mallarmé's thesis in his Oxford lecture, as it is Lévi-Strauss's when he states that the language of music, as a language without speaker, comes closest to being the kind of metalanguage of which the linguists are dreaming. If the radical position suggested by Lévi-Strauss is to stand, if the question of structure can only be asked from a point of view that is not that of a subject using a privileged language, then it becomes imperative to show that literature constitutes no exception, that its language is nowise privileged in terms of unity and truth over everyday forms of language. The task of structuralist literary critics then becomes quite clear: in order to eliminate the constitutive subject, they have to show that the discrepancy between sign and meaning (*signifiant* and *signifié*) prevails in literature in the same manner as in everyday language.

Some of the critics who call themselves structuralists have consciously been doing this, while others, who may be quite unaware of the label, are doing something very similar. Contemporary practical criticism, in France and in the United States, functions more and more as a demystification of the belief that literature is a privileged language. One possible strategy consists of showing that certain claims to authenticity attributed to literature are in fact expressions of a desire that, like all desires, falls prey to the duplicities of expression. The so-called idealism of literature is then shown to be an idolatry, a fascination with a false image that mimics the presumed attributes of authenticity when it is in fact the hollow mask with which a frustrated, defeated consciousness tries to cover up its own negativity. Perhaps the most specific example of this strategy is the use made by structuralist critics of the historical term *romantic*; the example also has the virtue of revealing the historical scheme within which they are operating, which is not always stated in the open. The fallacy of the belief that, in the language of poetry, sign and meaning can coincide or, at least, be related to each other in the free and harmonious balance that we call beauty (*Anmut*) is said to be a specificaly romantic delusion. The unity of appearance (sign) and idea (meaning)— to use the terminology that one finds indeed among the theoreticians of romanticism—is a myth that appears in a variety of romantic *topoi* that function as the figural representation of such a language.

The work of René Girard represents a highly articulate example of this attempt to strip literature of its claim to be a privileged language. We can use it therefore as typical of the powerful trend that it represents and assert that, in dealing with the manner in which it attacks romanticism, we gain some insight into the entire structuralist approach to this problem.

Anyone coming from English or American methods of the criticism of fiction is likely to be shocked by Girard's utter disregard for problems of point of view. He makes no distinction whatever between the sentiments and the consciousness of the characters and those of the author: a mystified character is held up as sufficient proof for the existence of an equally mystified author. The fact that Julien Sorel or Charlus is obsessed by falsely mediated desires does not necessarily mean that Stendhal or Proust is, or has been deceived in the same manner; it could indeed be argued that a deceived character could only be created by an author who is not himself thus deceived: Stendhal cannot be a social climber when he describes Sorel, Proust no longer a snob when he invents Mme Verdurin, Legrandin, or Charlus. It is true that the actual Henri Beyle and Marcel Proust, in their own lives, were involved with social ambition and snobbishness; yet the relationship between these empirical experiences and the subsequent novels accounts, at most, for their acquaintance with the exterior aspects of the mechanics of social behavior, but hardly for the obsessive fascination that makes them concentrate on this theme to the near exclusion of all others.

The objection carries some weight, but leaves Girard's main insight untouched. For it is part of his contribution to have removed the problem of point of view from mere narrative technique and to have integrated it within a truly intentional description of the novelistic consciousness. He no longer represents the relationship between the consciousness of the narrator who constitutes the fiction and the (fictional) consciousness of his creations as a purely formal one, a mere device that enables narrative to originate, so to speak, for its own sake. There can, indeed, be no narrative without point of view—but an intentional theory of the novel will have to turn this truism around and ask instead: since the correlative of all narrative is the constitution of a "point of view" to be occupied by the narrator, what then is the subjective necessity that prompts the creation of such a privileged viewpoint? Instead of showing that point of view exists for the sake of narrative—which is tautological—one should ask why and how narrative (in itself useless) exists for the sake of point of view. And although Girard does not approach the problem exactly in those terms, but in a more dramatically confessional manner, he provides us with an answer most worthy of being debated. For the relation between the narrating consciousness (of the author) and the narrated consciousness (of the character) is not for Girard a formal but a temporal one: the consciousness of the character necessarily precedes that of the narrator, and the latter only comes into being when the former has run its full course. At the outset of the novel (or in the earlier versions of certain texts, such as the early drafts for *The Red and the Black*, or Proust's *Jean Santeuil*) there is in fact no distinction between author and character; the objectivation implied in the third-person narrative is purely illusory, and the author gives un-critical expression to his wishful desire to belong to the chosen world inhabited by the mediator. The point of view is that of the mediator, and the author occupies it as if it were his own, with a bad faith that is as total as it is blind. Gradually, as the work develops, or as he revises the original statement, the process of demystification starts to take place, at first perhaps in the form of an increased insight into the sordidness of a world that only seemed glittering and desirable when it belonged to others. But the real revelation, the actual conversion can only occur at the very end, in the conclusion of the novel, when the author not only realizes that the world of the other is not better than his own but understands the self-deceit that made his desires tributary to an interpersonal substitution that enslaved his own judgment. At that moment, a genuine "point of view" becomes possible and the self of the author separates into two parts: a former self, which existed in darkness and in error, and a new, present self, capable of suddenly seeing the entire past in the right perspective. But this second self only exists as a single moment, an apocalyptic flash of lightning that concludes a book which, up till now, has consisted of nothing but falsehood and deceit. It exists only *for* this concluding moment, which also marks, in a radical and absolute way, the disappearance of the former self, which can be said, literally, to die at this instant. The language that exists in the novel is then, in fact, always an inauthentic language, and the further it reaches back in memory, the falser it becomes. However, it can be said of this language that it moves toward the truth of its own demystification, that its *telos* is an authenticity which it never names but in which it culminates as the final, consuming moment when it can disappear in the knowledge of its own falsehood.

The temporal pattern of this movement is relatively simple and recognizable: it goes from absolute error to truth by ways of an event that establishes a radical discontinuity between them. It separates a totally inauthentic past from a totally enlightened present by means of a revelation that reduces the past to the ashes of sheer falsehood. We can call this pattern, which we will find again in various forms in the course of these lectures, an *apocalyptic* form of temporality.

The term *apocalyptic* may seem forced when we think of it in reference to a single person, such as Proust or Stendhal. But the pattern here described exists on a collective as well as on an individual level, and one may assume, although René Girard only hints at this, that it exists in a general historical framework as well as in the history of literature. It does not just describe a certain group of novels but lays bare the unavoidable pattern of all novels as such; a novel is defined by its adherence to this pattern of apocalyptic self-discovery. And, beyond this, it describes the life of societies and civilizations, all of them mystified in similar ways and growing increasingly destructive, violent, and irrational as they come closer and closer to the moment when their true motives will be revealed. Romanticism represents the moment of maximum delusion when the mediator, who up till then had occupied a transcendental status at a godlike distance from man, is secularized and placed in man himself—when, in Girard's terms, "men will be gods for each other (*les hommes seront des dieux les uns pour les autres*)" (59). Since then, the development of Western thought turns around in the ever-narrowing circle of a false internal mediation of which the humanistic existentialism of Sartre and Camus is one of the last versions. The unstated implication is that of a romantic agony leading to an apocalyptic moment of self-destruction and self-renewal, a new, postromantic dispensation of which the nineteenth- and twentieth-century novelists are the prophetic precursors—not because their own language is free of delusions but because it acts out, on the level of fiction, the future liberation from deceit.

This scheme, which recurs with individual variations in many literarily oriented structuralists, is particularly satisfying to the modern consciousness; it seduces by its combined appeal to our desire for lucidity and to our impatience with a difficult present. It calls, however, for many qualifications and revisions.

Our criticism of Girard, rather than starting explicitly from the historical question of romanticism, takes as a point of departure the structure of the constitutive subject that appears in the novel, what is sometimes referred to as the unifying "voice" of the author. Since Girard refuses to give this voice a privileged status, he will not treat a literary consciousness in a manner that differs from the way in which he treats a simple empirical consciousness involved in the cares of everyday existence, in the contingent chaos of economic, intersubjective, and psychological concerns in which we live. The same bad faith and deceit govern our relationship to literature as to other activities or entities. This is apparent, for instance, in the many scenes from Proust's novel in which the main character comes into contact with art or with writers: the scenes at the theater, the episodes involving the writer Bergotte or the painter Elstir, etc. Girard can easily show how, in several of these scenes, art and literature represent a particularly vicious form of false mediation, in which the character is misled into a belief in its own independent judgment when, in reality, it merely echoes a desire that is artificially instilled into a passive mind. False mediation by means of fiction, also called *bovarysme* in reference to Flaubert's novel, is a particularly striking case of Girard's triangular desire since it explicitly involves the false claim for the autonomy of literature.

Novelists like Flaubert or Proust, however, have always distinguished sharply between the status of art and the empirical *use* that can be made of art when it is placed, as it cannot fail to be, in the world of everyday facticity in which books, pictures, plays, and movies exist as empirical entities among others (such as natural objects, tools, and other people). From the moment they become part of the empirical world, works of art become the prey of various intentionalities that are not necessarily related to the intent that brought them into being. This is true for the author as well as for the consumer. The self that uses the work for purposes of personal fame can be essentially different from the self that invented the work in the first place. Nor is the discovery of this distinction between an empirical and an authentic self a striking revelation that occurs as a flash of lightning; it has been part of the novel from the beginning, as if the author took pains to distinguish the attitudes toward art of the nonliterary figures that appear in the novel from his own attitude as it appears in the book as a whole. It is not difficult to distinguish, in Proust, the moments when he talks about art in his own terms from the moments when art is being used and abused by the characters acting out their dramatic destiny. And for all the misleading claims to identity between Madame Bovary and her author, Flaubert is careful to point out, from the start, the absolute distinction beween a bovarystic and a novelistic imagination: "She had to gain some personal profit from things and she rejected as useless whatever did not contribute to the immediate satisfaction of her heart's desires—being of a temperment more sentimental than artistic, looking for emotions, not landscapes."[8]

This distinction is of crucial importance, for it defines the self of the author as disinterested, as a self that, in the fiction, has renounced his empirical status in the world for an altogether different project. A disjunction has taken place between an empirical self and a new kind of subject which entertains a newly problematic relationship toward this empirical self. For Girard there are also two selves present in the fiction, that of the mediator and that of the mystified character. But the relationship that exists between them is purely intersubjective; the two subjects are engaged in a dialectic of desire and hatred which resolves itself with a bang at the end of the novel when a single and authentic self shines for one ineffable moment. This is not the case, however, in the relationship that exists between the empirical and literary self. This relationship is apparently one of distance, and far from being governed by jealousy and envy, it is remarkably neutral in sentiment. So detached does Flaubert seem from Madame Bovary that five generations of critics have not yet been able to decide whether he likes her or not. She is ambiguously both himself and what is most remote from him—though never as if she were a former, abandoned self that he has outgrown. Nothing in the temporality of the novel suggests such a one-directional *dépassement*. Nothing in the relationship suggests the intersubjective involvements of our daily existence which Girard then wants to transpose into the aesthetic sphere of the novel. Yet it is this problematic relationship which is constitutive for the novel and that we have to understand if we want to understand the authentically literary consciousness that appears in romanticism. If the relationship between the empirical subject Rousseau, or Flaubert, or Proust and the authors of *Julie*, *Madame Bovary*, and the *Recherche* is not one of false mediation, of desire, or of intersubjective involvement, what then is its nature?

The temporality of the structure will (as always) provide the answer. It allows for a better formulation of the difference between Girard's scheme and the one to be found in romantic and postromantic literature. Girard's description is obviously inadequate in that it accounts, to some extent, for the end of the novels but fails to account for the much more delicate moment of their beginning. In *Mensonge romantique* this beginning is nothing—sheer error, total delusion, the point farthest removed from true novelistic insight, etc. At the conclusion it will, at most, be a bad memory of a past aberration, forever left behind. From the reading of the novels we know that the opposite is true. The miracle is not that the end of the work has progressed so far beyond the beginning, but that the beginning already contains everything essential that the end will confirm. Whatever the profound dissimilarities between *Jean Santeuil* and the *Recherche*, they seem unimportant compared to the fact that the first novel has a beginning emphatically stressed to be the beginning of a fiction by the traditional trick of printing it as a posthumously published manuscript that is virtually identical with the beginning of the later novel. And there is nothing in the earliest section of *Madame Bovary*, which deals with the youth of Charles, that does not prefigure the later developments of the novel. For that matter, the earliest scenario in existence shows that Flaubert had practically conceived the totality of his novel at the very moment of its inception. The temporal structure of all these novels is prefigurative and prospective, rather than being founded on the retrospective pattern that Girard stresses to the exclusion of all others. The literary self seems to originate with a foreknowledge of its own destiny that no empirical self can ever possess. As such it dominates the action from a point of view that looks out in both directions, past and future, and that constantly creates new links between the two temporal directions. It acts as a constitutive center that engenders its own temporal structures, and it can only do so because it somehow knows its end at the very instant when it comes into being. This does not mean that the novelist actually and literally knows the detailed circumstances of his conclusion when he embarks on his novel, but rather that there could be no progress toward this end without unfolding the foreknowledge contained in the beginning. The relationship of the eighteenth-century novel of total contingency to the later type of novel is a genuine problem to which we shall briefly allude toward the end of this series. But Girard's description, needless to say, is not founded on eighteenth-century novels.

The determining structural importance of the beginning as a constitutive center leads to a temporal pattern that differs entirely from Girard's. It is the opposite of apocalyptic. The present "moment" does not stand at the end but at the beginning of the history; regardless of the grammatical tense used, the present of the novel is that of the beginning, the moment at which we enter into contact with a literary self that exists in its own fictional, nonempirical world. This moment is the constitutive center of the novel and defines the literary subject as a constitutive and not as the "virtual" center that we know from Lévi-Strauss's anthropological model. This center, unlike Girard's, is essentially prospective, oriented toward a future that it prefigures and, as such, already contains. The burden of the novel is not the constitution of a present and a future, but much rather that of a past, which Girard grants it so willingly. The fiction is all present and future, but has no past since, unlike empirical existence, it has a self-determined source prior to which it has neither existence nor memory. The constitution of a pastness (the *recherche du temps perdu*) ensues, however, from the novel's capacity to reverse, as it were, its own temporality and to link beginning to end by a movement that can travel in both directions. Starting point and end point are linked by a duration that the mind can encompass in both directions; the reader of the novel is in fact constantly making such temporal reversals each time he "understands" a plot as the unfolding of a prefigurative system of signs that become meaningful once their prefigurative function is revealed.[9] The duration of the fiction becomes articulated in these temporal reversals which confer upon the two-dimensional world of fiction an illusory dimension of pastness. All events in the novel are located at the intersection of this double temporal movement that takes place between beginning and end interacting upon each other.[10]

This total duration of the fiction can only be understood and interpreted from the point of view of a subject capable of encompassing within its scope a consciousness of its beginning as well as of its end. Because the character of a fiction appears in the guise of an empirical person, it does not possess this knowledge which only the author can bring to light. Therefore, the relationship between author and character is not governed by intersubjective feelings such as desire or envy but solely by an act of understanding. The temporality is not oriented toward a single culminating moment but follows instead the temporal movement of interpretation: the gradual bringing to light of a foreknowledge that existed at the beginning and that is recaptured by a circular movement of return to the source. This pattern is interpretative or hermeneutic rather than apocalyptic. Since it is not interpersonal, it does not matter whether it takes place between two subjects or within a single self; when another is chosen as a model of literary identity, as in the case of certain literary influences, the relationship takes on the form of an encounter (as between Dante and

Virgil) and a recognition (anagnorisis) of the other as a temporal precursor. Nothing could be more remote from Girard's pattern of external or internal mediation.

By the very strength of the evidence, Girard himself is ultimately recaptured by this very movement and, in essays written after *Mensonge romantique*, formulations occur that come very close to stating a hermeneutic instead of an intersubjective conception of the work of art. Thus, in an article from 1965 entitled "Expérience romanesque et mythe oedipien,"[11] Girard comes close to conceding the circular nature of the work: "In the round of successive versions, the omega immediately precedes the alpha. Nothing, in the order of creation, is closer to the conclusion than the beginning (*commencement*), which from now on will be understood as a repetition (*recommencement*). If inspiration originates at one end of the work, its effect will be felt most quickly and most directly at the other extremity." But he goes on to say,

> From another point of view, however, the beginning of the work is the point most distant from the novelistic experience. It remains caught, imprisoned in the spirit of this beginning. And when, contrary to what happens in myth, this beginning is recaptured in the perspective of the end, this recapture is never total enough to eliminate the original perspective. This means that the novel is an act of transition, a spiritual "translation," never the result of a finished transcendence (*un dépassement acquis*), of a transcendence that has made the full inventory and organized all its results, of a transcendence that is itself transcended. It is the act of transcendence itself.

It is clear that Girard has gone further in his formulation but has not changed his original premise: if the movement of the work is always from error to truth, then the truthful conclusion can never really establish contact with the beginning without falling itself back into error. But if the pattern is not one of error and truth but one of understanding a truth that was already there, albeit in a hidden form, then the circle, also, will never close perfectly, but exactly for the reverse reason than that given by Girard. For him, the circle remains open, remains spiral, because the end surpasses the beginning. In a hermeneutic structure, the circle never closes because all the end can achieve is an *understanding* of the beginning; it can never equal it in positing the truth that gave the beginning the power of being a source. In Girard's system, there is no reason why a first novel would ever have been written, since nothing has the strength to originate in the absence of a conclusion. Like all apocalyptic systems, his thought degrades and bypasses the constitutive power of time.

No wonder then that his historical and temporal perspective remains entirely different from ours. He calls conclusion what we call beginning; literature begins at the far side of the point where he claims that it reaches its apocalyptic climax. And this beginning occurs at the point which he considers to be the point of maximum error. His entire analysis applies, with a high degree of validity, to the empirical person who uses literature for its own purposes, like Emma Bovary. This self, as we all know, never produces literature, and the novelists Girard mentions had gone well beyond it even before they put their first words on paper; otherwise they would never even have started to write. The problems of the self that appear in literature are not empirical, and Girard's insights into the mechanics of intersubjectivity do not apply to them; the actual domain of literature lies beyond his reach. He has misconstrued the temporal relationships that exist between a transcendental self and its source as if they were interpersonal relationships between two empirical subjects.

This type of error is characteristic of all thought as it begins to reestablish contact with its source. It becomes obscured by exactly the same blindness that Girard attributes to the close presence of the mediator. One of his most perceptive insights describes the mixture of insight and blindness that comes over a person when he patterns himself on someone who is very similar to his own self. He develops a considerable insight into others, but "this lucidity is accompanied by a redoubled opacity toward his own self" (79). This opacity takes on the form of a blind hatred toward the envied mediator. The same process is in fact taking place in Girard himself, except that what is drawing near him is not a mediator, but his own intellectual origin, namely romanticism. The point is approaching at which the temporal movement will reverse itself and the origin can be understood as it really is. Girard's hostility toward romanticism, which takes on exactly the tone he describes so well in his mystified characters, is clear proof of the privileged, originary relationship that exists between him and his romantic precursors. Many of the structures he describes will turn out to be stated, more clearly and with greater understanding, in the romantic writers he considers mystified—but by whom he is in fact in the process of being demystified. Instead of appearing in a falsely interpersonal form, these structures will appear in their true light. The nature of the distinction between the self that appears in the work and the empirical self of the author, the problem of the relationship, within the work, between origin and totality, the temporality of literary language as a language of interpretation—these are the very problems we will find in evidence in the "romantic" authors with which we have chosen to deal, Rousseau, Hölderlin, and Wordsworth. Modern criticism has made us aware of their prevalence even when, as in the case of René Girard, it has cut itself off from the source of its own insight.

2

Rousseau and the Transcendence of the Self

*U*SING RENÉ GIRARD as a more or less docile straw man, we pointed to some of the problems that contemporary criticism has found prevalent in romantic literature: the problem of the self (or, more precisely, of the relationship between the empirical self of the author and the self that appears as the speaking voice in the work), the formal problem of the relationship between origin and totality in the work, the notion of literary language as a temporal structure. The contemporary study of romanticism has, at times, been able to describe some of these problems in broad historical terms, showing how they appear throughout the entire romantic movement, as writers and critics of the period seem to converge toward some of these central themes: thus we get a historical picture of the emergence of expressive concepts of the self in a book such as Meyer Abrams's *The Mirror and the Lamp*.[1] But most of the time, it is in studies of individual romantic writers that these insights appear most clearly. The fact that some of the most original recent works in the area of romanticism tend to cluster around the same figures—that Wordsworth, for instance, has received more sophisticated critical attention in the last decade or so than Shelley or Keats, Rousseau more than Chateaubriand, Hölderlin more than Schiller or Tieck—would indicate that they are the authors in whom these themes are most explicitly present.

René Girard performed still another service for us: he revealed how the work of some critics who claim to be antiromantic often allowed for a keener insight into the romantic mind than would be found in outspoken defenders of the movement. The particular mistake in which we found him trapped, that of locating a cause of error his own judgment seems able to dispel in the source from which he is, in fact, receiving the very light that allows him to judge correctly, is characteristic of all thought that occurs in a state of crisis, that is reestablishing contact with its own origin. It states its own birth in the mode of error, and remains radically blind to the source of the light it emits. It is mystified by its own claim at demystification. But this kind of thought, erroneous as it may be, is more revealing than the naive acceptance of values which, like those of the romantic consciousness, assert the impossibility of naiveté. The split, the disjunction between the empirical and what we have called the literary, or poetic self, means precisely that the judgments and pronouncements emitted in romantic poetry cannot be transferred to the world of empirical experience. A naive reading of romanticism turns to the period to find values by which it can live, examples of past strength by means of which it can sustain its own particular dejection and uncertainty. Since the main affirmation of the period is precisely the need to renounce the hope that a truer insight into the nature of existence (*Dasein*) will be of direct benefit to the empirical world, it is no wonder that a return to romanticism as a source of practical values is likely to miss the mark. The path that travels from aesthetic judgment to practical reason is labyrinthine, not straightforward.

More suggestive than a bland admiration that makes examples out of figures who spoke as voices of mourning rather than as voices of hope is Girard's type of error when he turns against the source of whatever wisdom he possesses. The history of the critical interpretation of romanticism is rich in examples of that kind, to the point where there seems to be no better way to interpret the movement than by understanding the misunderstandings it created among its interpreters. And in this history of misunderstandings, which should some day be written, there will be no richer chapter than the one dealing with Jean-Jacques Rousseau.

For here we are faced, at once, with a fatal confusion between two selves: the one specific, particular, historical, and chaotic, the other capable of the lofty lucidity of total self-understanding. The gap between the two is so wide as to have become comically proverbial. I remember that the first thing I was told about Rousseau in the lower grades of high school was that he had written a treatise on education but given away his children to charity. Among his contemporaries, one aspect of Rousseau achieved, almost at once, mythical dimensions that made it impossible to speak about the most basic facts of his life without distortion. People quite close to him and who personally knew several of his contemporaries are entirely unreliable on facts: Mme de Staël, for instance, does not hesitate to report, for her own philosophical satisfaction, that Rousseau committed suicide, and the myths about his life would fill many more volumes than M. Etiemble was able to collect on Rimbaud. He is admired, to the point of having comparisons of Rousseau with Socrates and Christ become commonplaces of later eighteenth-century occasional verse, and he acted so powerfully as a mediator, in Girard's sense of the term, that he shaped individualities more than Napoleon did and weighed much more heavily on history. On the other hand, the actual man has rightly been called a pathological liar, a thief, a paranoiac; it is true that his life contains some of the most intricate examples of bad faith to be found anywhere. It was suggested recently, for instance, that the entire story of the abandoned children was an invention of Rousseau to hide the, to him, much more embarrassing fact of his impotence; certainly, the assumption goes, anyone claiming fatherhood in such a disreputable fashion could never be suspected of feigning it in the first place. The theory is in all likelihood false, but it would nevertheless be perfectly in character; only Rousseau could trap one in a situation where proving that he actually disposed of his children would somehow turn out to be a defense of his moral character; only he could make one doubt the good faith of his sincerity even when he is revealing the most sordid weaknesses of his own behavior. The presence in Rousseau of a double self, not in terms of good and evil, but in terms of self-knowledge and self-deception, dramatizes the problem with which we are concerned in a manner that makes it as concrete as can be.

Still, even more remarkable than the discrepancy between the man Rousseau and his literary language is the ease with which one forgets the former for the sake of the latter: the rapid mythologization which occurred even during his lifetime indicates this, and created the near-tragic gap between Rousseau's intellectual authority and the personal circumstances of his life. The same phenomenon occurs not only with reference to the person of Rousseau but extends at times to the reader, causing an identification between author and reader of which there are few equivalences. The striking characteristic of these identifications, however, is that they precisely do not follow the pattern outlined by Girard in his description of triangular mediation. Far from leading the reader to betray his own spontaneity, far from blinding him to the real makeup of his soul, Rousseau serves as a mediating consciousness by means of which the greatest degree of self-insight can be achieved.

Examples abound among his immediate successors in the late eighteenth century. One thinks of figures that are close to Rousseau in their own poetic temperament, such as Joubert or Hölderlin, whose critical insight into their precursor coincides with the highest flights of their poetic imagination. But even in readers of a different temper, cruder or more extroverted, less prone to the inwardness of reverie, something similar happens. A good example is that of Madame de Staël, herself a personality tyrannized by the relentless power of her own self-deception and inconstancy, which made her life and most of her work into an opaque muddle of erotic and moral confusion. Yet, in the midst of this chaos, there are moments of remarkable insight. A near-Kantian respect for the clarifying power of the mind stands behind some of her statements, as when she asserts that "[l'élévation de l'âme—PdM] naît de la conscience de soi [(the elevation of the soul) is born of self-consciousness]"[2]—that the source of the moral dignity of the soul is found in the consciousness of the self. The statement is made in direct reference to Rousseau, in the early text about Rousseau with which she began her career as a critic. And this emphasis on self-knowledge always remains associated for her with the figure of Rousseau: "Only Rousseau (and Goethe)," she writes in *De la littérature*, "were able to depict the passion of self-reflection, the passion which can judge . . . its own action, even when it is unable to control it (Il n'y a que Rousseau (et Goethe) qui aient su peindre la passion réfléchis-sante, la passion qui se juge elle-même . . . sans pouvoir se dompter)."[3] Whenever Madame de Staël achieves a similar lucidity with respect to her own passions, it is impossible to say whether she refers to herself or to Rousseau. Rousseau and her own self act in a perfectly interchangeable manner, as if the one could substitute for the other without influencing in the least the content of the truth of which they are the source. She can forget, find relief from, the relentlessly driving power of aberration that dominates her existence in this identification with a consciousness that is certainly not that of the empiri-cal Rousseau—of whom she has neither knowledge nor understanding—but that of the voice that speaks to her through the language of the *Nouvelle Heloïse*.

Another example, closer to home, is that of Hazlitt. Hazlitt was temperamentally as remote from Rousseau as can be; we know of his dislike for solitude, of his gregarious sympathy for others, his preference for the spectacle and animation of the city, his passion for the theater, for actors, for museums, his contempt for nature and Wordsworthian rural bliss—all in all, a person much closer to Diderot and the spirit of the *En-cyclopédie* than to Rousseau. And it seems indeed to be by dif-ferentiation from his own nature that Hazlitt was one of the very few to see the affinity between Rousseau and Words-worth, and to locate this affinity in their comparable self-centeredness: "both create an interest out of nothing, or rather out of their own feelings; both weave numberless recollections into one sentiment; both wind their own being round what-ever object occurs to them."[4] In Hazlitt's literary typology, this kind of imagination would certainly stand at the antipodes of his own, and we would therefore expect him to talk about Rousseau with considerable detachment, as from the outside. This is indeed how he begins his article "On the Character of Rousseau," speaking perceptively but distantly about his author. But as the essay progresses, the tone undergoes a curiously revealing change. Hazlitt starts to speak about the *Confessions* and he singles out the passages that pleased him most: with unfailing discernment, he picks out the passages that are the most intimate, the most inward in the text, the closest to reverie and to self-centered states of consciousness—the most typical, in other words, of the literary temper this Shakespearian critic would consider overegotistical. But it doesn't take Hazlitt long to fall under the spell, and before we know it, he is no longer talking about the *Confessions*, but reminiscing, in a purely Rousseau-like fashion, about the past moment when, in the act of reading Rousseau, he could forget the presence of his own actual identity and lose himself in dreamlike moods of impersonal recollection. "We spent two whole years in reading these two works [the *Confessions* and *Julie*] and (gentle reader, it was when we were young) in shedding tears over them. . . . They were the happiest years of our life. We may well say of them, sweet is the dew of their memory and pleasant the balm of their recollection! There are, indeed, impressions which neither time nor circumstances can efface" ("Rousseau" 91). This last sentence is a near literal quotation of Rousseau: "Dans les situations diverses où je me suis trouvé, quelques uns ont été marqués par un tel sentiment de bien être, qu'en les remémorant j'en suis affecté comme si j'y étais encore. [Of the diverse situations in which I found myself, some were marked with such a feeling of well-being that upon recollecting them I am affected as if I were still there]."[5] But the chosen circumstance, the perfect moment is precisely the one at which Hazlitt, by reading Rousseau, has his own consciousness transformed into Rousseau's to such an extent that it becomes hardly possible to distinguish between them. And it is in this state that Hazlitt's critical insight into Rousseau is indeed so astute that he could write, about the author of *Julie*, some of the most perceptive sentences in his entire work—sentences that transcend the idiosyncracies of his own likes and dislikes and reach toward true generality.

The same man who was capable of awakening such insight into others, an insight directed toward him as well as toward themselves, also caused many of his readers to misunderstand him as radically as anyone can be misunderstood. This, despite the clarity of his style and a remarkable inner consistency of his thought that even some of his most sympathetic contemporary critics still refuse to grant him. Critical statements about Rousseau have a recurrent, obsessive way of stating the precise opposite of what he himself asserted with a minimum of ambivalence. Schiller reproached him for having underestimated man's power to change himself, when Rousseau had made this very power the basis of his social and political thought. Goethe accused him of confusing art and life in a text (*Pygmalion*) which, as we shall see in a moment, is one of the clearest statements about the need to keep them rigorously apart. Generations have considered and continue to consider Rousseau as an exponent of a naturalistic primitivism which, for him, is repeatedly stressed to be the most dangerous temptation to which man can succumb. All he stated to be error has been laid on his doorstep as if he were its advocate, and what he holds up as true is forgotten, or restated less well as a criticism of its originator. If, as in our Girard pattern, this kind of paradox is indeed revelatory of a proximity to origin, then Rousseau must be very close to the source indeed.

This makes of him, of course, a test case for all critical examination. We saw how Mme de Staël's or Hazlitt's most lucid statements about their own selves were also critical statements about Rousseau, statements by which they expressed their understanding and interpretation of Rousseau's own literary language. Critical insight seems to occur at the moment when the consciousness of the reader and that of the writer merge to become a single Self that transcends the two empirical selves that confront each other. This encounter forces the reader to leave behind his own everyday self, as it exists at this particular moment of his history, to reestablish contact with the forgotten origin of this self, and to gauge the degree of conformity he has maintained with this origin. Rousseau's *Confessions*, writes Hazlitt, "relate[s] entirely to himself; and no one was ever so much at home on this subject as he was. From the strong hold which they had taken of his mind, he makes us enter into his feelings as if they had been our own, and we seem to remember every incident and circumstance of his life as if it had happened to ourselves. We are never tired of this work, for it everywhere presents us with pictures which we can fancy to be counterparts of our own existence" ("Rousseau" 90). Hazlitt is careful to stress that this identification is imaginary, not literal, an act of the fancy and of the mind, by which the mind returns to the source of its own self-awareness.

This process of return to the source, through the mediation of a subject that has itself risen above its empirical status, strikes us as the best possible description of the critical process. Hence the particular, exemplary importance of Rousseau for literary criticism up to the present day. He is a test case. He demands a method that is a balanced combination of genuine subjectivity and rigor—that is, a method that does not, on the one hand, allow false claims of historical or philological objectivity to stand in the way of the highly subjective process of self-forgetting and self-remembering that we encountered in Hazlitt's text, nor allow, on the other hand, the empirical personality of the critic to infringe upon an understanding that can only originate in the author's voice, considered to be the exclusive source of this understanding. There is some poetic justice, from a Rousseauistic point of view, in the fact that a contemporary trend that dreams of a criticism ideally able to live up to these demands is being referred to, somewhat misleadingly, as the Geneva school of criticism. Rousseau has indeed played an important part in the work of such critics as Marcel Raymond and Georges Poulet, who are associated with this trend; in their picture of French literary history Rousseau occupies perhaps a more pivotal position than even they (especially Poulet) would be willing to grant him. On the other hand, any suggestion that, among these critics, a uniform method is to be found that could in turn be applied by others to a variety of topics (be it Rousseau, romanticism or any other literary topic) is misleading. The main merit of this group (if group it is) is precisely their awareness that method is the result, and not the tool, of understanding and that therefore the task of inventing a critical method is an endless project that each of us has to begin all over again, each time in his own terms. If this is what the Geneva critics stand for (in contradistinction to the structuralists, for instance, whose claims to objective knowledge allow them to teach a well-defined and authoritative body of subject matter and terminology), then I hope that we can all call ourselves Geneva critics. But it commits us to little more than sharing with them an initial attitude toward literature of disinterested and infinitely attentive expectation.

And as if it were necessary to demonstrate my independence from this group, I propose to use a text of one of their most distinguished representatives in somewhat the same manner I used René Girard's essay last time. Jean Starobinski's essay on Rousseau, written after his masterful full-length study of this author entitled *La Transparence et l'obstacle*[6] will serve as a critical mediator to approach the problem of the self in Rousseau. For this is indeed the problem we were describing when we spoke of the curious relationship that develops between Rousseau's language and the reader; it reflects an initial relationship that must exist, in Rousseau's own consciousness, between himself as an empirical subject and another entity, who still bears his name but who appears in the works. That Rousseau was eminently aware of this duplication within himself is clear from the numerous texts in which he has dramatized this very process. He used the device of the dramatic dialogue, which we find for instance in Diderot's *Neveu de Rameau*, in various places (such as the preface to the *Nouvelle Heloïse* and parts of *Emile*), but he pushed it the furthest in the so-called *Dialogues* (a text that follows the *Confessions*), in which the division is hypostatized into two actual, autonomous characters who confront each other in discussion about a common subject: themselves. Both are emanations of the same original self, called Rousseau and Jean-Jacques, respectively, and stand in judgment of each other. But the same relationship is present, with fewer overtones of paranoia and bad conscience, in earlier texts such as *Pygmalion* (which dates from 1762, after the *Nouvelle Heloïse*, but before the confessional writings), where we have a simpler confrontation between the artist and his work, dramatized in terms of problems of selfhood. Such a text will allow us to state in greater detail the relationship between empirical and poetic self that we consider constitutive of romanticism.

Starobinski's analysis, or description, of Rousseau, in conformity with the phenomenological leanings of much recent French criticism after du Bos, Sartre, and Bachelard, takes on the form of a description, not of particular works, but of a consciousness. It uses the works as the linguistic signs of an intentionality that can be recaptured by a correct interpretation of these signs. Because the critical reader knows this work as a panoramic totality and is able to detect connections and structures that the author, engaged in the process of elaborating the work, cannot always perceive, he is able to round off the picture of the trajectory of this consciousness as it progressed through the work, and present the writer "tel qu'en Lui-même enfin l'éternité le change [such as into Himself at last eternity changes him]."[7] This attempt is, in itself, altogether legitimate and corresponds to a need for totalization that is present at all times in the work itself. It allows a learned and sensitive critic such as Starobinski to organize a sequence of developments that is infinitely more informative and less arbitrary than a mere chronological enumeration of the positivistic type. For the ordering principle by means of which the critic organizes his narrative (and such essays have indeed a narrative structure, as we speak of historical narrative) is derived, as rigorously as possible, from the ordering principle explicitly or implicitly stated in the work itself. It is, moreover, an organization that is purely heuristic and at no moment claims to account for things as they actually happened; Starobinski, unlike [Raymond] and, at times, Poulet, is persistently careful at not letting his tentative point of view, which is there solely for the sake of continuous exposition, take over, so to speak, and substitute itself for the writer's. He can therefore, in the space of remarkably few pages and with great economy of philological and historical means, offer a great amount of insight, not only into Rousseau's main themes but into the manner in which they are articulated and interconnected. The central tensions that exist in the work (tension between origin—in a state of nature—and progression toward a state of full consciousness, tension between the mechanical passivity of natural matter and the constitutive, dynamic power of the imagination; tension within the imagination itself between the nothingness of its substance and the absolute claim made for fiction as the main depository of being; moral tension between a guilt caused by persistent bad faith and deceit and the claim to exemplary self-knowledge) all these tensions are shown to have a consistent pattern, rooted in Rousseau's psyche or affectivity.

The problem is best summarized in Rousseau's ambiguous position toward the act of reflection: according to Starobinski, Rousseau is never willing to enter into the dialectical process of inwardness and objectivity that is involved in a genuine process of self-discovery, as we would have, for instance, in Hegel's *Phenomenology of the Spirit*. He alternates instead, without mediation, between the two extreme antithetical poles of this process. He either considers himself as pure object, as a totally opaque entity that lies outside himself and that resists all attempt at understanding from the inside: this entity is pure *obstacle* to the light of consciousness and can therefore only be passively imitated, reproduced in terms of its material appearances as a camera reproduces a thing. Or, at the other pole, he coincides with his own consciousness with unmediated abandon, achieving a total continuity, a perfect transparency between his natural self and the self that tries to observe and interpret its own being. "Rousseau," writes Starobinski, "seems most of all to want to convince us that he was able to reach the truth without exposing himself to the dangers of reflection. We see him finding refuge before or beyond the domain of reflective thought: at times, he claims to be entirely separated from his own existence, pushing the reflexive disjunction (*dédoublement*) to the point where the reflected image would become, for the reflecting consciousness, an objective figure, kept at a distance and observable as from the outside; at other moments, he claims to be unable to depart from the undivided unity of unreflected feeling ("Péril" 166).

If this is granted, then the fundamental incoherence of Rousseau, on the level of his philosophical and moral ideas, necessarily follows. Leaving temporarily the subjective, critical point of view that he adopted at the outset of his study, Starobinski also considers Rousseau from the point of view of the intellectual historian and discusses his place in the history of eighteenth-century theories of consciousness, starting with Locke. And he finds here the same discrepancy that he detected in Rousseau's own consciousness with regard to reflection. On the one hand, Rousseau's naturalism remains materialistic, asserts a passive continuity between the biological and the superstructural (moral and social) pattern of human needs; on the other hand, the claim to unmediated contact with Being through an act of pure feeling stresses a purely transcendental, prereflexive intuition centered no longer in a consciousness but directly in Being, or rather in the perfectly transparent identification between them. Between the two attitudes, there is no synthesis possible, merely oscillation. In this view, one can explain Blake's contempt for the naturalistic aspect of Rousseau's "religion naturelle" as well as Babbitt's contempt for him as a mythical egomaniac. What one cannot explain, however, is the particular lucidity of Rousseau that attracted Kant, Hölderlin, and a long, persistent tradition of nineteenth- and twentieth-century writers and thinkers.

It is not difficult to see how Starobinski reaches his negative diagnosis about Rousseau and reflection. The claim to self-transparency made at times by Rousseau is indeed not the result of mere reflection, in the sense of an observation patterned after an object-subject relationship, but of another activity of the mind more closely akin to what we call imagination; Rousseau's own term for it is primarily that of *fiction*. This faculty allows not only for such philosophical operations as the fictional reconstruction of originary states—as in the state of nature in the *Discourse on Inequality*, or the birth of language in the *Essay on the Origin of Language*—but also for confessional operations such as the reconstruction of memories in the *Confessions* or the *Rêveries*, or the aesthetic operation of inventing entirely fictional worlds, as in *Julie*. The problem, therefore, is that of the relationship that exists between the self that makes use of this fiction-engendering faculty and the self that lives in the world of material and pragmatic substances. The manner in which Starobinski, in the first part of this essay, describes the origin of imagination in Rousseau leaves no doubt as to his view: for him, the imaginary function originates in the short-comings of the pragmatic subject and in attempts either to remedy these shortcomings or, more frequently, to shield it from a reflection that it might very well not be able to face. At any rate, the imagination comes into being *for the benefit of* a pragmatic self which *uses* it at once for its own empirical pur-poses. This assumption is built into Starobinski's language, which is that of the observer eager to catch the moment at which his patient reveals the flaw that his false consciousness is trying to hide; the intent of his analysis is to seize the precise instant at which Rousseau's consciousness begins to *use* its imaginative insights to its own advantage. He gives us, for instance, a very shrewd and subtle description of the prefer-ence, in Rousseau's characters as well as in himself, for the fictional contemplation of beloved objects over their actual sex-ual possession. "If there is originally something of the voyeur in St. Preux (and in Rousseau)," he writes, "he quickly be-comes the spectator of his own visions" ("Péril" 115)—in itself an excellent description of the aesthetic consciousness as self-reflective. But this contemplation, Starobinski goes on to say, does not exist for its own sake, but serves the empirical pur-poses of Rousseau. It allows him, in particular, to conceal the shameful, guilty intent, the perversity of the original passion: "The aggression of the voyeur becomes an innocent reverie. There is a double advantage to this: on the one hand, the concupiscent look, which can no longer be caught in the act, is protected against all punishment; on the other hand, the in-ward spectacle can now freely indulge in a luxury of intimate details, remembered and invented. All the more since Rous-seau, as we know, attributes a greater intensity to the mental image than to the sensory impression" ("Péril" 115).

We have then, in Starobinski, a pervadingly *interested* view of the origin of Rousseau's imagination. It leads indeed to a disjunction of the original self, but the new self that becomes the center of the fiction is not really autonomous and credita-ble. It exists merely for the sake of the former self, to protect it from the censure of others, or from its own guilt. Art is a fetishistic, substitutive activity that replaces an unavowable desire by a pseudoinnocent but, in fact, even more self-indulgent imaginary gratification. And this erotic fetishism "is the product of a disjunction, of a *dédoublement* forced upon us by a feeling of guilt: the unreachable object of desire is not profanely assaulted in the flesh, and moreover, the desire can satisfy itself on the symbolic substitute of the desired person" ("Péril" 116). The example should suffice to indicate Starobinski's strategy. He adopts a point of view not too different from that of the analyst toward his patient, assuming a possibility of deciphering, by means of the latter's language, states of consciousness of which the patient himself refuses to be fully aware. He does so with no hostile intention whatever, granting entirely that the source of information resides in the writer himself and that the clarity with which he confronts his own case becomes aesthetically admirable by the very subtlety of its inherent bad faith.

That Rousseau, perhaps even more than other writers, used his imagination at times in this fashion is certainly true. But it is misleading to derive from there that the original impulse of the imagination and the actual content of the statement that it makes are necessarily to be explained in these terms. The result, of course, is that Rousseau's claim to self-transparency is entirely discredited and that his system becomes a naturalistic empiricism disguised in the misleading appearance of a pseudoidealism. The oscillation is not even a true polarity, but merely a succession of flights from self-knowledge. There is no real disjunction, since it is in fact always only the empirical self who governs the activity of the imagination for its own purposes. To clinch his argument and show that Rousseau's subjectivity is in fact a passive adherence to the demands of his mystified self, Starobinski quotes a very important passage from the *Confessions* in which Rousseau describes the particular point of view used in this work: "By abandoning myself simultaneously to the memory of the impression I received and to the present sentiment, I will paint the state of my soul in a double perspective (*je peindrai doublement l'état de mon âme*), namely at the moment when the event happened to me and at the moment I described it (*Confessions*, in *Oeuvres* 1:1154; quoted in "Péril" 167).

This is a very curious quotation to select as an illustration of what Starobinski describes, in his comment introducing the quotation, as "a spontaneity without control" or "emotion invad[ing] him in an unpredictable and chaotic manner" ("Péril" 167). For, certainly, Rousseau's description of a double temporal perspective is much closer to Wordsworth's poetry "tak[ing] its origin from emotion recollected in tranquillity"[8] than to the total passivity suggested by the Geneva critic. If the description of the event has to take in the temporal distance that Rousseau suggests, then it will necessarily be mediated by a consciousness that has understood and interpreted the original emotion: it will never pretend to render this emotion in its unmediated intensity. An element of distance, of disinterestedness is introduced from the start, and the confessional statement is admittedly fictionalized, changed by an imaginative act of writing, which prevents it from coinciding entirely with itself. It could be shown that the *Confessions* comes indeed into its own as the imaginative work of literature that seduced Hazlitt as long as it maintains the distance of this double perspective, but that it turns at times into a near-paranoid document of self-justification when the distance is allowed to disappear, taking the literary status of the work along. Starobinski's reading no longer seems to coincide with the text. We can take this as a sure sign that a return to the text is indeed necessary if we want to understand the manner in which Rousseau understood himself.

Starobinski's contention about the pragmatic and psychological origin of Rousseau's imagination should at least be weighed against Rousseau's own statements on this point. There are numerous places in the work that treat explicitly this very problem and dramatize the relationship between author and work in considerable detail. Already in his first book on Rousseau, Starobinski had pointed to the importance of the brief lyrical scene entitled *Pygmalion*, which dates from 1762, and related this text to the very early play *Narcisse* and to the preface that Rousseau wrote for *Narcisse* in 1753, after the play had been publicly performed. *Pygmalion* is indeed a key text for our problem. It was written in the interval that separates the philosophical and literary part of Rousseau's work, culminating in the *Nouvelle Heloïse* (1761), from the confessional part (*Confessions, Dialogues* and *Rêveries*), which begins in 1766. In the figure of the sculptor Pygmalion contemplating his handiwork, Galathea, we thus have a clear equivalence of Rousseau reflecting on the feelings that develop between the author of *Julie* and the fictional character he has invented in that work. And the preface to *Narcisse* marks the beginning point of the creative period on which *Pygmalion* looks back, since it immediately precedes the productive years during which Rousseau completed the main bulk of his work: the *Social Contract, Emile,* and *Julie.* We can capture then, in these texts, Rousseau's prospective as well as his retrospective meditation on his relationship to the fictional self that gets expressed in the work, and on the nature of the relationship that develops toward this self.

The character at the center of the very early play, *Narcisse*—which Rousseau claims to have written when he was only eighteen years old (he is probably lying)—is not an artistic type, not even an anticipation of such a type. Instead, he is the classical comic figure of the man mystified by vanity to the point of distorting reality entirely. The comic symbol of this mystification is that of Narcisse falling in love with his own portrait, disguised just enough to make his image appear as that of a woman. Narcisse's vanity is such that he is at once mystified in all possible ways by the portrait: first, in believing that a woman who leaves her portrait in his room can only do so because she is madly in love with him; second, in failing to notice what everyone else notices at once, namely that the portrait represents his own image; and third, in mistaking his own feeling of delight in being thus pursued for love directed toward the pursuer. The self-interest of Narcisse is such, his vanity (*amour-propre* in Rousseau's terminology) so strong, that he cannot identify the portrait as his own, just because he stands to gain everything from believing it is somebody else. He is fascinated by his image to the point of complete blindness toward his own feelings; his genuine love for an actual other person, the girl he is about to marry at the beginning of the play, is temporarily forgotten for a self-fascination which is merely an objectified projection, an acting out, of the false consciousness that has always inhabited him. Vanity is a

false, mystifying consciousness because it reduces any outward event to the interested function of serving the designs of
the original self. This self constantly needs others to reassure it
about its quality and beauty: therefore, it goes so far as to
mistake itself for another, just to have an echoing voice that
will confirm what it wants to hear. Thus is Narcissus mystified
in the first part of the Ovid myth until the point where he
recognizes that the image he loves is his own: ["Iste ego sum:
sensi, nec me mea fallit imago; uror amore mei: flammas
moveoque feroque (Oh, I am he! I have felt it, I know now my
own image. I burn with love of my own self; I both kindle the
flames and suffer them").][9] But Rousseau's Narcisse never gets
that far, and he has to be demystified by the concerted efforts
of others and brought back to his senses by the natural love
which Rousseau benevolently grants him for the sake of a comic dénouement.

The interest of the play, from our point of view, is that the
only relationship that can develop between Narcisse and the
portrait is one of mutual mystification. The portrait has been
made for that specific purpose, and he is all too willing to let it
fulfill its function. The self here never really becomes another,
but remains all too much its own interested self. The portrait is
not a genuine work of art, and Narcissus is the opposite of an
artist; it takes a consciousness entirely incapable of disinterested judgment to be thus confused. Although an artifact
appears in the play (the portrait), it can be said that the relationship between Narcisse and the portrait is the one furthest
removed from the relationship that should exist between the
artist and his creation. Yet because it is involved with problems
of self-reflection, the play introduces the main elements that
will enter into the complex dialectical relationships of *Pygmalion* (of which several can be found as far back as in the Ovid
text on Narcissus): the dialectic of self and other in the act of
reflection, the dialectic of self-love and desire, the question of
the ontological status of the reflected image. In *Narcisse*, this
image has neither substance nor identity, and it can be thrown
away as the nothing that it is after it has served its function.

It is still the problem of *amour-propre*, of vanity, that is up-
permost in Rousseau's mind when he writes a preface for the

same little play many years later, after he has achieved literary fame as the author of the *First Discourse*. But here the vanity is no longer about physical appearance, but about the conceit of the man of letters. With a characteristic mixture of lucidity and bad faith, Rousseau shows how the insight into human nature achieved by authors or philosophers, far from adding to their wisdom or to that of society, leads them to an attitude of contemptuous self-isolation. As part of a culture, of a corrupt civilization, art is used only for reasons of deceit or, at the very best, to soften the harshness of the utter estrangement that self-love has created between all men. No writer can write with a good conscience in this situation, and Rousseau is hard put to give any reason why he should write at all. There are, however, he writes "some sublime geniuses who can penetrate beyond the veils that hide truth, some privileged souls capable of resisting the stupidity of vanity, the baseness of jealousy, and the other passions engendered by a taste for literature" (preface to *Narcisse*, in *Oeuvres* 2:970; de Man's translation). The only reason for writing is to put oneself to the test in the solitude of one's own consciousness: "It is only in observing myself [in the act of writing—PdM] that I can judge if I can count myself among the small group. . . . I needed this test to bring the knowledge of my own self to completion" (2:973). Clearly, there is a great deal of apparent conceit in this very assertion, but next to a genuine insight into the disinterested character of the work of art—for Rousseau clearly recognizes that the authenticity of an aesthetic consciousness is defined by the ability of the self *not* to use the product of its aesthetic activity for its own gratification. In terms of Starobinski's description of Rousseau's imagination, he would certainly not have withstood this test, and by Rousseau's own definition, the products of his productive years would not have been considered genuine art.

The play *Pygmalion*, however, looking back upon the past creation of *Julie*, claims full artistic success for the work: the beauty of Pygmalion's handiwork is flawless, and the fact that it actually comes to life at the end of the scene symbolizes the full authenticity of the fictional figure. Pygmalion's attitude toward her is therefore to be considered exemplary of the proper relationship between himself and the created statue.

Seen from Pygmalion's point of view (which is, it must be remembered, that of the successful, authentic artist considered as an empirical person), this relationship is anything but a clear and tranquil one. Pygmalion is not only in a persistent state of frantic excitement, but he keeps vacillating between contradictory attitudes of which several are clearly shown to be in error. This explains, be it said in passing, why this text lends itself so well from Goethe on down to the present, to being misused: many of the statements that occur in it, highly quotable in themselves, are supposed to be said in error; removed from the dramatic context, which gives at least some orientation as to whether they are meant to be statements of truth or of error, they allow for an easy distortion of Rousseau's intent. Nor does Pygmalion progress simply, in the course of the development, from error to truth. In his last statement, "Oui, cher et charmant objet [: oui, digne chef d'oeuvre de mes mains, de mon coeur et des Dieux . . . C'est toi, c'est toi seule: je t'ai donné tout mon être; je ne vivrai plus que par toi (Yes, lovely and beloved object: yes, worthy masterpiece of my hands, my heart and the Gods. . . It is you, you alone: I have given you my whole being; from now on I shall only live through you)"] (2.1231),[10] he is again as mystified as he was at the start of the scene, though the nature of his mystification is not like that of Narcisse in the early play. The progression has taken place, not in Pygmalion, but in the figure of Galathea, who, at the end of the scene, has not only come to life but has been able to define the nature of her own selfhood in relation to herself, to Pygmalion, and to the natural world. And a similar progression has taken place in us as readers, who are now able to understand the entire complex relationship that exists between the three entities (the artist, the live sculpture, and the piece of marble); this progression is a correlative of a progression that has taken place in Rousseau himself as the author of the play, who controls the patterns of truth and error, of insight and blindness, that organize the action. Thus the vacillations of Pygmalion are not meaningless, mere repetitions that leave things exactly as they were: certain truths and falsehoods are undoubtedly revealed by the action seen as a whole, even if they do not appear explicitly in the character of Pygmalion himself.

It is clear, for instance, from the first movement, the first exchange in the play, that Pygmalion is in error when his attitude toward the work is one of blind admiration: "Vanité, faiblesse humaine," he exclaims, "je ne puis me lasser d'admirer mon ouvrage; je m'enivre d'amour propre, je m'adore dans ce que j'ai fait [Vanity, human frailty! I can never tire of admiring my work; I am drunk with self-love; I worship myself in what I have made]" (2:1226). This admiration leads him to cover the statue with the veil that symbolizes his distance from its true significance; it stifles and paralyzes him in a fascination that is not too different from that of Narcisse contemplating his counterfeit image. The belief that it is his own, actual self that has created the work and that, therefore, in prostrating himself before its near-divine beauty he is worshiping his own glorious talent, is presented as ridiculous, a notion that has to be cleared away as the falsest possible justification for the artistic project. Pygmalion progresses beyond it when he says: "Eh, je ne l'ai point encore examinée, je n'ai fait jusqu'ici que l'admirer (I have never really looked at it; all I have done is admire it till now)" (2:1226). The distance involved in "examiner" as opposed to "admirer" is a first step toward insight into her true nature.

In the next episode, it is no longer pseudodivine admiration that governs his feeling toward his work but openly sexual desire. The gestures with which he approaches her clearly mimic, in somewhat painful detail (for the play *Pygmalion* itself, interesting as it is, is certainly not a highly successful work of art), sexual aggression: "Pygmalion! Je vois un défaut. [Ce vêtement couvre trop le nu; il faut l'échancrer davantage; les charmes qu'il recele doivent être mieux annoncés] (Pygmalion, I see a defect! This robe hides too much of her body; I must cut it lower; the charms it covers ought to be revealed)" (2:1226), Rousseau's treatment of sexual desire as an analogon for the type of relationship between artist and work is complex and subtle, very distinct from the one-sided feeling of guilt and shame that Starobinski attributes to him. When Pygmalion realizes the nature of his feeling, recognizes it to be sexual desire, he is at first indeed ashamed of himself. To have claimed that one was worshiping a goddess and to discover that this worship was in fact sexual desire is, at least to some extent, to have made a fool of oneself: "Je n'ose voir dans mon coeur: j'aurais trop à m'en indigner. . . . Voilà donc la noble passion qui m'égare! (I dare not look into my heart: I would be too shocked by what I found there. . . . This then is the noble passion that has brought me to such a pass!)" (2:1227), etc. But Rousseau has Pygmalion recover almost at once from this self-reproach and shame: "Non, je n'ai point perdu le sens; non, je n'extravague point, non, je ne me reproche rien (No, I have not lost my mind; I am not raving; I have no cause for self-reproach)" (2:1227), and what follows is to be taken as a true understanding of the way in which a poetic consciousness has at least some affinity with the structure of desire.

To the extent that desire is a movement of consciousness toward something that it has lost, toward something that it wants to possess in order to be complete, its pattern is truly aesthetic. The desire of an aesthetic consciousness is oriented toward its authenticity, which it lost in the fallen world of empirical experience. It experiences this desire as a lack, as a shortcoming in itself, which it tries to remedy. There is nothing wrong about this, nothing that would warrant feelings of guilt. The error is to believe that the possession of a particular person could be sufficient to fill a void that does not exist on an interpersonal but on an ontological level. The erotic mode is not contrary to the pattern of authentic consciousness, it is merely inadequate, it does not go far enough. To give in to the sensuous aspects of beauty is never, in Rousseau, a weakness to be punished by guilt. His guilt does not originate in a tension between needs that are of the senses and conflicting needs that could be said to be of the soul, or of the mind. Guilt always takes for him the form of a guilt about truth and falsehood, about sincerity and bad faith—not the kind of sexual guilt that Starobinski attributes to him. Body and soul are for him harmoniously united in the symbolical figure of the "beautiful soul," and there is no reason to renounce the desire that such a figure can inspire. Any particular incarnation of such a "beautiful soul" in an actual person, however, only exists as a prefiguration of an imaginary entity, and the possession of this person, sexually or otherwise, can never begin to satisfy a desire that transcends it.

For the desire is not the result of a dualism, of a body and soul or a subject-object relationship. Instead, it is a temporal predicament, the feeling of loss experienced at being removed from the source of one's own being. The text of *Pygmalion* makes clear that this source is not located in the self of the artist, but that it exists in the work that he has created: "Quels traits de feu semblent sortir de cet objet pour embraser mes sens, et retourner avec mon âme à leur source! [What lines of fire seem to emanate from this object in order to enflame my senses and return with my soul to their source—PdM]" (2:1228); the movement clearly originates in the work and returns to the work after having been reflected into Pygmalion's consciousness. The temptation arises, then, to join at all costs this source of truth from which one feels so painfully separated—but since the source exists outside the empirical self, such a union would imply the disappearance of the self, namely death. "Je crois, dans mon délire, pouvoir m'élancer hors de moi; je crois pouvoir lui donner ma vie et l'animer de mon âme. Ah! que Pygmalion meure pour vivre dans Galathée! (In my delirium I believe that I can escape outside myself; I think that I can give her my life, and animate her with my soul. Ah! that Pygmalion would die so that he might live in Galathea!)" (2:1228). The moment is an apocalyptic one, where unity is sought as the result of an absolute and future negation. It also corresponds to the moments of total, unmediated coincidence that Starobinski finds at the two endpoints of Rousseau's consciousness: the entire coincidence with nature or the entire coincidence with the self, points at which there is no distance between the consciousness and its intent. In this text, however, this moment only appears as a momentary temptation which is at once overcome: "Que dis-je, o ciel! Si j'étais elle, je ne la verrais pas, je ne serais pas celui qui l'aime! Non, que ma Galathée vive et que je ne sois pas elle. Ah! que je sois toujours un autre, pour vouloir toujours être elle, pour la voir, pour l'aimer, pour en être aimé. (Heavens! What am I saying! If I were she, I would no longer see her, I would not be the one who loved her! No, I would that my Galathea lived and that I were not she. Ah, let me always be another that I may forever desire to be she, that I may see her, that I may love her, that I may be loved by her" (2:1228). This is as close as Pygmalion will ever be allowed to come to the truth in the course of this text, as close indeed as any particular consciousness, even the most successfully creative one, ever can come. It [Pygmalion's consciousness] remains caught in the paradoxical dialectic of selfhood and otherness, apparent in the linguistic complexity of the sentence, which echoes a complexity very similar to what was already present in Ovid's Narcissus scene: "Que je sois toujours un autre pour vouloir toujours être elle." The paradox names as rigorously as possible the ambiguous nature of reflection and defines the nature of the aesthetic consciousness, contrary to Starobinski's assertion, as a reflective one. On the one hand, the figure of Galathée exists as a self; when she finally comes alive, in the last episode of the play, the first and only thing she can say is indeed "Moi"—I am a self (2:1230). And she distinguishes her mode of existence at once from that of natural objects, by touching a piece of marble and exclaiming: "Ce n'est plus moi (This is no longer I)" (2:1230). She exists, then, as an autonomous consciousness, distinct from the self identity that exists in nature, originating in the *cogito* of her awareness of herself as a consciousness. In this respect, she is indeed like Pygmalion, who can echo her "Moi" by a more anxious *"moi!"* which expresses his longing for entire identification.

But, on the other hand, and unlike Pygmalion, she exists *only* as an authentic consciousness, without any of the fallen and empirical attributes that make Pygmalion into an actual person. From an empirical point of view, she is nothing, and as this awareness grows, the word "rien" indeed appears more and more crucially in the text. The mystified Pygmalion exclaims, "Déesse de la beauté, épargne cet affront à la nature, qu'un si parfait modèle soit l'image de ce qui n'est pas (Goddess of beauty, do not insult nature by permitting such a perfect model to be the reflection of what is not)" (2:1229)— unaware of the fact that, at a moment when he is in error, he is stating the truth in a negative mode. When he comes back to his senses, he can restate the same insight more positively: "Hélas! en l'état où je suis on invoque tout, et rien ne nous écoute (In my state, alas, one invokes everything, and nothing listens)" (2:1229). We will have the opportunity to come back to the importance of this "rien" in the romantic consciousness in subsequent lectures. Here it refers, among other things, to the imaginary nature of the work that exists for us as a reflected source, beyond our grasp, lost in a past from which we are separated or away in a future that we cannot reach. To identify with this "rien," with this nothingness, is impossible, a death by mystification—a giving in to a hope that must be renounced since it is misleading. "L'espoir qui nous abuse est plus insensé que le désir (The hope which leads us on is more unreasonable than the desire itself)" (2:1229), says Pygmalion, speaking at this moment for Rousseau.

At no point is Pygmalion deeper in error, in this text, than at the moment when he thinks of Galathea as Venus, as a goddess of plenitude and stability "par qui tout se conserve et se reproduit sans cesse (through whom all things are conceived and endlessly reproduced)" (2:1228). This would be the form of naturalistic primitivism so frequently equated with Rousseau and with a certain type of romanticism even by as enlightened a contemporary critic as Starobinski. Rousseau's own immediate successors frequently made the same mistake, and the kind of language we hear in statements such as these: "L'ordre est troublé, la nature est outragée; rends leur empire à ses lois, rétablis son cours bienfaisant et verse également ta divine influence (Order is disturbed, Nature is outraged; restore its laws to their rightful sovereignty, reestablish its beneficial course, and distribute your divine influence again in equal measure)" (2:1228) will be heard in Herder, in Bernardin de Saint-Pierre, still in the early Chateaubriand, often with reference to Rousseau. *Pygmalion* is particularly clear evidence of the fact that, for Rousseau, this kind of naturalism, of belief in the harmonious economy of natural processes, is an aberration that spells death to an individual and to societies. For fallen man, there is no way back to a natural paradise, and art least of all pretends to be such a way. Nor can it be said of art that it achieves the ultimate triumph of consciousness by an act of imagination that would, in its turn, recapture the fullness of Being. At the end of the play, in a scene [prefiguring] the episode in the *Confessions* with Mme Basile from which Starobinski takes off, Galathée puts her hand on Pygmalion's head, sighs, and says: "Encore moi (This too is I)" (2:1231). This sigh, comparable to Alkmene's ambiguous "Ach!" at the end of Kleist's play *Amphitryon*, sets the mood of ironic renunciation that characterizes, for Rousseau, the reflective project of the artist. His entire effort has been directed toward freeing himself, by reflection, from the burden of his own empirical contingency. In his attempt, he has indeed transcended his actual self into a language, a work that now exists outside himself. The future project announced in the preface to *Narcisse* has, in a way, succeeded. But when, as he cannot help doing, he starts to reflect upon the work that he has created, he realizes that it only records his failure really to transcend his own selfhood. The work is "encore moi," the half-resigned, ironic mood of self-reflection that predominates in Rousseau and in the readers who recognize themselves in him. The romantic artist is still Narcissus, though a Narcissus who has come back alive from his trip to the other side of the mirror— perhaps what Rilke will call later, in one of his French poems, *le Narcisse exaucé*—the demystified Narcissus.

3

Patterns of Temporality in Hölderlin's
"Wie wenn am Feiertage . . ."

*T*HE OBSERVATIONS that have been made up till now would tend to suggest that romantic literature appears primarily as a dialectic between an empirical and an ideal subject, and that it dramatizes a persistent conflict between fiction and reality. This is not the case. The empirical element, in the two preceding lectures, did not stem primarily from the romantic writers but from the contemporary critics. The confrontation of the two selves, and the conflicts that result from it, is a modern rather than a romantic theme, and its importance for contemporary criticism corresponds to its predominance in twentieth-century poetry and fiction. It is a postromantic development. Even in Rousseau, perhaps the most "modern" of the romantics, such dramatized confrontations, as in *Pygmalion* or in the *Dialogues*, occur in minor works that comment on the other, major literary achievements. In these, the empirical experience is entirely subsumed in the fiction, even when the work is cast in an autobiographical mode. Starobinski's problem, whether this fiction is invented to serve the personal, social, and moral interests of the self, is left far behind, as if it mattered very little what the answer is. The writer knows the use that he and others can make of the work for their own purposes, and he cautions against it at times. But he has few illusions that he can prevent this degradation, and turns away from it toward things that matter more to him. "Tel est le néant des choses humaines qu'hors l'Etre existant par lui-même, il n'y a rien de beau que ce qui n'est pas [Such is the nothingness of human matters that outside self-sufficient Being the only beautiful thing is the one that does not exist],"[1] Rousseau has Julie say near the end of *La Nouvelle Heloïse*. This kind of insight is only allowed to those who have indeed left the problems of the empirical self behind, and the truth of the work is obscured by reintroducing them surreptitiously.

The situation is different with poets, romantic or other, who have not reached a point of self-transcendence and who base the generality and apparent impersonality of their language, not on a real *dépassement* of their empirical consciousness, but on a flight from its insights. Keats, as I see him, would be a case in point, where self-encounter and self-transcendence occur in one single, destructive moment that puts the entire strategy of the work into question.[2] The later, confessional Rousseau, is certainly not free from relapses into a similar predicament, although his prose remains curiously intermingled with the more tranquil light of the earlier wisdom. In general, it can be said that the romantics were less, not more mystified by their empirical self than we are, partly because they had fewer illusions about their impact on the practical world. Our own great demystifiers, Freud, Marx, and Nietzsche, are much more naive than their romantic predecessors, especially in their belief that the demystification can become a praxis beneficial to the personality or to the society. In most romantic writers, this belief is overcome quite soon in their development—in Rousseau certainly as early as in the *Second Discourse*, in Wordsworth in the personal and political crisis of his visit to France, in Hölderlin in a similar pattern of sentimental and political disappointments recorded in the novel *Hyperion*. It matters little whether they were themselves, as persons, able to maintain and to live with this knowledge; whatever the personal adjustment, the works grew out of it.

For the transcendence of the self occurred for them, much more consistently than for us, in their exclusive concern with *poetic* language, the medium in which the transcendence fulfilled and preserved itself. I probably could have spared you—and myself—a certain amount of distress and resistance if, instead of using the Kantian term of *a transcendental self*, I had directly spoken in terms of poetic language or even of poetic form. With this terminology, we would have felt on much more familiar terrain. Yet there is, I believe, some virtue in the distress created by speaking of poetic form in terms of a self. It helps to dispel, from the start, a fallacy that underlies much of the critical writing on romanticism: the reification of form into an object, a thing that can be described independently of its intentional structure.[3] It obliges us to be aware at once of the difficult problem of form as a consciousness, as a constitutive project that exists temporally. The idea of a consciousness that is not empirical, that exists regardless of its own gratification, that is directed toward being instead of being directed toward particular entities, is perhaps difficult to conceive—yet it is this effort that aesthetic understanding obliges us to make. Moreover, by speaking of a self that is transcendental in relation to actual experience, we guard ourselves against any suspicion of psychologism or aestheticism. The dimension of generality that is always present in a poetic statement removes the particular psychological concern that may be present from the immediate pursuit of its aims and makes it, at the very least, into an object of reflection instead of into a project of gratification. Neither can the reflection, as in aestheticism, become an end in itself, for this would let the consciousness repose tranquilly within a static self-immanence that is contradictory to its very nature.

Transcendence means that the self has to get outside its own immanence, that it has to find another entity in which it can structure its own intentionality in such a manner that it can contemplate it as a total figure, instead of being caught up in the inevitable shortsightedness of lived desire. The intention takes on the pseudo-objective aspect of a total entity, centered on a point of origin and circumscribed by an outer limit. But this entity is never allowed to remain static and self-sufficient, like a natural object, or like the perfect artifact that exists for art's sake. For it has to transcend itself anew each time it has achieved a temporary totality in the never-ending process of preserving its autonomy as a self. This is symbolized, in part, by Rousseau's image of Galathea's statue coming to life, not as a part of "this living universe" but in contradistinction to the static totality of nature. The term *form* has become so thor-

oughly reified as the basis of a formalism that ha
with the organic unity of nature or with the object
ization of the world that it can no longer be trusted
the process of totalization that takes place in the l
the romantic poets. Yet a correct reading of romai... poetry
would make it possible to restore a term that phenomenological criticism had discarded perhaps all too quickly. We will
henceforth be speaking about the poets in terms of their language, not in terms of their selves; this was, in fact, what we
had been doing all along when we phrased our disagreement
with Girard and Starobinski not in terms of a general psychological or philosophical argument but simply on the basis of
their alleged misreading of the texts.

For if language is the medium in which the aesthetic self is
constituted, then there is no reason to look beyond this language in the hypothetical regions that precede or follow its
existence as a poetic work. We are interested primarily and
exclusively in the truth of this language, much less in the
genesis that leads to it (except insofar as it is part of the truth it
asserts), less still in the subsequent empirical application of
this truth. The aesthetic self transcends the empirical to the
precise extent that it rejects as irrelevant whatever experience
is not of its language. As such, it can go much further than any
empirical act in terms of understanding, but it will remain
narrow and apparently reduced in terms of experience. The
self-centeredness for which romantic poets are so often blamed
is the outward aspect of this exclusive concentration on language. And no poetic work of the romantic period is more
exclusively language-centered in this manner than that of
Friedrich Hölderlin.

The multiplication of highly specialized critical work on
Hölderlin makes it almost impossible to speak about this poet
in an intelligible manner, even to an audience of Hölderlin
specialists. It has been possible to give a very complete survey
of the developments in German criticism from Dilthey to the
present merely in terms of Hölderlin research; a work by an
Italian historian of criticism, Alessandro Pellegrini, recently
translated in an expanded German version, does just that.[4]
The particular circumstances of the rediscovery of Hölderlin's

work at the period of the First World War, followed in turn by the discovery of a crucially important poem entitled "Friedensfeier" in 1954, have unleashed such a storm of methodological and critical debate that by now, even when (which is not always the case) the commentator is free of pedantic traits, he has to find his way in such an elaborate forest of hypotheses, contestations, cross-references, cruxes, and problems that he may seem far removed from the understanding of Hölderlin's actual poetry.[5] The philological problem, particularly arduous in the case of a poet whose entire work had remained practically unpublished, hangs heavily over Hölderlin studies, since here the close and difficult relationship between text and interpretation became concretely noticeable in specific decisions about the establishment and the presentation of the texts. On the other hand, the relevance of Hölderlin's thematic statements for our own times is so striking that it is very tempting to adopt the poet, at the exclusion of all others, as a prophetic prefiguration of our own predicament and to approach him with the uncritical awe and urgency that is reserved for oracular pronouncements. Hölderlin criticism thus becomes a somewhat unholy mixture of extreme philological pedantry with some of the most turgid, pseudoprophetic prose to be found on any literary subject. What makes matters worse is that these extremes of rigor and of fervor cannot be simply dismissed or demystified as passing aberrations: both are to some extent legitimate and necessary. The interpretation of the later Hölderlin is indeed as difficult as the interpreters make it appear; one could even say that none has been found yet who is rigorous and detailed enough for the task. And it is, on the other hand, a sufficiently important task to warrant the effort, for every progress made into the understanding of the work contributes not only to the definition of poetry as such, but brings new insight into the historical destiny of poetic consciousness, which this writer exemplified with extraordinary rigor.[6]

Appearances to the contrary, contemporary criticism of Hölderlin in Germany and abroad is still dominated by the direct or indirect impact of Heidegger, despite the fact that Heidegger's own Hölderlin studies, that go back in some cases as far as 1936 and appeared in book form in 1951,[7] have been discredited in their specific details. The textual emendations he suggested, especially in the case of the poem "Wie wenn am Feiertage . . . ," which we are using as our main text today, have nowhere been adopted, and his claim that his version had been "checked anew against the original manuscripts" was rightly dismissed as a blatant case of pseudoscientific bad faith. The political overtones of the commentaries (especially when juxtaposed with the Rectoral Address of 1933) are far from reassuring and have done the cause of Hölderlin no service. From a stylistic point of view, Heidegger's own language has come in for severe criticism, not without reason, for the manner in which it reduces the original text to a relentless philosophical discourse that bypasses the complexity and the nuances of the statement; at no point does Heidegger reveal an awareness of the expressive value of Hölderlin's highly deliberate formal structurization.

But yet, although they are philologically, historically, and stylistically discredited, Heidegger's interpretations remain of considerable methodological importance. For he remains one of the first to have reoriented the interpretation of poetry toward its real objective: instead of seeing it as a paraphrase that transposes a poetic statement into a context that is no longer poetic—for instance, into a historical, or a theological, or a psychological context—he discards, in principle, any consideration that is not aimed at an understanding of poetic language in terms of its own essence. Each poem, or every work seen as a whole, is a particular version of the understanding that a poetic consciousness possesses of its own specific and autonomous intent—or, to put it differently, each work asks the question of its own mode of being, and it is the task of the interpreter not to answer this question but to make explicit in what manner and with what degree of awareness the question is asked. The intent of poetic language is certainly not directed toward empirical insight, nor is it transcendental in the sense that it leads to a closer contact with being in general; its intent is ontological, that is, directed toward an awareness of its own particular being. In principle then, when Heidegger comes across the use of certain key terms in the work of his poet, such as *Nature* or *das Heilige* (to take examples from our text), he will not try to recapture what such words may mean in the context of the intellectual history of the later eighteenth century, or in terms of the religious experience that was prevalent at the time, but will ask instead how these terms can be understood as the signs that allow the poem to exist as it does. The poetic context within which they function as cornerstones of a linguistic structure that strives to exist as a total, monadic entity will be the main source of information for an understanding of these key terms. For it is in the interaction between these words and the total structure (or poem) within which they operate that they mutually clarify each other.

Heidegger's commentaries thus take on the form of an ontological understanding of Hölderlin's key concepts as they are seen to operate within the limits of particular poems. Because they make explicit the ontological intent (the intent at total self-understanding) that informs the poem, the commentaries are destined to bring out with greater analytic clarity what is already present and stated in the poem. They do not pretend to add anything to it. "The last, but also the most difficult step in any exegesis," says Heidegger, "takes place when all its explications must disappear before the mere presence of the poem. Standing within its own right, the poem will then in its turn cast its light directly on other poems. Therefore, we have the feeling, in rereading the poems, that we had always understood them in this manner. It is right that we should think so (Der letzte, aber auch der schwerste Schritt jeder Auslegung besteht darin, mit ihren Erläuterungen vor dem reinen Dastehen des Gedichtes zu verschwinden. Das dann im eigenen Gesetz stehende Gedicht bringt selbst unmittelbar ein Licht in die anderen Gedichte. Daher meinen wir beim wiederholenden Lesen, wir hätten die Gedichte schon immer so verstanden. Es ist gut, wenn wir das meinen)" [*Erläuterungen* 8].

In the history of German criticism (and even in a wider European context) this reorientation of literary interpretation toward an ontological understanding represents a step of major importance. It gives a much firmer foundation, rooted in the work itself, to the concept of experience (*Erlebnis*), which Dilthey had placed in the empirical person of the poet, or of the historical moment. It avoids the mythologized aestheticism that stands behind the approach of the George circle as well as the implicit, naive antihistoricism that is to be found in the topological criticism of someone like Curtius. It does allow, in principle, for the combination of a sense of form (or of totality) with an awareness that poetic language appears as the correlative of a constitutive consciousness, that it results from the activity of an autonomous subject. Neither American formalist criticism nor European phenomenological criticism has been able to give a satisfactory account of this synthesis: the former had to give up the concept of a constitutive subject, the latter that of a constituted form. This despite the fact that, in romantic poetry, the synthesis is without doubt not only implicitly achieved but also explicitly, thematically accounted for by the poetic devices that give the poems their unity (even when they may appear, on the surface, fragmentary or unfinished). It would seem (again in principle) that Heidegger's radical "ontologization" of the language of interpretation would give a better opportunity to account for the effectiveness of a poet like Hölderlin, whose significance as a conveyor of general truth, as a source of light for general anthropological insight (using the term again in the Kantian sense), is so clearly linked with the formal rigor of his control over the language of poetry

As the author of *Sein und Zeit*, Heidegger seemed particularly qualified to undertake this renewal of critical method, or to instigate others to undertake it since literary interpretation was not his own academic field. For although *Sein und Zeit* nowhere deals with literature, except for some passing references, it does contain insights that can give a more concrete direction to an ontological interpretation of texts. *Sein und Zeit*, indeed, stresses not only the privileged, determining importance of language as the main entity by means of which we determine our way of being in the world, but specifies that it is not the instrumental but the interpretative use of language that characterizes human existence, as distinct from the existence of natural entities. And this interpretative language possesses a structure that can be made explicit. This structure is in essence temporal—a particular way of structuring the three dimensions of time that is constitutive for all acts of consciousness. The main task of any ontology thus becomes the description of this temporal structurization, which will necessarily be a phenomenology of temporality (since it is the description of consciousness) as well as a phenomenology of language (since the manner in which temporality exists for our consciousness is through the mediation of language). One understands that, as the "purest" form of interpretative language, the one least contaminated by empirical instrumentality and reification, poetic language is a privileged place from which to start such a description. And conversely, one sees that an approach to poetic language that would, by a description of its temporal structure, bring out its interpretative intent, would come closest to the essence of this language, closest to accounting for what Heidegger calls "das Wesen der Dichtung." We could thus legitimately expect from the Heideggerian premises a clarifying analysis of poetic temporality, as it is seen to act within the poetic form.

Approaching Heidegger's commentaries on Hölderlin with such expectations, one is disappointed not just by the inevitable shortcomings of any method that is in the process of finding itself but in a more fundamental manner. The nature of this disappointment is worth considering because it throws light not only upon certain problems inherent in contemporary criticism but also upon the link between these problems and their origin in romanticism. We will have to confine ourselves to the example of one single text.

Because it is a poem in which "the poets" and their function are explicitly named, the fragmentary hymn that begins "Wie wenn am Feiertage, das Feld zu sehn . . ." is particularly suitable for our purposes. It is a relatively early poem, Hölderlin's first attempt, in 1799, to write a hymn in a Pindaric mode. The commentary that Heidegger gives on this text is typical of the merits and shortcomings of his method, although, in this case, the latter overshadow the former perhaps more than is usual. But we can well afford, in the case of a figure of Heidegger's stature, to forgo fairness for the sake of economy of exposition.

This poem is not, as Hölderlin poems go, particularly difficult, and since it is not my intention to give a "reading" of the text but to use it for more general considerations, I will forgo a detailed explication. Its main difficulty for the editors and interpreters of Hölderlin has to do with the concluding section. The poem comes to what seems like a very satisfactory ending in line 66, which speaks of the steadfastness with which the poets are able to endure the approach of the gods, an event which has been represented throughout by the unifying metaphor of the thunderstorm:

> bleibt in den hochherstürzenden Stürmen
> Des Gottes, wenn er nahet, das Herz doch fest.[8]

> [yet in the far-flung down-rushing storms of
> The God, when he draws near, will the heart stand fast.[9]]

This ending is not just satisfactory because it strikes a positive note, but it seems formally satisfactory to see the final statement of the poem corroborate what had been stated symbolically at the onset of the first stanza in the simile. For the poem opens, like many of Hölderlin's poems, with the description of a natural scene, a landscape that is very general in its outward aspect but very specific at capturing the inner mood of a particular moment:

> [Wie wenn am Feiertage, das Feld zu sehn
> Ein Landmann geht, des Morgens, wenn
> Aus heisser Nacht die kühlenden Blize fielen
> Die ganze Zeit und fern noch tönet der Donner,
> In sein Gestade wieder tritt der Strom,
> Und frisch der Boden grünt
> Und von des Himmels erfreuendem Reegen
> Der Weinstok trauft und glänzend
> In stiller Sonne stehn die Bäume des Haines
>
> (2[1]:118)[10]]

> [As on a holiday, to see the field
> A countryman goes out, at morning, when
> Out of hot night the cooling flashes had fallen
> For hours on end, and thunder still rumbles afar,
> The river enters its banks once more,
> New verdure sprouts from the soil,
> And with the gladdening rain of heaven
> The grapevine drips, and gleaming
> In tranquil sunlight stand the trees of the grove
>
> (Hamburger, 373)]

The moment here recaptured is that of a danger that has been avoided, of a disturbance that could have been catastrophical but that has mercifully turned out to be harmless—somewhat like the transition to the *Durchsegnung nach dem Sturm* in the concluding section of Beethoven's Sixth Symphony. Before any more detailed consideration, this certainly is the general suggestion that emanates from the pastoral palingenesis evoked by the beginning stanza. Whatever the dangers and the complexities contained in the middle part of the poem, beginning and end seem to tie it up very neatly in a circle that is as reassuring as the circular pattern of the weather.

One of the troubles with this reassuring picture is that Hölderlin never intended line 66 to be the end of his poem. We know so not only from the triadic Pindaric construction, which would have required a ninth stanza, but also from the prose draft which Hölderlin wrote for the poem.[11] This draft is clearly legible and had been mentioned by several of the earlier editors. This draft indicates a much more negative, tentative statement than that of line 66; it speaks of a self-inflicted wound upon the "heart" that was named as steadfast just before, of lost peace, of unrest and dearth (*Mangel*). And the beginning of execution that Hölderlin gave to a verse version of this prose outline still heightens the tone of despair since, unlike the prose outline, it begins with the anguished outcry, twice repeated, "Doch weh mir! . . . / Weh mir . . . (Woe is me)" (2[1]:120). When the poem was first printed by George and Wolfskehl, these final lines were not included;[12] Norbert von Hellingrath, the first editor of Hölderlin, gives part of them in a note but does not include them in the printed version of the poem as such. Heidegger follows Hellingrath, makes no mention of the additional lines, and orients much of his reading implicitly against their inclusion. This purely philological problem exemplifies for us the manner in which Heidegger failed to live up to the demands of his own method—certainly not because this method would have required the inclusion of the final lines for reasons of objective information, but because the hermeneutic totality of the work is not enforced, but destroyed, by their omission. A somewhat more detailed discussion of the poem is necessary to bring this out.

Simple and straightforward as the opening stanza may seem, interpreters have not been able to agree on the exact manner in which it works as a simile. One is certainly tempted, at first reading, to see the countryman who appears in line 2 as the equivalent figure to that of the poet first named explicitly in line 16 (So trauert der *Dichter* Angesicht auch [The *poets'* faces also mourn]); the grammatical connective "Wie" . . . so," at the beginning of stanza 2, suggests the pattern, "Wie . . . ein Landmann geht . . . so stehen sie [the poets—PdM] unter günstiger Witterung [As the countryman goes . . . so the poets stand in favorable weather]" (2:[1]:118). Like the countryman, the poets have not been themselves directly involved in the storm; they have been concerned with the damage that it might have done to others rather than threatened by it in their own persons, and now, after the danger is past, they leave the shelter of their home to survey the damage done to the land. Heidegger, who pays very little attention to the first stanza and clearly sees it as altogether unproblematic, reads it in this manner: "As a countryman on his walk, happy that his world has been preserved, wanders around his field, so the poets stand in favorable weather" (*Erläuterungen* 51). A recent commentator on this poem, Peter Szondi, pointed out, with some justification, that in the [rest] of the poem the poets' experience of the thunderstorm seems to be much more direct than that of the farmer.[13] Stanza 7, line 57, speaks of the necessity for the poets to stand bareheaded beneath God's thunderstorms, not to be like those who, at daybreak, survey the damage, but like those who, during the night, have been as exposed as the trees and the vineyards that are described in the first stanza. The simile would then not link the poets with the countryman but with the exposed trees, objects that were never sheltered from the direct impact of the lightning. The temporality is different in each case: in the reading suggested by Szondi, the poet stands within the *Jetzt*, the immediate present of the flash of light; in the other instance, which comes more naturally to any reader and which Heidegger adopts without being aware that there could be a question, the poet stands outside and comes after the moment of greatest danger.

In terms of the syntax of the first stanza, it is impossible to decide on this particular point, except to say that a naive, spontaneous reading would tend to identify the poet with the countryman, a more involved reading that takes the full sequence of the poem into account, with the trees and the vine. It also might seem to the reader of the entire poem (leaving the problematic conclusion for the moment outside consideration) that no important problem is raised by this possible ambiguity of metaphorical reference. The significance of the thunderstorm, for instance, can be deduced from the poem without having to settle the question of the first stanza. It appears, in the poem, on levels of increasing generality. It first appears, within a context of natural events, as a literal thunderstorm in nature. Then, in the third stanza, the association of the storm with a heroic, military imagery ("Die Natur ist jetzt mit Waffenklang erwacht [Nature now awakens to the clamor of arms]"), as well as such later references as "die Taten der Welt (the deeds, the actions of the world)" suggest a historical reading that is frequent enough in Hölderlin. It refers to the political turmoils that agitated Europe in the wake of the French Revolution through the Napoleonic Wars. It is well known that Hölderlin, like his friends and fellow Tübingen students Schelling and Hegel, was deeply involved with these events. The point, however, is not that the thunderstorm works here as a metaphor for a historical event but that both the literal thunderstorm and the historical turmoil are treated, on the same level, as manifestations of an entity that contains and transcends them. It would be entirely wrong to say that the natural thunderstorm in stanza 1 represents the revolutionary wars in stanza 2, or vice versa; both are equally literal, or equally symbolic in reference to the actual event, which is located not in physical nature or in historical events but in what Hölderlin here still calls, in line 23, Nature, *die Natur* ("Denn sie, sie selbst, die älter denn die Zeiten / Und über die Götter des Abends und Orients ist, / Die Natur ist jetzt mit Waffenklang erwacht [For she, she herself, who is older than all times, and above the gods of Orient and Occident, Nature now awakens to the clamor of arms]"). If associated with the landscape of stanza 1, the term *nature* would be misleading and hardly compatible with the heroic tonality that comes later, let alone with the claim that this awakening of nature is in fact the open reassertion of divine strength in the world (lines 35–36).

But here Heidegger's commentary helps us to avoid such a mistake. For the emphasis throughout is indeed, as he points out, on the all-encompassing, the absolute totality of the concept Nature, of which the actual, pastoral nature of trees, vineyards, and thunderstorms is only one manifestation among others. Nature is indeed here the disclosure of being as that in which all entities, including the gods, exist and are grounded.[14] The poets can derive their language from natural events, as in stanza 1, or from heroic, historical events, as where it is said in stanza 4 that the deeds of the world have kindled the fire of inspiration in their souls. Beyond that, they could even take divine events like the birth of Dionysos or the death of Christ as their subject. None of this is mutually exclusive, and Hölderlin will himself juxtapose such a span of events in later poems. This is possible because all these events, when considered poetically (i.e., in reference to a language that strives to name them in their essence) have a common source in what in this poem is called "Natur," or "das Heilige." The direction toward this common source becomes manifest in the poem's ability to encompass such widely divergent entities within its own language. Because of his ontological bent, Heidegger is able to see this. Heidegger's ontological orientation allows him to avoid a falsely naturalistic or analogical reading of the term *nature* and to discard a tendency to read the original landscape as a kind of *paysage moralisé* expressing a unity between the natural and the historical world of man.

But if, in this poem, the flash of lightning is indeed the disclosure of being in some of its authentic manifestations, it could by no means be said that the poem names this disclosure, that it somehow represents its poetic equivalent in the realm of language. As far as actual events are concerned, the disclosure occurs, in the poem, in two instances: that of the actual thunderstorm in stanza 1, and that of the revolutionary wars in stanza 2. Neither of these events is in itself poetic; both take place outside the realm of language. On the other hand, the poem speaks in some detail about the relationship of language toward these privileged events. And this is where the degree of proximity of the poet to the lightning—the question of whether the poet is *like* the trees or *like* the countryman—becomes of importance. As the poem progresses, the movement seems more and more to diminish the distance that separates the poet from what are called "the deeds of the world" and that we know to be, for Hölderlin, a direct manifestation of the authentic presence of being. His poem not only understands the full significance of these events as such a manifestation, but it seems to take its fire directly from them. Capable of seeing the acts of nature, the historical acts of man, and the acts of the gods as common manifestatations of the same source, he himself is capable of reaching this source. Moreover, whereas the effective action of the divine source is dispersed and lost in natural events, or in the flattening effects of practical history, it can be maintained in poetic language. The poet becomes a mediator between being and history, the continuator and preserver of the heroic deeds that he records, exposed to divine presence like the trees but as solicitous of the common good as the countryman. He becomes the one who calls and keeps the gods down among men, and Heidegger defines the hymnal mode not as a praising but as a *calling* of the sacred back to earth. "It is the sacred that donates the word and that comes to us in that word (Das Heilige verschenkt das Wort und kommt selbst in dieses Wort)" (74).

On this level of experience, there can be no real tension, in the poem, between the beginning and the end. The totality that is expressed here is absolutely all-encompassing, *allgegenwärtig*,[15] and has to be equally present in all parts of the work. The opening scene may seem more restricted, more particularized than the very general statements that are made later; but this is merely due to the fact that the explicit awareness of its full significance is not immediately stated. By its gradual widening out from particular physical nature to history, to the gods, and finally to being itself, the poem dramatizes a process of all-encompassing totalization that stretches from the beginning to the end of the text. The progression takes place without discontinuity and moves in one single direction, toward the full disclosure of being. The pattern is apocalyptic, a temporal movement that culminates in a transcendence of time. The temporal tension that might be contained in the metaphorical ambiguity of the opening stanza is completely resolved in the description of the poet as someone who stands in the presence of being in the past (when he is waiting for the disclosure), in the present (when it takes place in the heroic acts of history), and in the future (when, like the countryman caring for his land, the concern of his work will maintain, for others, a mediate form of contact with being). Neither is there a tension between the violence of heroic action, which takes place, in line 23, "to the clamor of arms," and the inwardness with which the same experience is said, in line 44, to end quietly in the soul of the poets. The relentless progression of the apocalyptic pattern unifies these apparent discrepancies. It is not surprising that Heidegger, in describing this pattern, sees Hölderlin as an eschatological figure, the precursor who, during a period of temporary alienation from being (*Seinsvergessenheit*), announces the end of this barren time and prepares a renewal. The eschatological pattern can be extended, beyond Hölderlin, to embrace an entire development originating in romanticism and that (to confine ourselves to German names) would lead to Nietzsche, to George, to Rilke, and to Heidegger himself.

In such a vision, there would indeed be no room for the negative lines that Hölderlin had planned as a conclusion to his poem; they had to be discarded as a passing weakness, a fit of discouragement that prevented Hölderlin from maintaining the tone, after the poem had in fact reached its real conclusion in line 66. The embarrassing fact remains that they always had been destined to be the concluding part. Their suppression means, in fact, that the truth of the poem, as Heidegger understands it, expresses a totality that does not coincide with the mode of totalization of the poem's own language; it is of course particularly important, in this respect, that it is precisely the concluding section, the part that delimits the horizon the poem is able to reach, which resists Heidegger's claim for absolute totality. The source of the truth of the text then no longer resides in the text but in an awareness that lies beyond it; the commentary, the interpretation, really adds something to the poetic statement, and this addition becomes apparent in the interpreter's right to suppress what he now considers to be irrelevant.

A closer look at the suppressed material may be helpful at this point. It had frequently been regarded as a mere cry of despair, barely articulate and close to incoherence. At least one critic, Peter Szondi, was curious enough to consider it with more care and to propose an interpretation that restores a connection between the theme Hölderlin meant to introduce at this highly sensitive moment, near the end of his poem, and other Hölderlin themes that appear in neighboring works. The lines suggest in fact a theme that appears over and over again in Hölderlin and that is far from being an isolated outcry, an accidental intrusion.

In his study of the end of the poem, Peter Szondi focuses on the "self-inflicted wound" from which the poet suffers, and contrasts this personal, individual suffering with line 64— "sharing the sufferings of him who is stronger than we"—in which the sympathy of the poet is not directed toward himself but toward someone who stands above him in the hierarchy of beings. Basing himself on an emendation in the prose outline, he interprets the apparent hesitations of the end as an awareness in Hölderlin that his participation in the heroic actions and sufferings of his period was not sufficiently disinterested. They were not sufficiently detached from the personal sufferings that play a prominent part in the Diotima episode of the novel *Hyperion* and in elegiac poems that derive from Hölderlin's unhappy love affair with Suzette Gontard. His claim at participating in the revolutionary enthusiasm of the period (which is for him indeed the historical manifestation of a divine will) would then not have been altogether genuine. Still caught in a personal, sentimental misfortune, Hölderlin would not have felt himself worthy of the claims made for poetry in a true hymn, which is aimed at the gods, not at the self. Only after he had detached himself sufficiently from his own tragedy could he develop a truly hymnal style; this poem begins to make the transition. "It is the moment of personal suffering," writes Szondi, "that is excluded from the hymnal mode. When Hölderlin began to write this poem he had not entirely freed himself from this suffering; this is clear from the fact that, at the end of the poem, his own self interrupts the hymnal self and claims his rights. This is why he could not bring the hymn to a satisfactory conclusion" ("Der andere Pfeil" 61).[16]

Convincing as this may sound, it misses a more important point. The passage from an experience of personal love to an experience of heroic action occurs frequently in Hölderlin and is in fact the basis of the entire Diotima cycle, including the novel *Hyperion*. He never, in fact, wrote a personal love lyric, for the love experience is always transcended toward a heroic tonality of a more general nature. Neither is this transcendence in bad faith; the continuity which makes the love for Diotima preparatory to a higher calling is genuine and not problematic. The temptation to write in a more personal vein never was a very strong one for Hölderlin; he could never have felt very close to the problem that Szondi mentions as crucial.

The danger mentioned in the final lines of "Wie wenn am Feiertage . . ." is of a somewhat different nature, and threatens the poet as much in the experience of love as it threatens him in moments of revolutionary upheaval. It is precisely the danger of believing that he can accomplish the kind of proximity to being which Heidegger detects in the rest of the poem. The mythological insertion in stanza 6, the story of Semele, which was the point of departure of the poem, speaks of the danger of wanting to see the god without mediation ("sichtbar / Den Gott zu sehen begehr[en]"); this wording is almost literally repeated in the planned conclusion: "ich sei genaht, die Himmlischen zu schauen, / Sie selbst, sie werfen mich tief unter die Lebenden [I approached to look upon the Heavenly, and this is why they have cast me down, as a false priest, below the living]." In this poem, the particular form which this danger takes is that of confusing the function of the poetic word with what is called "the deeds of the world"—in purely stylistic terms, to think that the poem could come to a satisfactory conclusion in the heroic tone that has been prevalent from the second stanza on. Transposed to a more thematic level, the end cautions against the belief that the kind of enthusiasm that animates a heroic act is identical with the predominant mood of a poetic consciousness. It can be said, of the heroic action, that it indeed establishes an unmediated contact with being, but it does so necessarily in a tragic mode, in the form of an apocalyptic death, alluded to in this poem in the death of Semele. This death is far from meaningless: out of Semele's death, Dionysos is born—but Dionysos never does appear, in Hölderlin's work, as a figure of the poet, as little as Christ does. Dionysos is the founder of what Hölderlin calls, in derivation from Rousseau, the general will (*Gemeingeist*): he is a political force connected with the practical organization of a society in as close as possible an accordance with the true being of man. He is the political organization that results from the sacrifice of heroic action; his main concern, unlike the poet's, is not with language.

The poet's relationship to the heroic sacrifice that makes history possible is more complex. It holds for him an almost irresistible temptation. Because of the immediacy that characterizes it, the heroic deed has a temporal priority over his own activity: its impact on the destiny of humanity is such that the hero can almost be said to be the agent of the divine will on earth. The hero's situation is much closer to that of the trees that stand directly under the divine fire of the storm. Because his own medium, language, has a mediate relationship of a self-conscious, reflective type toward actions and deeds, the poet never achieves the same proximity to being. Hence the attraction that the heroic holds for him: Hölderlin's elegiac longing goes to entities that have achieved heroic status; his conception of the Hellenic world, for instance, which plays such a prominent part in his work, is primarily a heroic one. The heroic tonality, however, is for him inseparable from a tragic outcome: the kind of near-Divine immediacy achieved by certain figures in history who seem to bring about a reconciliation of humanity and the gods necessarily involves a sacrificial destruction as the consequence of the more-than-human status achieved at that moment.

The tragedy *Empedokles* develops this sacrificial theme, which anticipates another form of sacrifice in the late, Christ-oriented hymns. The tragic death of the heroic ruler, however, is to some extent legitimate, for caught up in action as he is, he cannot be fully conscious. He does not fully know what he is doing when he abandons himself to a will that seems to come from beyond himself. In the fully conscious figure of the poet, however, such a sacrificial urge is a form of hubris and has to be resisted. Indeed, the main poetic theme becomes the necessity of moving beyond the heroic to a state of consciousness that recognizes and contains the heroic dimension in all its grandeur but that warns of its inherent danger. Our poem explicitly mentions, in the last lines, the necessity to "sing, to those eager to learn, my warning song (dass ich / Das warnende Lied den Gelehrigen singe)." It does so by describing the destiny of those who, through heroic action, tried to approach divine status and were cast down like Tantalos. They misunderstood tragically their own poetic function, which demands a conscious renunciation of the heroic stance. The heroic becomes for them a tonality among others that poetry can adopt, a theme it can and should use, but with the distance of a consciousness that has, in a sense, gone beyond it—although this going beyond implies the necessity of maintaining a distance from divine presence. This new metaheroic tonality is what Hölderlin calls the "ideal" tone.

The dramatic (or tonal) structure of the poem thus becomes entirely different from Heidegger's scheme. It begins by naming, in the form of a pseudoidyllic scene, a potential tension: that between two ways, temporally different, of relating to the divine presence represented by the storm: to stand directly exposed to it, like the trees, or to make its danger the subject of one's concern at a time that comes *after* the moment of crisis (like the countryman). The ambiguity we had noted as to which of the two attitudes corresponds to the poet's thus becomes the central concern of the text. But it is first stated without explicit awareness of the conflict, in a manner that in Hölderlin's own terms would be referred to as naive. The entire development from the second through the seventh stanza, which is predominantly in a heroic mode, names the tendency of the poet to be identical with the active men that are shaping the destiny of the contemporary world. But the concluding two stanzas, which remain unfinished, put this entire middle section in an ironic light and define it as an error, a temptation to be avoided. It is a false totalization that has to be replaced by the more restrictive, negative conclusion that Hölderlin planned but failed to develop fully; a full poetic control over the "ideal" tonality was to be the most arduous stylistic task he had to solve, and it is only achieved in the later hymns. In these later texts (as I have tried to show elsewhere in interpretations of "Der Rhein" and "Mnemosyne"),[17] the parallel but distinct destinies of the poet and the titanic, heroic man are clearly apparent. But the same theme is already the organizing theme of this poem and was already present in various forms even earlier in the work.

For our more limited purposes, the manner in which this "ideal" ending relates to the "naive" beginning is of particular importance. The relationship is quite different from the simple, circular corroboration that Heidegger found, in which the final statement repeats in fact, in more general language, what the beginning landscape stated implicitly. We have instead a considerable tonal tension, almost a contradiction, between the seductive nature imagery of the start and the negative, anxious warning uttered at the end. But it is not, in fact, a genuine contradiction, for what the ending does, in conjunction with the temptation described in the middle part, is bring out a tension that was latent from the start but that was stated in a nonproblematic, naive tone. The ending makes the hidden meaning of the beginning explicit; it interprets it in a language that has accumulated the experience necessary to bring out what was there from the beginning, but in a neutral, nonconscious state. As Heidegger claimed that the commentary could disappear to let the poem speak fully in its own right, so the last part of the poem, which is the most purely interpretative, could disappear after revealing the full potential content of the naive beginning. It is indeed these openings of Hölderlin poems that stay most prominently in the mind and by which the poet becomes part of one's own consciousness. They contain in fact all that the development of the poem will bring out and they could not have been composed if the poet had not had a certain foreknowledge of his final, ideal insight. In the final analysis, the ideal and the naive statement seem to coincide; beginning and end come together within the tension of the radical discontinuity that seemed to keep them apart. But the temporal and ontological priority of the beginning is maintained as that of a foreknowledge, a prefiguration that the later, "ideal" statement makes explicit but never supersedes. The totality of the poem is rigorously included within the hermeneutic circularity that thus connects its beginning with its end and constitutes its form; its source is not to be sought outside, whether in Hölderlin's empirical existence or, as in Heidegger, in an experience of being that would precede the language of the text. The source of the poem is exactly the naive first stanza, its *telos* the ideal last one, its form the temporal process that brings both together in an act of interpretative reading which is an extension of the interpretative act that takes place in the poem itself. At no time do we have to leave the realm of the language that constitutes the poem in order to understand it.

That Heidegger had to do so indicates a flaw in his method that leads to a misinterpretation of Hölderlin as an apocalyptic poet, when Hölderlin's main theme is precisely the non-apocalyptic structure of poetic temporality. The flaw is the substitution of ontological for what could well be called formal dimensions of language. The ontologization of literary interpretation, which seemed so promising in the Heidegger of *Sein und Zeit*, does not mean that literature can be read, so to speak, from the standpoint of being, or from that of a poet who is said to act as a direct spokesman for being. The standpoint can only be that of a consciousness that is ontologically (and not empirically) oriented but that nevertheless remains a consciousness, rooted in the language of a subject and not in being.

We could then well agree with the substance if not with the polemical tone of Theodor Adorno when he attacks Heidegger's method as alien to its real function. "The corrective should be found," says Adorno, "where Heidegger breaks off, namely in the question of the relationship that the content, including the intellectual content, maintains with the form."[18] And he goes on to suggest that the key to this relationship is to be found in the paratactic constructions that, especially in the later hymns, interrupt the logical movement of the thought and the regular pattern of the rhythm, thus establishing a principle of organization that is no longer based in an identity, a continuity, or even an analogy between the different parts of the poem. Sketchy and overhasty as Adorno appears in his interpretation of this discontinuous element, his remark nevertheless touches on an important aspect that other commentators had also noticed and brought out in a different terminology. Hölderlin passed indeed from the different tonal levels that exist in his poetry without transition; the brusqueness of the change at the end of "Wie wenn am Feiertage . . ." is such that the end almost seems like another poem. And, as we saw, it is the tension between the different tonal units that brings out the final meaning of the poem, not the isolated statements that are made in each of them. "The tension between two moments, not a thesis, is the vital element in Hölderlin's work" (201), Adorno writes in reference to the nature-spirit antithesis, but the statement would apply to all the tensions that appear in Hölderlin's work, especially the tension between the different tonalities. The totalization, the unity that is achieved in spite of these discontinuities, is certainly not an organic one; nothing could be more remote from Schelling's philosophy of identity, with its latent pantheism, than the strict emphasis on difference, discontinuity, and mediation that we find in Hölderlin's world. Nor is it purely dialectical, in the Hegelian sense, for time itself, which remains unproblematically forward-directed in Hegel, here becomes itself a discontinuous element of a structure that consists of a series of temporal reversals—as when, in the *Feiertagshymne*, we observed a tension between simultaneity and succession. Hölderlin's own term for what Adorno calls parataxis is the caesura referred to in the commentaries on the Oedipus tragedies, which marks a reversal of tone as well as a reversal of time and in which the end reestablishes with the beginning a contact which it seemed to have lost. The principle of totalization is indeed ontological, in that it has to be sought in the discontinuous structure of being itself.

Such an ontological orientation is perfectly compatible with the notion of parataxis. Well before Adorno, Auerbach had pointed out that parataxis in a style indicates "the dramatization of an inner event, an inner about-face" and that it is a specifically Augustinian type of diction: "for no one ever more passionately [than Augustine—PdM] pursued and investigated the phenomenon of conflicting and united inner forces, the alternation of antithesis and synthesis in their relations and effects."[19] Auerbach went on to link parataxis with what he calls a figural style, a style in which the temporal relationship between parts is no longer based on the order of natural succession but on a relationship of priority between figural entities, types of consciousness that correspond to what Hölderlin calls "tones" of diction, forms of language. In a religious context, this means the ultimate dependence of poetic language on the revealed language of Scripture; in the secular context of romanticism, it means that the language originates with a consciously ontological concern. This does not imply the kind of unmediated proximity to being that we find in the later Heidegger, but much rather the specifically romantic warning against the danger of this delusion that we found in Hölderlin, and of which we will find another version in the poetry of Wordsworth.

4

Time and History in Wordsworth

U P TILL NOW, the double-barreled topic of these lectures has rather prevented us from reading our romantic authors with the kind of receptivity, the self-forgetting concentration, that we have been describing (in the case of Rousseau) as the proper state of mind for critical insights. The need to keep one eye on the text and another eye on the critical commentator has forced us into the rather tiresome grimace well known to anyone who has ever played in an orchestra, where one has to keep track simultaneously of the score and of the conductor. The grimace becomes even more painful when the directives of the score and those of the interpreter are pulling in different directions, as we found to be the case, to some extent, in the three preceding examples. The result often is that because of the unavoidable simplifications involved in a polemical discussion, one fails to do justice to both the writer and the critic. I probably had to overstate the degree of my disagreement with Girard and Starobinski, critics for whom I have a great deal of sympathy and admiration, and I was clearly not being critical enough, to your taste, with Heidegger, when I suggested that there might be perhaps something of merit in an imaginary figure, one that never existed in the flesh, who would have approached literature with some of the insights that appear in *Sein und Zeit*. More distressing are the one-sided readings given to some of the texts, in order to use them as a rebuttal of methodological assertions. Such overanalytical approaches are certainly not attuned to catch the subtle nuances of temporality and intent that a valid commentary should bring out.

Fortunately, my topic today will allow for a more relaxed kind of presentation in which the voice of the poet might come through in a less garbled manner. Geoffrey Hartman's study of Wordsworth awakens in me no trace of methodological dis-agreement.[1] I read whole parts of it with the profound satisfaction of full agreement, only marred by the slight feeling of jealousy that I did not write them myself. The much hoped-for synthesis between the best qualities of American and Continental criticism certainly begins to come true in a book like this. It is based on a wide knowledge of the tradition in which the poet is writing, in this case true familiarity with Words-worth's antecedents in Milton and in eighteenth-century poet-ry, combined with an ear that is finely attuned to the slightest nuances of Wordsworth's language. Moreover, by interpreting Wordsworth from the inside, from the phenomenological point of view of his own consciousness, Hartman can trace a coherent itinerary of Wordsworth's poetic development. His achievement will make it possible for us to limit ourselves to some indications derived from the reading of a few very short but characteristic texts, thus tracing, in turn, an itinerary through Wordsworth by means of some of those larger themes that Hartman has pursued. These themes, in the case of Wordsworth and Wordsworth scholarship, are quite obvious, and Hartman does not depart from a well-established custom when he makes the relationship between nature and the imag-ination into Wordsworth's central problem. The Arnoldian tra-dition of reading Wordsworth as a moralist has, for quite a while now, been superseded by a concern for the implicit poet-ics that are present in his writing and that have to be under-stood prior to the interpretation of a moral statement that seems conventional. This leads inevitably to such abstractions as nature, the imagination, self-knowledge, and poetry as a means to self-knowledge, all of which figure prominently in recent Wordsworth studies, not only because Wordsworth himself talks at times openly about them, but because his poet-ry, even at its most trivial, always seems to be supported by and to relate back to them.

As will be clear to all of you, the path I'll try to trace by this direct commentary overlaps with that proposed by Hartman in more places than I will have time to mention. It diverges from it in at least one point of some importance, and I will comment on this disagreement later, as a way to summarize a tentative view of Wordsworth's poetry.[2]

Let me start out with a very well known poem to which Hartman devotes a chapter, the text that Wordsworth placed at the head of the section of his *Collected Poems* entitled "Poems of the Imagination." He later incorporated it into *The Prelude* and seems to have, in general, attached a special importance to it. It was written in Goslar, during his stay in Germany, together with several of the childhood memories that went into the two first books of *The Prelude*. "The Winander Boy" is divided into two sections separated by a blank space, and all readers of the poem have been struck by the abruptness of the transition that leads from the first to the second part. Problems of interpretation tend to focus on the relationship between the two parts. (I would add that that these problems were solved in a definitive but somewhat peremptory fashion in a fine recent anthology of English literature in which the second part has simply been suppressed.)

> There was a Boy, ye knew him well, ye Cliffs
> And Islands of Winander! many a time
> At evening, when the stars had just begun
> To move along the edges of the hills,
> 5 Rising or setting, would he stand alone
> Beneath the trees, or by the glimmering Lake,
> And there, with fingers interwoven, both hands
> Press'd closely, palm to palm, and to his mouth
> Uplifted, he, as through an instrument,
> 10 Blew mimic hootings to the silent owls
> That they might answer him.—And they would shout
> Across the watery Vale, and shout again,
> Responsive to his call, with quivering peals,
> And long halloos, and screams, and echoes loud
> 15 Redoubled and redoubled; concourse wild
> Of mirth and jocund din! And when it chanced
> That pauses of deep silence mock'd his skill,
> Then, sometimes, in that silence, while he hung
> Listening, a gentle shock of mild surprize

20 Has carried far into his heart the voice
   Of mountain torrents; or the visible scene
   Would enter unawares into his mind
   With all its solemn imagery, its rocks,
   Its woods, and that uncertain Heaven, receiv'd
25 Into the bosom of the steady Lake.
         This Boy was taken from his Mates, and died
   In childhood, ere he was full ten years old.
   —Fair are the woods, and beauteous is the spot,
   The Vale where he was born; the Churchyard hangs
30 Upon a Slope above the Village School,
   And, there, along the bank, when I have pass'd
   At evening, I believe that oftentimes
   A full half-hour together I have stood
   Mute—looking at the Grave in which he lies.[3]

The first part of the poem introduces us into a world that is, in the words of the text, both "responsive" and, as in the gesture of the hands, "interwoven." Voice and nature echo each other in an exchange of which the exuberance expresses a stability, a firm hold on a universe that has the vastness of rising and setting stars, but nevertheless allows for an intimate and sympathetic contact between human and natural elements. Not the "vaste et profonde unité" of Baudelaire's *Correspondances* should come to mind, but a more innocent, more playful, pleasure at finding responses, satisfying possibilities of relationship even for someone who, like the boy, "stands alone." The "watery Vale" that might separate him from an alien natural presence is easily bridged by the cry of the owls; it is, by itself, an eerie enough noise on a dark night, but little of this eeriness is allowed to enter the poem. If we mimic it well enough to engage the response of its originators, the gulf between ourselves and nature need not be unbridgeable. "The poet . . . considers man and nature as essentially adapted to each other, and the mind of man as naturally the mirror of the fairest and most interesting qualities of nature." This statement from the Preface to the *Lyrical Ballads* would be a good commentary on the opening scene of the poem.[4] Much Wordsworth criticism still today, considers this frequently as the fundamental statement not just of Wordsworth but of romantic naturalism as a whole, and refuses to go beyond it. Yet, even in this first section of the poem, one finds some strain at keeping up a belief in such an "interwoven" world. "Mimic hootings" is not the highest characterization imaginable for the human voice, and we have somehow to be told explicitly that this is "concourse wild / Of mirth and jocund din" to convince us of the persistent cheer of the scene.

As soon as the silence of the owls allows for the noise to subside, what becomes audible is poetically much more suggestive than what went before. The deepening of the imaginative level is not announced with any fanfare or pointed dramatic gesture. The "surprises" that Wordsworth's language gives are indeed such *"gentle* shocks of *mild* surprize" that the transition from stability to suspense can be accomplished almost without our being aware of it. Yet certainly, by the time we come to *"uncertain* heaven," we must realize that we have entered a precarious world in which the relationship between noun and epithet can be quite surprising. Coleridge singled out the line for comment, as being most unmistakably Wordsworth's: "Had I met these lines running wild in the deserts of Arabia, I should instantly have screamed out, 'Wordsworth.' "[5] The line is indeed bound to engender wonder and meditation. The movements of the stars, in the opening lines, had seemed "certain" enough, and their reflection in the lake was hardly needed to steady the majesty of their imperceptible motion. But the precariousness that is here being introduced had been announced before, as when, a little earlier, in lines 18 and 19, it was said that when "pauses of deep silence mock'd his skill, / Then, sometimes, in that silence, while he (the boy) *hung* / Listening, a gentle shock of mild surprize. . . ." We would have expected "stood listening" instead of the unusual "hung / listening." This word, "hung" plays an important part in the poem. It reappears in the second part, when it is said that the graveyard in which the boy is buried *"hangs* / Upon a Slope above the Village School." It establishes the thematic link between the two parts and names a central Wordsworthian experience. At the moment when the analogical correspondence with nature no longer asserts itself, we discover that the earth under our feet is not the stable base in which we

can believe ourselves to be anchored. It is as if the solidity of
earth were suddenly pulled away from under our feet and we
were left "hanging" from the sky instead of standing on the
ground. The fundamental spatial perspective is reversed; instead of being centered on the earth, we are suddenly related
to a sky that has its own movements, alien to those of earth and
its creatures. The experience hits as a sudden feeling of dizziness, a falling or a threat of falling, a *vertige* of which there are
many examples in Wordsworth. The nest-robbing scene from
book 1 of *The Prelude* comes to mind, where the experience is a
literal moment of absolute dizziness which disjoins the familiar perspective of the spatial relationship between heaven and
earth, in which the heavens are seen as a safe dome that con-
firms at all times the earth's and our own centrality, the steadfastness of our orientation toward the center which makes us
creatures *of* earth. But here, suddenly, the sky no longer relates
to the earth

> Oh! at that time,
> While on the perilous ridge I *hung* alone,
> With what strange utterance did the loud dry wind
> Blow through my ears! the sky *seem'd not a sky*
> *Of earth*, and with what motion moved the clouds!
>
> [*1805 Prelude* 1:335–39 (bk. 1, ll. 335–39), 291]

Later, when in the Preface to the 1815 edition of his *Poems*,
Wordsworth gives examples of the workings of the highest
poetic faculty, the imagination, as it shapes poetic diction, he
chooses three passages, from Virgil, Shakespeare, and Milton,
in which the italicized key word is the same word, "hang," not
used literally as in the last instance from *The Prelude*, but used
imaginatively. The Milton passage begins

> As when far off at Sea a Fleet descried
> *Hangs* in the clouds, by equinoxial winds
> Close sailing from Bengala
>
> . . . .
> so seem'd
> Far off the flying Fiend.
>
> [Preface to *Poems* (1815), 248]

Wordsworth comments: "Here is the full strength of the imagination involved in the word *hangs*, and exerted upon the whole image: First, the Fleet, an aggregate of many Ships, is represented as one mighty Person, whose track, we know and feel, is upon the waters; but, taking advantage of its appearance to the senses, the Poet dares to represent it as *hanging in the clouds*, both for the gratification of the mind in contemplating the image itself, and in reference to the motion and appearance of the sublime object to which it is compared" [248]. This *daring* movement of the language, an act of pure mind, corresponds to the *danger*, the anxiety of the moment when the sudden silence leaves the boy *hanging*, listening. In the second part of the poem, we are told, without any embellishment or preparation, that the boy died, and we now understand that the moment of silence, when the analogical stability of a world in which mind and nature reflect each other was shattered, was in fact a prefiguration of his death. The turning away of his mind from a responsive nature toward a nature that is not quite "of earth" and that ultimately is called an "uncertain heaven" is in fact an orientation of his consciousness toward a preknowledge of his mortality. The spatial heaven of the first five lines with its orderly moving stars has become the temporal heaven of line 24, "uncertain" and precarious since it appears in the form of a preconsciousness of death.

The uncertainty or anxiety is not allowed, however, to go unrelieved. In the prefigurative first section the uncertain heaven is, with a suggestion of appeasement, "receiv'd / Into the bosom of the steady Lake," and in the second part, at the moment when we would have expected an elegaic lament on the death of the boy, we hear instead a characteristically Wordsworthian song of praise to a particular place, the kind of ode to spirit of place of which Hartman has traced the antecedents in eighteenth century nature poetry:

Fair are the woods, and beauteous is the spot,
The Vale where he was born; the Churchyard *hangs*
Upon a Slope above the Village School
And, there, along that bank, when I have pass'd
At evening, I believe that oftentimes
A full half-hour together I have stood
Mute—looking at the Grave in which he lies.

The dizziness revealed in the "hung / listening" has indeed resulted in a fall, has been the discovery of a state of falling which itself anticipated a fall into death. Now become part of earth in the graveyard, the boy is part of an earth that is itself falling into a sky that is not "of earth." But the movement is steadied, the fall cushioned, as it were, when the uncertain heaven is received into the lake, when sheer dizziness is changed into reflection. The corresponding moment in the second part is the meditative half-hour, which introduces a long, extended period of continuous duration that exists outside of the ordinary time of daily activity, at the moment of a privileged encounter with a scene that merges the youth of the village school with the death of the graveyard, as boyhood and death merged in the figure of the Winander boy.

We understand the particular temporal quality of this slow half-hour better when we remember that the earliest version of this poem was written throughout in the first person and was referred to Wordsworth himself as a boy.[6] The text went: "When it chanced / That pauses of deep silence mocked *my* skill . . ." The poem is, in a curious sense, autobiographical, but it is the autobiography of someone who no longer lives written by someone who is speaking, in a sense, from beyond the grave. It would be banal and inadequate to say that Wordsworth is praising and mourning, in the poem, his own youth, the boy he used to be. The movement is more radical, more complex. The structure of the poem, although it seems retrospective, is in fact proleptic. In the second part, Wordsworth is reflecting on his own death, which lies, of course, in the future and can only be anticipated. But to be able to imagine, to convey the experience, the consciousness of mortality, he can only represent death as something that happened to another person in the past. [Dead] men,[7] as we all know, tell no tales, but they have an assertive way of reminding us of mortality, of bringing us eventually face to face with our own finitude. Wordsworth is thus anticipating a future event as if it existed in the past. Seeming to be remembering, to be moving to a past, he is in fact anticipating a future. The objectification of the past self, as that of a consciousness that unwittingly experiences an anticipation of its own death, allows him to reflect on an event that is, in fact, unimaginable. For this is the real terror of death, that it lies truly beyond the reach of reflection. Yet the poem names the moment of death in a reflective mood, and it is this reflective mood that makes it possible to transform what would otherwise be an experience of terror into the relative appeasement of the lines, ". . . that uncertain Heaven, receiv'd / Into the bosom of the steady Lake."

Another way of putting it is that what Wordsworth strives to conquer, on the relentless fall into death, is the time, the surmise that would allow one to reflect upon the event that, of all events, is most worth reflecting upon but hardest to face. This time is conquered at the end of the poem, in the curiously exact full half-hour that becomes available to him, a purely meditative time proportionate to the time it takes us to understand meditatively Wordsworth's own poem. But the strategy that allows for this conquest is temporally complex: it demands the description of a future experience by means of the fiction of a past experience which is itself anticipatory or prefigurative. Since it is a fiction, it can only exist in the form of a language, since it is by means of language that the fiction can be objectified and made to act as a living person. The reflection is not separable from the language that describes it, and the half-hour of the end also clocks the time during which Wordsworth, or ourselves, are in real contact with the poem. Hartman is quite right in saying that the poem "becomes an . . . extended epitaph" (20), though one might want to add that it is the epitaph written by the poet for himself, from a perspective that stems, so to speak, from beyond the grave. This temporal perspective is characteristic for all Wordsworth's poetry—even if it obliges us to imagine a tombstone large enough to hold the entire *Prelude*.[8]

Wordsworth himself gives us sufficient evidence to defend this kind of understanding. The first of the *Essays upon Epitaphs* describes, in prose, insights that are very close to what we have found in "The Winander Boy." What seems to start out as a simply pious statement about the consolatory power of a belief in the immortality of the soul turns very swiftly into a meditation on the temporality that characterizes the consciousness of beings capable of reflecting on their own death. The first characteristic of such a consciousness is its power to anticipate: "The Dog or Horse perishes in the field, or in the stall, by the side of his Companions, and is incapable of *antic- ipating* the sorrow with which his surrounding Associates shall bemoan his death, or pine for his loss; he cannot *pre-conceive* this regret, he can form no thought of it; and therefore cannot possibly have a desire to leave such regret or remembrance behind him" [605]. And Wordsworth characterizes a human being that, not unlike the Winander boy at the beginning of the poem, would have chosen to remain in a state of nature by an "inability arising from the imperfect state of his faculties to come, in any point of his being, into contact with a notion of death; or to an *unreflecting* acquiescence in what had been in- stilled in him" [606]. Very soon in the same essay, however, it becomes clear that the power to anticipate is so closely con- nected with the power to remember that it is almost impossible to distinguish them from each other. They seem like opposites, and are indeed at opposite poles if we think of time as a con- tinual movement from birth to death. In this perspective, the source is at a maximal remove from the final point of destina- tion, and it would be impossible to reach the one by ways of the other. In a more reflective, more conscious concept of tem- porality, however, the two poles will, in Wordsworth's phras- ing, "have another and finer connection than that of contrast" [608]. "Origin and tendency are notions inseparably co- relative," [606] he writes, and the essay develops this notion in an extended voyage image:

> As, in sailing upon the orb of this Planet, a voyage, towards the regions where the sun sets, conducts gradually to the quarter where we have been accustomed to behold it come forth at its rising; and, in like manner, a voyage towards the east, the birth- place in our imagination of the morning, leads finally to the quar- ter where the Sun is last seen when he departs from our eyes; so, the contemplative Soul, travelling in the direction of mortality, advances to the Country of everlasting Life; and, in like manner, may she continue to explore those cheerful tracts, till she is brought back, for her advantage and benefit, to the land of transi- tory things—of sorrow and of tears [608].

Stripped of whatever remnants of piety still cling to this language,[9] the passage summarizes the temporality of the "Winander Boy" poem. In this poem, the reflection on death takes on the form, at first sight contradictory, of a remembrance of childhood. Similarly, in Wordsworth, evocations of natural, childlike or apocalyptic states of unity with nature often acquire the curiously barren, dead-obsessed emptiness of non-being.[10] The poetic imagination, what is here called the contemplative soul, realizes this and thus encompasses source and death, origin and end within the space of its language, by means of complex temporal structurizations of which we found an example in "The Winander Boy."[11]

Another brief poem of Wordsworth's will allow us to take one further step in an understanding of his temporality; it may also make the concept less abstract by linking it to its more empirical mode of manifestation, namely history. The poem belongs to the later sonnet cycle entitled *The River Duddon*, which appeared in 1820.

> Not hurled precipitous from steep to steep;
> Lingering no more mid flower-enamelled lands
> And blooming thickets; nor by rocky bands
> Held;—but in radiant progress tow'rd the Deep
> 5 Where mightiest rivers into powerless sleep
> Sink, and forget their nature; *now* expands
> Majestic Duddon, over smooth flat sands,
> Gliding in silence with unfettered sweep!
> Beneath an ampler sky a region wide
> 10 Is opened round him;—hamlets, towers, and towns,
> And blue-topped hills, behold him from afar;
> In stately mien to sovereign Thames allied,
> Spreading his bosom under Kentish downs,
> With Commerce freighted or triumphant War.

> (699)

The *Essay upon Epitaphs* had already suggested the image of a river as the proper emblem for a consciousness that is able to contain origin and end in a single awareness. "Origin and tendency are notions inseparably co-relative. Never did a Child stand by the side of a running Stream, pondering within himself what power was the feeder of the perpetual current, from what never-wearied sources the body of water was supplied, but he must have been inevitably propelled to follow this question by another: 'Towards what abyss is it in progress? what receptacle can contain the mighty influx?' " (606). In this poem, we have what seems at first sight like a progression, a continuous movement that flows "in radiant progress" toward the triumphant ending:

> In stately mien to sovereign Thames allied,
> Spreading his bosom under Kentish Downs,
> With Commerce freighted or triumphant War.

Equally convincing seems to be the movement that leads, in the poem, from the idyllic setting of "flower-enamelled lands / And blooming thickets" to the political, historically oriented language at the end. The progression from nature to history, from a rural to an urban world seems to be without conflict. We move from a relationship between the personified river Duddon and its pastoral banks to a relationship that involves human creations such as "hamlets, towers, and towns," or human historical enterprises such as "Commerce" and "War." And this gliding passage, similar to what is called in *The Prelude* "love of nature leading to love of man" [in the title to book 8 of the 1850 version of *The Prelude*],[12] appears as a liberation, an expansion that involves a gain in freedom. The river is no longer restricted "by rocky bands" and now flows "with unfettered sweep." The order of nature seems to open up naturally into the order of history, thus allowing the same natural symbol, the river, to evoke the connection between them. The poem seems to summarize the "growth of a mind" as espousing this movement, and to prove, by the success of its own satisfying completeness, that language can espouse poetically this very movement.

Some aspects of the language, however, prevent the full identification of the movement with natural process and put into question an interpretation of the river, which a subsequent poem in the same series addresses as "my partner and my guide" ["Conclusion," l. 1, 699], as a truly natural entity. The beginning of the poem, for instance, casts a curious spell over the subsequent progression. It describes what the river no longer is in such forceful and suggestive language that we are certainly not allowed to forget what the river *has been* by the time we encounter it in its expanded form. The opening line, for example, cannot cease to haunt us, and no matter how strongly the italicized *now* (in "*now* expands") takes us to the present, so much has been told us so effectively about what came before that we can only seize upon this present in the perspective of its past and its future. The past is described as successive motions of falling and lingering. The dizziness of the Winander Boy poem and of the childhood scenes of *The Prelude* is certainly present in the image of the river "hurled precipitous from steep to steep," which introduces, from the start, a powerful motion that dominates the entire poem and that the various counterforces, including the initial *not*, are unable to stem. For the idyllic stage that follows, among flowers and blooming thickets, is a mere lingering, a temporary respite in a process that is one of steady descent and dissolution. The implications of this movement become clearer still when the radiant progress is said to be "tow'rd the Deep / Where mightiest rivers into powerless sleep / Sink, and forget their nature." This description of the sea is certainly far removed from the image of a pantheistic unity with nature that one might have expected. It is presented instead as a loss of self, the loss of the *name* that designates the river and allows it to take on the dignity of an autonomous subject. The diction of the passage, with the antithetical balance of "mightiest" and "powerless," is all the stronger since the apparent strategy of the poem does not seem to demand this kind of emphasis. It makes the forgetting of one's nature that is here mentioned into a movement that runs counter to the original progression; this progression, which first seemed to lead from nature to history while remaining under the dominant sway of nature, now becomes a movement away from nature toward pure nothingness. One is reminded of a similar loss of name in the Lucy Gray poems, where death makes her into an anonymous entity "Roll'd round in earth's diurnal course / With rocks and stones and trees!" ["A slumber did my spirit seal," ll. 7–8, 165]. Similarly, the river Duddon is first lost into a larger entity, the

Thames, which in turn will lose itself in still larger anonymity. There is no cycle here by means of which we are brought back to the source and reunited with it by natural means. No prospect of natural rebirth is held out, and the historical achievement at the end seems caught in the same general movement of decay.

Nevertheless, the poem can overcome the feeling of dejection that this irrevocable fall might suggest; it ends on a statement of assertion that is not ironic. Not altogether unlike the uncertain heaven in "The Boy of Winander" that was steadied in reflection, the fall here is not prevented, but made tolerable this time by the assertion of historical achievement. There seems to be an assertion of permanence, of a duration in what seems to be an irrevocable waste, a falling away into sheer nothingness. It is based on a certain form of hope, on the affirmation of a possible future, all of which makes it possible for man to pursue an enterprise that seems doomed from the start, to have a history in spite of a death which Wordsworth never allows us to forget.

In this poem, the possibility of restoration is linked to the manner in which the two temporalities are structurally interrelated within the text. If taken by itself, the progression toward history would be pure delusion, a misleading myth based on the wrong kind of forgetting, an evasion of the knowledge of mortality. The countertheme of loss of self into death that appears in the first and second quatrain introduces a temporality that is more originary, more authentic than the other, in that it reaches further into the past and sees wider into the future. It envelops the other, but without reducing it to mere error. Rather, it creates a point of view which has gone beyond the historical world of which we catch a glimpse at the end of the poem, but which can look back upon this world and see it within its own, relative greatness, as a world that does not escape from mutability but asserts itself within the knowledge of its own transience. We have a temporal structure that is not too different from what we found in "The Winander Boy." Instead of looking back upon childhood, upon an earlier stage of consciousness that anticipates its future undoing, we here look back on a historical consciousness that existed prior to the truly temporal consciousness represented by the river. This historical stage is named at the end of the poem, but this end is superseded by the authentic endpoint named in line 5. We see it therefore, with the poet, as destined to this same end. Like the boy experiencing the foreknowledge of his death, history awakens in us a true sense of our temporality, by allowing for the interplay between achievement and dissolution, self-assertion and self-loss, on which the poem is built. History, like childhood, is what allows recollection to originate in a truly temporal perspective, not as a memory of a unity that never existed, but as the awareness, the remembrance of a precarious condition of falling that has never ceased to prevail.[13]

Hence, in the concluding sonnet of the same cycle, the emphasis on the italicized word *backward* in "For, *backward*, Duddon! as I cast my eyes, / I see what was, and is, and will abide" ["Conclusion," ll. 3–4, 699]. As a mere assertion of the permanence of nature, the poem would be simply pious and in bad faith, for we know that as soon as we think of the river as analogous to a self, as a consciousness worthy of engaging our own, that it only reveals a constant loss of self. Considered as a partner and a guide, it has indeed "past away" [l. 2] and never ceases to do so. This is the "Function" it fulfills in the line, "The Form remains, the Function never dies" [l. 6], in which the Form corresponding to this Function is the trajectory of a persistent fall. The entire poignancy of the two sonnets is founded on the common bond between the *I* of the poem and its emblematic counterpart in the Duddon, which makes the river into something more than mere nature. Instead of merely letting ourselves be carried by it, we are able to move backwards, against the current of the movement. This backward motion does not exist in nature but is the privilege of the faculty of mind that Wordsworth calls the imagination, asserting the possibility of reflection in the face of the most radical dissolution, personal or historical. The imagination engenders hope and future, not in the form of historical progress, nor in the form of an immortal life after death that would make human history unimportant, but as the persistent, future possibility of a retrospective reflection on its own decay. The 1850 version of

The Prelude makes this clearest when it defines the imagination as being, at the same time, a sense of irreparable loss linked with the assertion of a persistent consciousness.

> I was lost
> Halted without an effort to break through;
> But to my *conscious soul* I now can say—
> "I recognise thy glory."
>
> [*1850 Prelude*, 6:596–99]

The restoring power, in Wordsworth, does not reside in nature, or in history, or in a continuous progression from one to the other, but in the persistent power of mind and language after nature and history have failed. One wonders what category of being can sustain the mind in this knowledge and give it the future that makes imagination dwell, in the later version of *The Prelude*, with "something evermore about to be" [6:608].

This may be the moment at which a return to Hartman's book is helpful. Like all attentive readers of Wordsworth, he reaches a point at which the nature of this restorative power has to be defined as the main assertive power in Wordsworth's poetry. And the understanding he has of Wordsworth's own mind allows him to give a very full and penetrating description of the complexities involved. He has noticed, more clearly than most other interpreters, that the imagination in Wordsworth is independent of nature and that it leads him to write a language, at his best moments, that is entirely unrelated to the exterior stimuli of the senses. He has also noticed that there is a kind of existential danger connected with this autonomy, and that when Wordsworth speaks about the *daring* of his imagery in the 1815 Preface, this risk involves more than mere experimentation with words. Hartman refers to this danger as an apocalyptic temptation, in his words, "a strong desire to cast out nature and to achieve an unmediated contact with the principle of things" [x]. Carried by the imagination, Wordsworth would at certain privileged moments come close to such visionary power, although he reaches it without supernatural intervention and always in a gradual and gentle way. Still, in the climactic passages of *The Prelude*, and in the main poems generally, the evidence of a moving beyond nature is unmistakable. What characterizes Wordsworth, according to Hartman, and sets him apart from Milton, for instance, and also from Blake, is that the apocalyptic moment is not sustained, that it is experienced as too damaging to the natural order of things to be tolerated. Out of reverence, not out of fear, Wordsworth feels the need to hide from sight the vision he has glimpsed for a moment; he has to do so, if his poetry is to continue its progression. And he finds the strength for this avoidance of apocalyptic abandon in nature itself—a nature that has been darkened and deepened by this very insight, and that has to some extent incorporated the power of imagination. But it has naturalized it, reunited it with a source that remains in the natural world. "The energy of imagination enters into a natural cycle though apart from it" [69], writes Hartman. The return to a natural image at the end of the famous passage on imagination in book 6 of *The Prelude* "renews the connection between the waters above and the waters below, between heaven and earth. Toward this marriage of heaven and earth the poet proceeds despite apocalypse. He is the matchmaker, his song the spousal verse" [69]. The road apparently beyond and away from nature in fact never ceased to be a natural road, albeit nature in a negative form, the *via naturaliter negativa*.

We cannot follow him in speaking of an apocalyptic temptation in Wordsworth. The passages that Hartman singles out as apocalyptic never suggest a movement toward an unmediated contact with a divine principle. The imagination [in book 6 of the 1805 version] is said to be "like an unfather'd vapour" [l. 527] and is, as such, entirely cut off from ultimate origins; it gives sight of "the invisible world" [l. 536], but the invisibility refers to the mental, inward nature of this world as opposed to the world of the senses; it reveals to us that our home is "with infinitude" [l. 539], but within the language of the passage this infinity is clearly to be understood in a temporal sense as the futurity of "something evermore about to be" [l. 542]. The heightening of pitch is not the result of "unmediated vision" but of another mediation, in which the consciousness does not relate itself any longer to nature but to a temporal entity. This entity could, with proper qualifications, be called history, and it is indeed in connection with historical events (the French Revolution) that the apostrophe to imagination comes to be written. But if we call this history, then we must be careful to understand that it is the kind of history that appeared at the end of the Duddon sonnet, the retrospective recording of man's failure to overcome the power of time. Morally, it is indeed a sentiment directed toward other men rather than toward nature, and, as such, imagination is at the root of Wordsworth's theme of human love. But the bond between men is not one of common enterprise, or of a common belonging to nature: it is much rather the recognition of a common temporal predicament that finds its expression in the individual and historical destinies that strike the poet as exemplary. Examples abound, from "The Ruined Cottage" to "Resolution and Independence," and in the various time-eroded figures that appear throughout *The Prelude*. The common denominator that they share is not nature but time, as it unfolds its power in these individual and collective histories.

Nor can we follow Hartman in his assertion of the ultimately regenerative power of nature. His argument returns to passages like the passage on imagination in book 6 of the [1850] *Prelude* in which, according to him, after having shown the "conscious soul" as independent, Wordsworth has to return to a natural image. The soul is said to be

> Strong in herself and in beatitude
> That hides her, like the mighty flood of Nile
> Poured from her fount of Abyssinian clouds
> To fertilize the whole Egyptian plain
>
> [*1850 Prelude*, 6:613–16; Hartman 69]

Perhaps enough has been said about the river Duddon to suggest that Wordsworth's rivers are not to be equated with natural entities. We don't even have to point to the further distancing from nature suggested by the exotic reference to an entity richer in mythological and literary than in natural associations; the abyss in "abyssinian" maintains the source far

beyond our reach, at a dizzying distance from ordinary perception and certainly not in "any mountain-valley where poetry is
made" [69], as Hartman would have it. The fertile plain at the
end occupies the same position that the historical world occupies in the last lines of the Duddon sonnet and is thus not a
symbol of regeneration. Hartman reads the "hiding" as naturally beneficial, as the protective act of nature that makes possible a fertile continuation of the poem and of life, in contrast to
the "unfathered vapour" that rejects the source in a supernatural realm. The hiding rather refers to the invisibility, the
inwardness, the depth of a temporal consciousness that, when
it reaches this level, can rejoice in the truth of its own insight
and find thoughts "too deep for tears." If rivers are, for Wordsworth, privileged emblems for the awareness of our mortal
nature, in contrast to the natural unity of echoes and correspondences, then the use of an allegorical river at this point
can hardly be the sign of a renewed bond with nature.

Hartman speaks of the need for Wordsworth "to respect
the natural (which includes the temporal) order" if his poetry
is to continue "as narrative" (46). The equation of natural with
temporal seems to us to go against Wordsworth's most essential affirmation. He could well be characterized as the romantic
poet in which the separation of time from nature is expressed
with the greatest thematic clarity. The narrative order, in the
short as well as in the longer poems, is no longer[14] linear; the
natural movement of his rivers has to be reversed as well as
transcended if they are to remain usable as metaphors. A certain form of narrative nevertheless persists, but it will have to
adopt a much more intricate temporal movement than that of
the natural cycles. The power that maintains the imagination,
which Hartman calls nature returning after it has been nearly
annihilated by apocalyptic insight, is time. The key to an understanding of Wordsworth lies in the relationship between
imagination and time, not in the relationship between imagination and nature.

A late poem of Wordsworth's that appears among the otherwise truly sterile sequence of the *Ecclesiastical Sonnets* can
well be used as a concluding illustration. Like all other romantic poets, Wordsworth claims a privileged status for poetic

language—a formula which was most legitimately put into question during our last session as standing in need of closer explanation. In Wordsworth, the privileged status of language is linked with the power of imagination, a faculty that rates higher than the fancy, or than rhetorical modes such as imitation, which, unlike the imagination, are dependent on correspondence with the natural world and thus limited by it. The language of imagination is privileged in terms of truth; it serves no empirical purposes or desires other than the truth of its own assertion:

> The mind beneath such banners militant
> Thinks not of spoils or trophies, nor of aught
> That may assert its prowess, blest in thoughts
> That are its own perfection and reward
> Strong in itself . . .
>
> [*1805 Prelude* 6:543–47, 372]

This truth is not a truth about objects in nature but a truth about the self; imagination arises "before the eyes and progress of my Song" [l. 526], in the process of self-discovery and as self-knowledge. A truth about a self is best described, not in terms of accuracy, but in terms of authenticity; true knowledge of a self is knowledge that understands the self as it really is. And since the self never exists in isolation, but always in relation to entities, since it is not a thing but the common center of a system of relationships or intents, an authentic understanding of a self means first of all a description of the entities toward which it relates, and of the order of priority that exists among these entities. For Wordsworth, the relationships toward time have a priority over relationships toward nature; one finds, in his work, a persistent deepening of self-insight represented as a movement that begins in a contact with nature, then grows beyond nature to become a contact with time. The contact, the relationship with time, is, however, always a negative one for us, for the relationship between the self and time is necessarily mediated by death; it is the experience of mortality that awakens within us a consciousness of time that is more than merely natural. This negativity is so powerful that no language could ever name time for what it is; time itself lies beyond language and beyond the reach of imagination. Wordsworth can only describe the outward movement of time's manifestation, and this outward movement is necessarily one of dissolution, the "deathward progressing" of which Keats speaks in *The Fall of Hyperion*. To describe this movement of dissolution, as it is perceived in the privileged language of the imagination, is to describe it, not as an actual experience that would necessarily be as brusk and dizzying as a fall, but as the generalized statement of the truth of this experience in its universality. Dissolution thus becomes mutability, asserted as an *unfailing* law that governs the natural, personal, and historical existence of man. Thus to name mutability as a principle of order is to come as close as possible to naming the authentic temporal consciousness of the self. The late poem entitled "Mutability" comes as close as possible to being a language that imagines what is, in essence, unimaginable:

MUTABILITY

From low to high doth dissolution climb,
And sinks from high to low, along a scale
Of awful notes, whose concord shall not fail;
A musical but melancholy chime,
Which they can hear who meddle not with crime,
Nor avarice, nor over-anxious care.
Truth fails not; but her outward forms that bear
The longest date do melt like frosty rime,
That in the morning whitened hill and plain
And is no more; drop like the tower sublime
Of yesterday, which royally did wear
Its crown of weeds, but could not even sustain
Some casual shout that broke the silent air,
Or the unimaginable touch of Time.

[780]

5

Fragment of the Fifth Gauss Lecture

If we try to move from the study of particular authors to a more general view of "romanticism," we run at once into a series of quite irrelevant questions. We start wondering whether the authors we have considered are either more or less properly "romantic" than others; we wonder if the kind of insight we have found in them is more or less generally prevalent among their contemporaries, etc. From the moment we start asking such questions, we lose contact with the actual significance of this insight and we cease to respond to the formal attributes of the language. We fall prey to the aberration of believing that historical facts exist for the benefit of a clear historical scheme, and that the intrinsic interest of a writer can be measured by the contribution he makes to the elaboration of a cogent historical outline. The validity of a historical term such as *romantic* can only be evaluated heuristically, by the contribution it can make to the understanding of statements, not to the ordering of data. Intellectual history seems to have had a great deal of difficulty escaping from the reification that threatens all historical narrative. Events or changes in the history of consciousness, in the historical process of the act of understanding, are not like events in nature, and no objective correlations can ever be found to prove that such events have actually taken place, as when we speak of a change in the weather or a change in a biological organism. The change does not occur as something that happens factually at a definite time and place, but in the increased self-understanding that takes place in the historical observer as he interprets the event. The history of romanticism is therefore not to be separated from the interpretation of individual authors, and the validity of the term does not depend on its greater or lesser inclusiveness, on its ability to set up a type to which a large number of particulars conforms more or less closely. It rather depends on the truth value of the knowledge that the term can be made to bear.

Some of the current writing on authors of the period indicates that the critics are deepening and refining their insight into this knowledge, and that they do so more successfully in dealing with some writers than with others. Contemporary criticism of romanticism has given up attempts at so-called synthesis for the study of particular texts and authors. It has directed its attention toward the texts most likely to contribute to genuine insight and has performed useful revisions in the established hierarchies of romantic authors. It seems now more fruitful, for instance, to approach a poet like Keats or Shelley, or even Coleridge, on the basis of the knowledge one can derive from Wordsworth rather than vice versa—and not for chronological reasons. Not only are [contemporary critics of romanticism] concerned with the right authors, but they reveal the high level of their understanding by the choice they make of the passages they select for major emphasis. The quality of quotation is always extremely high, even when the commentary sometimes remains a little below it. And the changes which the study of romanticism brought about in the conventional methods of literary history are of far-reaching importance. This is not surprising, for in stressing the predominance of a hermeneutically structured temporality in authors of the period, we implied that the poets, conceiving of themselves as the reflective interpreters of experience rather than as the originators or the imitators of unmediated experience, have in fact the concerns of the historian more closely than those of the visionary or the prophet. One can think of these writers as historians of the self; their main works—one thinks of Wordsworth's *Prelude*, of Keats's *Hyperion*, of Hölderlin's late hymns but also of *Faust*, of Hegel's *Phenomenology of Spirit*, and even of Baudelaire's *Fleurs du mal*—are such histories. It is perhaps a good sign that no satisfactory histories of romanticism, in the traditional conception of literary history, are available and that the historical study of the movement, in terms of antiquated concepts of influence, form, and periodization, is bogged down in a maze of irrelevant side issues. It reveals the impossibility of reified concepts of history to deal with a truly historical consciousness. By the time a more valid history of romanticism will come to be written, it may well look very different from what we have come to expect literary history to be.

For all their considerable merits, we found in most contemporary critics of romanticism a curious turning back at the very moment when they seemed closest to their conclusive point. Thus we found in Girard a potential theory of fiction as the gradual explication of a prefigured foreknowledge—but the very opposite is stated as a thesis. Starobinski provides an astutely chosen documentation to establish the dissociation of the empirical from the transcendental self in Rousseau, but seems himself to relapse at times into an empirical psychologism. Heidegger rightly names the central problem of Hölderlin's poetry as being that of language as mediation, but by a terminological sleight-of-hand makes the poet say the opposite of what he actually says about this very problem. Hartman shows quite convincingly how the category of nature is superseded in Wordsworth, but then smuggles nature back in through the back door. In all these cases, the critics seem to have gone to the right kind of evidence but to have shrunk back before the full impact of their findings. We never had to go far beyond the texts they used to show their reversal of the original position: it is not that they loaded the scales by ignoring certain aspects of their authors, rather that they seemed reluctant to stay till the end with evidence they had themselves discovered.

One can attribute this recurrent pattern, of which I am certainly myself also a victim, to the feeling of crisis that comes over all thought when it comes into close contact with its own source. It happens frequently enough, in the case of philosophers as well as critics, that the very text in which a certain attitude of mind is convincingly shown to be conducive to truth fails to adopt, in relation to itself, the attitude it advocates. Among many possible examples, I think of Husserl, in his *Crisis of the European Sciences and Transcendental Phenomenology*, defining eloquently the proper philosophical attitude as a steady putting into question of its own premises, a steady philosophical doubt about the possibility of philosophy, and then proceeding to state, with entirely uncritical blandness, the *a priori* supremacy of Western posthellenic philosophy over all other modes of cognition. Something similar is certainly going on in the case of romanticism, and it proves, by itself, how powerful a source romanticism still is for our own consciousness. Put in more pragmatic historical terms, it seems as if the critics in question were hampered from reaching their conclusions by certain postromantic assumptions, reached in the course of the nineteenth century, from which they are not entirely able to free themselves—although they have come quite a way in doing so. It might be that between the later eighteenth century and ourselves stands a long period that is regressive, in terms of self-insight, in relation to romanticism, and that we have to overcome this obstacle before we can reestablish contact with the real source. Our two last lectures will deal with some aspects of this possible regression, first by examining a specific problem of romanticism, then by seeing how a nineteenth-century, postromantic poet like Baudelaire could be . . .

[At this point the page numbers indicate that some twenty-five pages are missing from the handwritten manuscript, which concludes in the following way:[1]]

The same problem exists in a different form in English and German romanticism, obscured, in the latter case, by the apparent opposition between Jena romanticism and Weimar classicism. The historians of English romanticism, however, have repeatedly raised the question of allegorical diction, but most of the time as a side issue. Wimsatt comes upon it, in the previously mentioned article, in connection with Blake.[2] He quotes two brief poems by Blake—"To Spring" and "To Summer"—and comments, "Blake's starting point . . . is the opposite of Wordsworth's or Byron's, not the landscape but a spirit personified or allegorized. Nevertheless, this spirit as it approaches the 'western isle' takes on distinctly terrestrial hues. . . . These early romantic poems are examples of the Biblical, classical, and Renaissance tradition of allegory as it approaches the romantic condition of landscape naturalism—as Spring and Summer descend into the landscape and are fused with it" (113). Rather than this continuous development from allegory to naturalism, the example of Rousseau shows us the rediscovery of an allegorical (or, better, figural) tradition beyond the analogical naturalism that stems from the eighteenth century. Starting out from the eighteenth-century local poem, Abrams can be even more precise. After having pointed out the thematic resemblance between romantic and metaphyiscal poetry, he goes on: "There is a very conspicuous and significant difference between the Romantic lyric and the seventeenth-century meditation on created nature. . . . The 'composition of place' was not a specific locality, nor did it need to be present to the eyes of the speaker, but was a typical scene or object, usually called up . . . before 'the eyes of the imagination' in order to set off and guide the thought by means of correspondences whose interpretation was firmly controlled by an inherited typology."[3] The distinction is made in terms of the determining importance of the geographical place as a link with natural experience.

As one watches the progress of a poet like Wordsworth, however, the significance of the locale tends to broaden into an area of meaning that is no longer literally bound to a particular place. The significance of the landscape is frequently made problematic by a succession of spatial ambiguities, to such an extent that one ends up no longer with a specific locale but with a mere name, of which the geographical existence has been voided of significance. "The spirit of the answer [as to the specific locale of a given symbol, that of the river—PdM]," says Wordsworth, "though the word might be sea or ocean, accompanied perhaps with an image gathered from a map, or from the real object in nature—these might have been the *letter*, but the *spirit* of the answer must have been, *as* inevitably,—a receptacle without bounds or dimensions;— nothing less than infinity."[4] Passages like the crossing of the Alps or the ascent of Mount Snowden in *The Prelude* can no

longer be traced back to the locodescriptive poems of the eighteenth century. In Abrams's own terms, the interpretation of
these passages is no longer dependent on a specific locale,
but is now controlled "by an inherited typology," exactly as
was the case in sixteenth- and seventeenth-century poetry—
except that the typology is not the same and that the poet first
has to renounce the possibilities and surmount the limitations
of a metaphorical diction. It is a short-lived victory, for before
long the temptation of a metaphorical style will return to English, as it did to French poetry, and create the style we generally refer to as "romantic," although it obscures the actual insight of the period. But this new . . .

[The rest of the manuscript pages are missing.]

6

Allegory and Irony in Baudelaire

T HE DESCRIPTION of romanticism to which we were led by a critical examination of some contemporary interpretations of the movement is difficult to grasp and to summarize. It is difficult from a conceptual point of view because it expresses a tension that doesn't easily lend itself to philosophical paraphrase. A dialectic between subject and object can find, in the vocabulary of German and French idealism, a readily available terminology and a logic; even the presumably empirical vocabulary of English and American criticism is founded, in the last analysis, on unexamined premises that can be traced back to idealist conceptions. But the actual diction of the romantic poets, as we saw last time, is not based on a subject/object relationship only. The objective reference tends to vanish, reduced to grammatical articulations of language that have a purely structural function devoid of ontological significance. The tension is entirely located within a self that remains autonomous in its relation to the outside world; a rigorous investigation along idealist lines can go just far enough to reach this conclusion and then has to disqualify itself from further effectiveness. This point is being reached in a confused form in much of the critical writing of today: in the American interpreters of romanticism, in French phenomenological critics, as well as in German critics in the idealist tradition, whether they go back to Hegel or to Dilthey. But the problem had been stated with considerable philosophical clarity as early as 1917, in an insufficiently known article of Georg Lukács: "As the fulfillment of

an artistic activity, the work is fully transcendental in relation
to the constitutive subject. But the fact that it is . . . more than
an object, although it is the only adequate objective expression
of a subjectivity, is reflected in the infinite process of artistic
activity and in the leap in which this activity culminates."[1]

"The infinite process of literary activity and the leap in
which this activity culminates"—with this vocabulary, we are
no longer in the realm of a subject/object relationship but have
come back to the insight of the early romantic writers.[2] This
temporal process discloses the historicity of literary language,
engaged in a continued act of self-interpretation that is, in fact,
endless. We return here to what we referred to as the figural
conception of literary language in romanticism. The determining relationship is not oriented toward natural objects but toward other, anterior literary languages that appear as exemplary in that they proleptically foretell the act of renunciation
that allows for this temporal relationship to come into being.
We described this very relationhip when we tried to recapture
the intricate temporality of Wordsworth's poem on the Winander boy: Wordsworth retrospectively reflecting on a self
that is proleptically bringing him into contact with his authentic temporal destiny. The Winander boy appears in this poem
as Wordsworth's own *figura*. In the wider scale of literary history his place would be taken by the literary precursors whose
destiny, as it appears in their work, has an exemplary value for
the writer. The central articulations in the history of literature
occur when such moments of recognition take place, as between Dante and Virgil, between Milton and Virgil, between
Wordsworth and Milton. We have tried to show that romanticism was such a moment.

The distinctive character of such moments of temporal recognition is always determined by the nature of the obstacle
that has to be removed to make the recognition possible, by the
error which hid the true predicament from sight. In the case of
romanticism the error is that of a self that tries to forget its own
temporal fate by patterning itself on the eternal aspects of
nature; hence, a conception of the self as the pole of a subject/
object relationship becomes the illusion that has to be renounced. The somber light, the harsh serenity that prevails in

authentic romantic literature, expresses the difficulty of this renunciation. And the persistent intellectual refinement with which the successors of romanticism have pursued the dialectic of subject and object to its most extreme form indicates the increased strength with which this renunciation is being resisted. The major poets that come after romanticism are mostly impressive as negative figures, by the subtlety of the strategies they devised to avoid confronting the self-insight achieved by their predecessors. Some of them, however, came closer to this insight, though none, it seems, has recognized the romantic ancestors as clearly as the romantics were able to recognize their own precursors in the sixteenth and seventeenth century. Their relationship to the truth of romanticism is, at best, highly oblique and ironic. We have tried to document how this truth still remains elusive to the most perceptive of the contemporary critics. A comparable blindness can be found in post-romantic writers and poets as well, and nineteenth- or twentieth-century literary movements such as realism, symbolism, surrealism, etc. can be described as various forms of misunderstanding of romanticism, the most interesting ones being those in which the understanding comes close enough to the source to force the writer into a conscious attitude of bad faith. But the most complex case of all is that of the greatest poet since romanticism. Is the work of Charles Baudelaire a novel articulation in the history of literature of that which romanticism, in its turn, would have been a prefiguration? Or is he himself to be grouped with the writers we discussed as a later version, in somewhat different historical circumstances, of the same experience? Or is he, like other nineteenth-century poets and twentieth-century critics, mystified to the point of blindness about his actual understanding of his precursors? One's entire conception of postromantic literature will depend on the answer to this question, since Baudelaire's position is central to the whole of modern European literature.

Recent criticism of Baudelaire has been influenced by the interpretation that Sartre gave of Baudelaire in his 1947 essay.[3] Sartre rightly saw that in Baudelaire there is a disjunction between the self that appears in the work, the voice that speaks in the poems, and the actual person Baudelaire, and that this disjunction is rooted not in the accidents of Baudelaire's life but in the structure of his consciousness. Sartre then describes a strategy by means of which Baudelaire tried to heal this disjunction, using his poetry for this very purpose. His language would be the expression of a material imagination that represents his mental universe in sensory terms, thus making the whole of the objective world into an analogous extension of his consciousness. "Like Baudelaire," writes Sartre,

> we will describe as *spiritual* the thing which allows itself to be apprehended by the senses and which most resembles consciousness. The whole of Baudelaire's efforts were devoted to the recovery of his consciousness, to possessing it like an object in the hollow of his hand. . . . He was haunted by the desire to touch and feel thoughts which had become objects—his own incarnate thoughts. . . . His poems themselves are "corporealized" thoughts, not simply because they have assumed bodily form in the signs employed, but mainly because each of them . . . is a restrained, fleeting existence exactly like a scent . . . Such was the term of Baudelaire's efforts—to take possession of himself in his eternal "difference," to realize his Otherness by identifying himself with the whole world. Lightened, hollowed out, filled with signs and symbols, this world which enfolded him in its immense totality was nothing but himself; and he was himself the Narcissus who wanted to embrace and contemplate himself. (175–76, 179).

One recognizes in this language a popularized version of the problem Lukács described in his philosophical essay: the contradiction of the aesthetic self if it sees itself as engaged in a dialectic of subject and object. All the other commonplaces about Baudelaire, his dandyism, his fetishism, his theory of correspondences, his bad faith in his relations to others, all of which figure prominently in Sartre's essay, derive from this initial orientation of the consciousness toward the material sensation of the object. Another critic, Jean-Pierre Richard, who by no means shares Sartre's ambivalent hostility toward Baudelaire, describes the materiality of Baudelaire's language as giving density and consistency to the void of his consciousness: "Le substantif emplit la profondeur. En substituant à la viduité du gouffre la plénitude véritablement *substantielle* d'un sens, il lui donne épaisseur et densité [The substantive fills in the depth. By substituting the truly *substantial* plenitude of a meaning for the emptiness of the abyss it endows it with volume and density]."[4] Despite all the difference in value emphasis, Richard is in fact following in Sartre's footsteps.

We don't have to inquire into the motives that led Sartre to substitute his own obsessions for those of Baudelaire. That his description of Baudelaire's poetry has missed the outstanding characteristic of the poet's theme and diction will be clear from our subsequent remarks, and there will be no need to return to Sartre. Other critics have come closer to Baudelaire's real concerns. Perhaps the Baudelaire image furthest removed from Sartre's, and closest to the poet's actual consciousness, is that suggested by Walter Benjamin when he stresses Baudelaire's language as destructive of organic, sensory relationships and as predominantly allegorical. "Baudelaire's allegory," writes Benjamin, "in contrast to baroque allegory, shows the traces of anger, of wrath (*Ingrimms*), which was necessary to reduce the harmonious constructs of this world incessantly to ruins. . . . The signature of heroism in Baudelaire is to live at the heart of irreality (of appearance—*des Scheins*). It follows that Baudelaire has not really known nostalgia. . . . The renunciation of the magic attraction of distances is one of the decisive moments in Baudelaire's lyric poetry."[5] This characterization of Baudelaire goes against all the prevalent *idées reçues* describing him as a poet of nostalgic memories, of narcissistic, autoerotic sensuality and of material symbols. The stress on allegory is of particular interest to us since it suggests a possible proximity of Baudelaire to the kind of tension between symbolic and figural diction we found prevalent in early romanticism.

The notion of allegory, as applied to Baudelaire, tends to be confusing, and Benjamin's remarks are too cryptic to provide a firm basis. One would have to distinguish between at least two aspects of Baudelaire's poetry, both of which could be called allegorical. One thinks, of course, first of all of the notion of "analogie universelle," which occurs at different moments in the critical prose, as early as the Salon of 1846 and still prominently in 1861 in the articles on Hugo and Wagner, and which underlies the famous sonnet "Correspondances." To see the material and the spiritual world connected by a system of correspondences can reduce nature to a set of signs that refer, allegorically, to a unity of a greater order, the senses being, as it were, the key to this allegorical deciphering. Among Baudelaire's numerous sources for this conception many are of romantic origin; through Poe, Mrs. Crowe, and de Quincey, his description of the universe "as a storehouse of images and signs to which the imagination gives a place and a relative value"[6] is related to Coleridge, [who was] himself directly derived from Schelling. This assertion is a commonplace of romantic idealism, much more frequent, however, as a general assertion of faith than as a poetic practice. Baudelaire, in this respect, is no exception. For the assertions about an analogical universe of correspondences occur in the critical articles but find, in fact, very few equivalences in his poetic practice. The general impression one receives of Baudelaire's work is not at all that of an impersonal affirmation of a metaphysical unity between mind and matter. Very few poems, in fact, have the philosophical generality of texts such as "Correspondances," "L'Homme et la mer" or even "Elévation," all of them poems that date from well before 1855. Even in "Correspondances," the unity of mind and nature is based on the assertion that, in nature, "Les parfums, les couleurs et les sons se *répondent*," thus suggesting the model of a conversation, of language exchanged between human subjects, as the analogous link between the spiritual world and the world of the senses. But this intersubjective element is generally much stronger in Baudelaire's work than in this rather untypical poem.

The predominant impression is not that of an impersonal subject lost in oneness with nature but instead of a very specific and particular self in its relation to others. A great variety of human types appear throughout the work, individual human beings as well as groups (*les artistes, les amants, les chiffonniers, les petites vieilles*, etc.), and their main function is not so much to act as mediators between the poet's subjectivity and a world of external or natural objects, but rather to dramatize conflicts and tensions that exist within the self. This interpersonal, dramatic element seems to grow more and more prominent, to the point where the work becomes increasingly narrative in form, and the poems, especially the later ones, become short stories, *récits* with a very distinctive plot outline; not landscapes or scenes, but dramatic actions. These actions are by no means realistic but function as parables, allegorical tales illuminating the fate of a certain type of mind and its destiny in the world. The prose poems of the *Spleen de Paris*, Baudelaire's latest book, are certainly allegorical, but this allegory has nothing in common with the allegory of correspondences found earlier. It has nothing to do with a possible unity with nature, or with a cosmology of transparent signs. It has the clarity of outline of an arabesque, a sharp contour very different from the confused depth of a world in which "de longs échos . . . de loin se confondent." It is this later allegorical style which has to be interpreted if we wish to relate Baudelaire to his romantic predecessors.

The world of correspondences and analogies functions, in Baudelaire's poetic world, as a myth, as a conception that can only be admitted or rejected in terms of belief. A naive commentator on Baudelaire illustrates this well when he waxes earnestly indignant against anyone who would dare to question Baudelaire's faith in the myth. "A cette réalité métaphysique des correspondances, il croit de la façon la plus ferme, et il est inconcevable qu'on ait pu soutenir le contraire. Il y croit en 1856 . . . Il y croit plus que jamais en 1861 . . . etc. [He believes in this metaphysical reality with total conviction, and it would be inconceivable to suggest otherwise. He believes in it in 1856 . . . He believes in it more than ever in 1861 . . . etc.]."[7] All Baudelaire's assertions of pseudofaith are taken at face value, independently of a tone which draws explicit attention to the fact that they are precisely that, mere assertions of faith. Yet Baudelaire himself had warned: "the only concession which could reasonably be made to the partisans of the theory that considers faith as the only source of religious experience is that the poet, the comedian and the artist, at the moment they are engaged in the performance of their task, believe in the reality of what they represent, stimulated as they are by necessity. Therefore art is the only spiritual domain in which man can say: 'I'll believe if I wish, and if I don't want to, I will not believe (*Je croirai si je veux, et si je ne veux pas, je ne croirai pas*)'" ("Religion, Histoire, Fantaisie," *Salon de 1859* 2:628–29).

Transferring in this manner the decision of belief onto the will of the poet reduces in fact the myth to pure illusion. The depth, the infinite expansion of the universe of correspondences—*vaste comme la nuit et comme la clarté* [as spacious as night and clarity]—is a myth, a beautiful but arbirary construct that the consciousness of the poet can destroy at will. At all times, any intrusion from the outside (a knock at the door, the mere passage of time, as well as the decision of the author himself) can undo the harmony of the imaginative vision and shrink this universe down to the point where it becomes like a confining space in which the mind feels trapped. This moment of sudden demythification, when the artist awakens from his illusion, when the vision dissolves, is a recurrent and essential moment in Baudelaire. It is linked with a contraction of space, or with a sudden, shock-like discontinuity that, like a death, separates the mystified from the awakened self. In the late story entitled "Une Mort héroique," the comedian figure of the poet is brought to his immediate death when his performance is brutally interrupted by the deliberate intruding action of another allegorical figure, a ruler who is himself another incarnation of the poet's consciousness. The sudden contraction of the poetic universe is evoked in the opening lines of "Le Voyage":

> Pour l'enfant amoureux de cartes et d'estampes,
> L'univers est égal à son vaste appétit.
> Ah! que le monde est grand à la clarté des lampes!
> Aux yeux du souvenir que le monde est petit!

[For the child in love with maps and charts the universe is as big as his wants. Ah, but the world is grand in the light of a lamp! But through the eyes of memory it becomes so small!]

The "belief" in the unity of a world of correspondences is as vulnerable as all others to this awakening shock. One cannot understand the generic development of Baudelaire leading to his later allegorical style if one fails to see that this shock stands at the very beginning of his poetic itinerary; his work is not a strategy to avoid its effect, but an attempt to incorporate this very experience in a language that nevertheless remains poetic and refuses to let itself be destroyed by the destructive immediacy of the shock.

For Baudelaire starts out in the particular restlessness of the man who thus feels oppressed in a world in which all the myths that relate him, as a subject, to this world no longer give him any real assurance. A line of the poet Hugo von Hofmannsthal describes this predicament, as well as points to its possible transcendence: "Was Geist ist, erfaszt nur der Bedrängte."[8] *Der Bedrängte* is a word that is difficult to translate. It combines an impression of spatial oppression, of being locked in too narrow a space, with the temporal ordeal of being steadily harrassed, pressed by urgency, an impossibility of remaining motionless in the same place. One thinks of Pascal, of course, but also of man in Baudelaire's "Le Voyage" driven "like a top (*imitant la toupie et la boule*)":

> Singulière fortune où le but se déplace,
> Et, n'étant nulle part, peut être n'importe où!
> Où l'Homme, dont jamais l'espérance n'est lasse,
> Pour trouver le repos court toujours comme un fou!

> [Singular fate in which the endpoint moves and, being nowhere, can be anywhere at all! In which Man, whose hope knows no fatigue, in order to find peace runs constantly and madly about!]

Only the man who knows this feeling of harrassed confinement, says Hofmannsthal, can find access to spirit, can aspire to the tranquillity that only exists in the realm of the contemplative mind. Caught in this ontological "ennui," Baudelaire's first reaction will indeed be this voyage into space, what Binswanger calls the "march into the distance," the search for new experiences to which one can find access without leaving the horizontal space that stretches to the horizons of the world. But, because the confinement is not merely due to the spatial contraction of the universe, but is caused by the excessive presence of time, these movements of horizontal extension can never relieve the predicament. The disappointment, the failure is manifest in the fact that these horizontal movements fail to be more than a game, a way of killing time, as Baudelaire puts it in a prose poem. The poetic leap forced upon us by the temporal nature of our existence demands a different kind of act, a passing from a mere extension of the self to an altogether different kind of self that results from a radical change of the *level* of consciousness. One can think of it—although the spatial metaphor is misleading—as a vertical movement of climbing and falling rather than the horizontal motion of the voyage. Baudelaire ascends literally above the world of his *ennui*, which is the world of the exploded myth of the correspondences, by a movement of ascent that allows him to occupy a vantage point from which he can encompass the totality of the world that now lies underneath him. Such privileged viewpoints, high rooms from which one looks down upon Paris, balconies from which one contemplates a past or a future condition, become more and more prominent in his work as symbolic of the manner in which he relates himself to earthly experience:

> Le coeur content, je suis monté sur la montagne
> D'où l'on peut contempler la ville en son ampleur,
> Hôpital, lupanar, purgatoire, enfer, bagne,
> Où toute énormité fleurit comme une fleur . . .

[With a light heart I climbed the mountain from which one can contemplate the city in all its fullness; hospital, house of pleasure, purgatory, hell, penal colony in which every outrage blossoms like a flower . . .] ("Projets d'un épilogue pour l'édition de 1861," *Oeuvres* 1:191).

This privileged viewpoint is not an escape from the condition of restlessness by which he was originally threatened; it is, in fact, a more precarious state than ever. The possibility of falling, which is an event forced upon us by an exterior force and doesn't depend on our will, exists only in a vertical space, [like] such related experiences as dizziness (*vertige*) or relapse. This is another way of saying that in such experiences of verticality death is present in a more immediate and more radical way than in the experiences of the earthly, active life.

How can the poet constitute this other self that overlooks the former self caught in the world, as from a higher viewpoint? In Baudelaire, a variety of privileged experiences contribute to this gradual depersonalization which allows for a perspective of distance upon one's own consciousness, for the creation of a point of view which is that of an *observer* of the self. One of these experiences is that of the city and the crowd. "For the passionate observer," writes Baudelaire in "Le Peintre de la vie moderne,"

> "there is an immense satisfaction in housing himself within the number, in what is transient, mobile, unstable and infinite. To be outside oneself (*hors de chez soi*) and still to feel everywhere at home (*chez soi*); to see the world, to be at the center of the world and to remain hidden from the world, such are some of the lesser pleasures of these independent, passionate, impartial spirits for which it is difficult to find a descriptive term. One can compare them to a mirror as immense as the crowd itself; to a kaleidoscope endowed with consciousness of which each movement represents the multiplicity of life and the graceful motion of all elements of which life is made up. It is a self insatiable for a nonself which, at all times, expresses and reflects this self in images that are more alive than a life that always remains transient and fugitive (C'est un *moi* insatiable du *non-moi*, qui, à chaque instant le rend et l'exprime en images plus vivantes que la vie elle-même, toujours instable et fugitive)." ("Le Peintre de la vie moderne," *Oeuvres* 2:692).

The experience of the crowd, together with several other experiences that become Baudelaire's preferred themes—that of the child, of the woman, of the dandy, and many others—are all particular versions of experiences that allow for the origination of an *ironic* consciousness and diction. It is by means of irony that Baudelaire achieves the dominant overlooking position that represents his form of vertical transcendence.

The essay on humor entitled "De l'essence du rire" is therefore the text in which this multiplication of the self, by means of which the subject can come face to face with its own fallen condition and with the threat of a persistent falling, is most clearly expressed. Man is defined in this essay as the entity capable of irony, capable, that is, of perceiving the contradiction which is inherent in him: "Le rire est essentiellement contradictoire, c'est-à-dire qu'il est à la fois signe d'une grandeur infinie et d'une misère infinie, misère infinie relativement à l'Etre absolu dont il possède la conception, grandeur infinie relativement aux animaux [laughter is essentially contradictory, in other words it is simultaneously a sign of infinite grandeur and of infinite wretchedness; infinite wretchedness with respect to the supreme Being of which it has the conception, and infinite grandeur with respect to the animal world]" ("De l'essence du rire," *Oeuvres* 2:532).[9] And in what he calls philosophic man, *le philosophe*, which in fact designates the poet, irony is the possibility to name the contradiction, to make his own fall the object of his laughter; he can do so "because he has acquired, by habit, the strength of making himself *quickly* double (*la force de se dédoubler rapidement*) and to observe as a disinterested spectator the phenomenon of his own self. . . . For there to be humor"—which, in this text, is equivalent to irony—"two beings must be present, except in the case of men who make it their trade to develop within themselves the feeling of irony and to produce it for the entertainment of their fellow beings. This phenomenon enters under the general heading of all artistic phenomena which denote, in the human being, the existence of a permanent duality, the power of being at the same time oneself and someone else" (2:543).

This definition of irony is clearly a later version of romantic irony as it is stated theoretically in Friedrich Schlegel, or in Solger, or practiced in such writers as E. T. A. Hoffmann, to whom Baudelaire directly alludes. The use that Baudelaire makes of irony, however, indicates his genuine affinity with an insight that is deeply and personally his own. Irony becomes the structural principle by means of which his work develops. It does so in a very specific and concrete way, by the fact that many of Baudelaire's poems are later, ironic versions of poems that had originally been stated in a nonironic, or only potentially ironic tonality. Several later poems are interpretations of earlier versions of the same poems, interpretations that bring out an ironic potential that was always there but had been hidden from the reader's and perhaps even from the author's consciousness. And this kind of ironic "repetition"—using the word in the full Kierkegaardian sense of the term (Baudelaire and Kierkegaard's notion of irony being very closely related and having, be it said in passing, a common point of reference in Hoffmann's story "The Princess Brambilla")—this ironic repetition, then, is particularly in evidence when the original poem starts out from the theme of analogical correspondences.

I have time for only two very brief illustrations. The poem "Correspondances" has, as far as I know, not been dated exactly but is at any rate anterior to 1855.[10] A poem from 1860 entitled "Obsession" is clearly an amalgamation of the setting of "Correspondances" with a passing allusion to another previous poem founded on apparent analogy and entitled "L'Homme et la mer." Several direct verbal echoes establish the link with "Correspondances" beyond any possible doubt. But "Obsession" appears as an explicit demythification of the assertive positivity of the earlier poem, a demythification achieved by taking the symbolic assertion of "Correspondances" literally and showing what it means from the point of view of an actual self. Instead of being the sensory qualities of nature, sound, color, and perfume, that answer each other, it is now the hearts of particular men that *respond* to nature, that *answer*, when the sounds of nature are horrifying and chaotic enough to correspond to the bitterly ironic derision with which the self has to contemplate its own mortal condition. The language of nature which, in "Correspondances," stated an originary unity now becomes an obstacle to the kind of language the poet would want to use. For nature speaks a language that is all too familiar, not by itself, since the otherness of authentic nature resides in an area that no language can reach, but because we endow nature with the illusory correspondences that originate in ourselves. As such, they are the expression of our own regrets and nostalgias, of the beings real and imaginary, that existed in the past and that have been like the stations recording the fall into the present state of mourning and distress. The interpersonal element that was potentially present in "Correspondances" is now fully in evidence: what was presented as a relationship toward nature was in fact a relationship toward other human beings, that *we* projected into nature. The familiar glances that are forever looking at us are not in nature, but are aspects of our own past, of our own self in its involvements with others, which record our undoing. They have become obsessions that stand between us and true self-knowledge:

OBSESSION

Grands bois, vous m'effrayez comme des cathédrales;
Vous hurlez comme l'orgue; et dans nos coeurs maudits,
Chambres d'éternel deuil où vibrent de vieux râles,
Répondent les échos de vos *De Profundis.*

Je te hais, Océan! tes bonds et tes tumultes,
Mon esprit les retrouve en lui; ce rire amer
De l'homme vaincu, plein de sanglots et d'insultes,
Je l'entends dans le rire énorme de la mer.

Comme tu me plairais, ô nuit! sans ces étoiles
Dont la lumière parle un langage connu!
Car je cherche le vide, et le noir, et le nu!

Mais les ténèbres sont elles-mêmes des toiles
Où vivent, jaillissant de mon oeil par milliers,
Des êtres disparus aux regards familiers.

[Great woods, you terrify me like cathedrals; you shout like an organ; and in our accursed hearts, shelters for eternal mourning that resonate with ancient death rattles, respond the echoes of your *De Profundis.* I hate you, Ocean! Your leaps and bounds find their way inside my mind; I can hear that bitter laughter of the beaten man, full of sob and insult, in the outrageous laughter of the sea. How you would please me, o night! without those stars whose light speaks a well-known language! For I seek the void, and the dark, and the unadorned! But even the shadows themselves are canvases on which live, darting from my eye by the thousand, departed ones whose looks are all too familiar.]

Although the tone of the poem, despite its reference to "rire amer," is not ironic, the allusive reference to "Correspondances" certainly establishes an ironic attitude toward the assertion of this poem; correspondences now become an obstacle to authentic poetry, a way to hide the predicament of the self by a pseudo-objective myth that manipulates nature for the purpose of self-deceit.

Another example comes from the well-known poem "L'Invitation au voyage," in which Baudelaire addresses a woman and invites her to journey with him to a country "qui te ressemble [that resembles you]." The poem seems to move away from the theme of a resemblance, or an analogy between the woman and the country, and describes the region as a reconciled world, a state without tension in which a highly complex system of correspondences, much subtler than the synesthesia of the sonnet "Correspondances," achieves a suspended state of balance between potentially negative forces. Baudelaire returned to the poem later and wrote a prose version for the *Petits poèmes en prose* that curiously modifies the balance and the point of view. The emphasis on the theme of resemblance is now much more in evidence, and rather than an evocation of the ideal region, the text literalizes what was indefinite and symbolic in the early version. The country becomes a very specific and explicitly *named* Holland, the "luxe" of the early refrain ("Là tout n'est qu'ordre et beauté / Luxe, calme et volupté [there one finds nothing but order and beauty / Luxuriousness, calm, and voluptuousness])" becomes the economic reward of the hardworking burgher, the "ordre" the proverbial cleanliness of the Dutch housewife, the "volupté" the lavishness of a cuisine called "poétique, grasse et excitante à la fois [poetic, rich, and exciting all at once]." By thus giving to all the symbols a concrete, literal significance, Baudelaire also makes evident the interpersonal function of the analogy: the comparison with the foreign region is primarily a compliment addressed to the lady, perhaps in the hope of seducing her, but the carefully worked out details of the comparison make the poem into an ambivalent, ironic portrait, reminiscent in some respects of the portraits of La Bruyère, for which Baudelaire had considerable admiration. The analogies thus become a device to evoke the mood of an interpersonal relationship, in all its ambiguities and complexities. When the woman is compared to an analogical flower, this flower too has been made extremely literal by allusions to the prizes awarded in Holland to the growers of rare new species of tulips. The least one can say is that when Sartre quotes the following passage as representative of Baudelaire's mythical and deluded faith in an escapist analogism, he has entirely missed

the ironic context in which it appears; it could almost be reduced to a teasing comment on feminine vanity:

> Moi, j'ai trouvé *ma tulipe noire* et mon *dahlia bleu*! . . . Fleur incom-
> parable, tulipe retrouvée, allégorique dahlia, c'est là, n'est-ce pas,
> dans ce beau pays si calme et si rêveur, qu'il faudra aller vivre et
> fleurir? Ne serais-tu pas encadrée dans ton analogie et ne
> pourrais-tu pas te mirer, pour parler comme les mystiques, dans
> ta propre *correspondance*?

> [I have found *my black tulip* and my *blue dahlia*! . . . Incomparable
> flower, rediscovered tulip, allegorical dahlia, shouldn't we go live
> in that wonderful country, so peaceful and dreamy? Wouldn't you
> be surrounded by your own resemblance and couldn't you reflect
> yourself, to speak like the mystics, in your own *correspondence*?]
> ("L'Invitation au voyage," *Oeuvres* 1:301–3)

The tone of this kind of irony is not easy to catch. It does not
destroy the original beauty of the world of correspondences,
nor does it in any way depoeticize the original poem. One can
go back to it with increased insight and appreciation. For that
matter, the prose poem is as felicitous and suggestive as its
antecedent in verse. The irony is not destructive, but it sees the
original description from a different and higher point of view.
It has by no means introduced a realistic, empirical element
that would show the earlier vision as being in bad faith. The
point of view is, if anything, further removed from reality by
showing ironically how the earlier conception of beauty still
drew too heavily on material elements that belong to a fallen
world. The prose poems are more and not less allegorical than
the earlier poems in verse and acquire this element of irreality
that is an essential component of Baudelaire's language: "Deux
qualités littéraires fondamentales: surnaturalisme et ironie
[Two fundamental literary qualities: supernaturalism and
irony]" (*Fusées, Oeuvres* 1:658). Irony is the device by means of
which the excessive naturalism of the correspondences is exorcized and renounced in the hope of achieving a truly allegorical style, no longer dependent on references to entities
that lie outside the self. That still neglected masterpiece, the
prose poetry of Baudelaire considered as a whole, as a completed work of the same order as the *Fleurs du mal*, represents

Baudelaire's attempt to reach the level of language that we found sustained in some of the romantic poets.

But is it possible for irony to take us this far? Wordsworth, Hölderlin, the best passages in Rousseau are not ironic, but lay claim to being a straightforward expression of authentic wisdom. There is no element there of play, of the hoax and deceit that Baudelaire admired in Poe and in Hoffmann, and that feeds his irony. The self-reflection does not seem to need the ironic moment in order to achieve the distance from itself for which Baudelaire is striving. But Baudelaire himself never suggested that the highest poetic achievement had to be ironic. In the same essay on laughter, he writes: "If, in an ultracivilized nation, an intelligence inspired by a superior ambition wants to go beyond the limits of worldly vanity and to move decisively toward pure poetry, from this poetry . . . laughter will be absent as it is absent from the soul of Wisdom (*dans cette poésie, le rire fera défaut comme dans l'âme du Sage*)" (*Oeuvres* 2:532–33). It is not easy to decide whether Baudelaire ever achieved this metaironic "pure poetry" of which instances can be found among his romantic predecessors—although these instances are very different from what will later be referred to, in another context, as *poésie pure*. If one wanted to find such instances in his work, it would be in the poems in which the themes of human suffering and death coalesce, whether or not they are placed in an ironic context, in poems such as "La Servante au grand coeur," "Recueillement," "La Mort des artistes," or late prose poems such as "Le Tir et le cimetière," "Une mort héroique," etc.—all of which still await exegesis.

The same level of self-insight exists in these poems as can be found in Rousseau's sense of "le néant des choses humaines [the nothingness of human matters]" or Wordsworth's sense of mutability. In book 7 of the *Prelude*, Wordsworth describes his experience of what he calls the "blank confusion" of the crowds in the city, a confusion that transports him into a sense of irreality far removed from the everyday world but very close to the state of "supernaturalism" that Baudelaire reaches by ironic self-detachment. In this mood, the sudden encounter with a blind beggar causes him, with the suddenness of revelation, to discover all possible knowledge accessible to man mediated by this figure of suffering and imminent death. One is very close to the final theme of Baudelaire's late poetry in these lines, as one is close also to the reference from *Paradise Lost* that Wordsworth singled out in the 1815 Preface, in which the sky is weeping "at completion of the mortal sin":

> How often, in the overflowing streets
> Have I gone forwards with the crowd, and said
> Unto myself, 'The face of every one
> That passes by me is a mystery.'
> Thus have I looked, nor ceased to look, oppressed
> By thoughts of what and whither, when and how,
> Until the shapes before my eyes became
> A second-sight procession, such as glides
> Over still mountains, or appears in dreams,
> And all the ballast of familiar life—
> The present, and the past; hope, fear; all stays,
> All laws of acting, thinking, speaking man—
> Went from me, neither knowing me, nor known.
> And once, far-travelled in such mood, beyond
> The reach of common indications, lost
> Amid the moving pageant, 'twas my chance
> Abruptly to be smitten with the view
> Of a blind Beggar, who, with upright face,
> Stood, propped against a wall, upon his chest
> Wearing a written paper, to explain
> The story of the man, and who he was.
> My mind did at this spectacle turn round
> As with the might of waters, and it seemed
> To me that in this label was a type,
> Or emblem, of the utmost that we know,
> Both of ourselves and of the universe,
> And on the shape of the unmoving man,
> His fixèd face and sightless eyes, I looked,
> As if admonished from another world.[11]

In Baudelaire, such moments appear only by instants, as isolated shocks that can never be incorporated in a larger temporal duration. Unlike Wordsworth, he was never able to reestablish contact, through the figural dimensions of his language, with his real poetic antecedents. It was never given him to do so, and he remains for us the emblem of the tragic isolation of postromantic literature, on the rare occasions when its self-insight was of the same quality as that of the early romantics. A true interpretation of Baudelaire, in terms of the categories of temporality and figural language that were found operative in the works of his romantic predecessors, would help to alleviate this isolation and allow us, in turn, to recognize ourselves for what we are in our real precursors.

Part II

ESSAYS AND PAPERS

7

Hölderlin and the Romantic Tradition

VERY FEW OF Hölderlin's works were published during his lifetime: some poems, the novel *Hyperion*, and two translations of Greek tragedies. He received generous assistance from Schiller, but was rather icily dismissed by Goethe; his classmates from the Tübingen theological seminary, Hegel and Schelling, admired his poetic talent, but they had lost touch with him well before 1806, when insanity removed him forever from the literary scene. Although his work and the myth of his existence were not entirely forgotten during the nineteenth century, it was not until [1913–23[1]] that a first complete edition was published and that the main part of the poetry written between 1800 and 1806 became known.

Now, more than one hundred fifty years after the time they were written, Hölderlin's works receive more expert critical attention, in Europe, than those of any other poet. Four years ago a completed poem of his was discovered in London, and on this particular poem alone, there is now a bibliography of over fifty items. This is a staggering amount. Neither is quality inferior to quantity. It is no exaggeration to say that the best philological (and critical) talent of Germany has been concerned, in the last twenty years, with the publication and interpretation of Hölderlin. The leading critical schools of Europe have devoted a great amount of work to Hölderlin and, in some cases, they have originated in contact with this work.[2]

Two questions at once arise: (1) Is this sudden outburst of interest in a single, long unknown poet truly warranted?

(2) What has this intense critical effort accomplished; has it led to an increased understanding, to a fundamentally accepted interpretation of the work?

I will say very little about the first question. There are many apparent reasons to be suspicious of the extraordinary vogue created around Hölderlin—a vogue which, inevitably, will sooner or later reach the United States. His life history, like Rimbaud's, lends itself easily to being made into a myth: the totally alienated and inward poet driven to insanity by his utter solitude. The insanity introduces another ambiguous element and casts doubt on the intelligibility of the very difficult later poetry. (I am speaking only of that preceding the final breakdown of 1806. The poems written by Hölderlin while he was insane, of which several have been preserved, are clinical as well as literary documents.) One can be attracted to Hölderlin for the wrong reasons, use him as an external pattern on which to transfer personal frustrations or anxieties, or attempt identifications which his own statement and poetic code would never allow. This is more dangerous still when it happens on a collective, national scale and when Hölderlin is seen as an individual incarnation of the destiny of Germany. He has written a poem called "Germanien" and used words such as "vaterländisch" and "nationell"—terms which acquire highly disturbing connotations when they are used by some, in Germany, around 1940. In an article published during the war in his review, *Critica*, Croce with customary courage gave voice to the protest of European liberalism against the exploitation of Hölderlin's name for nationalistic and political ends, and he included a critical judgment that echoes Goethe's early rejection of Hölderlin as an excessively "subjective" poet.[3] Nowadays, very few, even among Croce's disciples, would subscribe to this evaluation, but his indictment of a messianic nationalism that makes use of Hölderlin's name is still altogether valid. (It is understandable that Croce's polemical intent, in the service of a good cause, blinded him to the quality of a poet who, more than any other, has satisfied his criteria for supreme poetry as pure expression. I will have to come back later to what "national" means in Hölderlin's poetry, and it should then be clear that it has nothing in common with the extreme forms of twentieth-century nationalism.)

Suspicions and misgivings about the motives behind the current Hölderlin vogue vanish at once upon contact with the work.[4] It speaks for itself and, unless totally distorted, allows no room for subjective aberrations of any kind, as little as does the music of Bach or the painting of Piero della Francesca; it leaves the reader in contact with a poetry upon which no impure critical language has any hold. Whoever comes to Hölderlin for the wrong reasons will either have to change his reasons or change poets. Therefore, the entire problem of relative evaluation—which is itself a highly impure problem—should not retain us any longer. Evaluation is a corollary of a correct reading; the understanding of the poetry in itself is the only right starting place.

This brings us to the second question: has the intensive study of Hölderlin in recent years produced tangible results? As far as the all-important problem of a correct text is concerned, the answer is doubtlessly affirmative. The complete Hölderlin edition now in progress under the direction of Friedrich Beissner benefited from earlier editions but marks a great improvement. Thanks to this edition, we have come to know Hölderlin's work more closely and intimately than that of most poets. (Precisely because so few of the writings were published during the poet's lifetime, the editor had to give us what practically amounts to a facsimile of the manuscripts, with a detailed description of all variants, handwritten corrections, revisions, and the like. The philological difficulties of establishing a correct critical edition of a work that exists only in manuscript are considerable. There are passages, even in Beissner's very careful edition, where room remains for disagreement and doubt. But on the other hand, whatever doubts remain, the difficulties are never caused by exterior causes—as is the case, for instance, in a writer like Diderot, whose clandestine works were often altered and disguised for obvious political reasons. Hölderlin's innumerable variants and rewritings always indicate changes and evolutions of his own mind or technique; they are therefore themselves a very fruitful source for interpretation.)

Recent commentators thus have had access to a reliable text. One could have expected a parallel progress in the field of interpretation and understanding—but it has not taken place.

If one compares an early work on Hölderlin, written without the benefit of a careful edition, such as the thesis by Böhm which dates from 1902,[5] with recent works, backed by Beissner's erudition and by thirty years of research, one is forced to admit that most of the early questions have remained unanswered. We know with a considerable degree of accuracy what Hölderlin has written, but we are still very ignorant as to the exact meaning of this poetry. The discrepancies and the confusion in Hölderlin criticism were dramatically illustrated on the recent occasion when the new poem I mentioned was discovered. The poem, entitled "Friedensfeier [Celebration of Peace]," is a finished version of a hymn of which fragments were known and had been included in most editions. Its importance in Hölderlin interpretation became at once apparent. It is one of the most positive of his statements, in which he describes a certain relationship between men and the gods that holds a promise of peace and stability. A poem in which an oracular poet explicitly states and describes the ideal landscape toward which his work has been striving is naturally of great significance; here was a wonderful opportunity for the interpreters to test their image of Hölderlin's ideal—which, up till now, they had been forced to reconstruct from fragmentary passages.

As it turns out, the interpretation of the poem hinges to a large extent on the identity of a figure which appears in the second stanza and to which Hölderlin does not allude by name; such figures, historical or mythological but always mythologized, often appear in his poems, sometimes designated by name, sometimes by a descriptive epithet which can be quite clear (*der Donnerer* for Zeus, *der Weingott* for Dionysos), but sometimes remain deliberately ambiguous. Here, the central figure is merely referred to as "Der Fürst des Festes, der Allbekannte (the king of the feast, known to all)." Because the epithet "Allbekannter" is used in a project for another hymn to designate Napoleon Bonaparte, the first interpreters of "Friedensfeier" took the king of the feast to refer to the emperor of France. The main proponent of this thesis is a Swiss philologist, a pupil of Staiger and disciple of Heidegger, Beda Allemann. But strong opposition arose at once against this reading. The editor of Hölderlin's works, Friedrich Beissner, took sharp issue with Allemann, and in the latest volume to appear in the Stuttgart edition, we are told, together with some very unfriendly things about Professor Allemann, that the "Fürst des Festes" can only be the "Genius of the [German— PdM] people" (*Genius unsers Volks*). It may be pointed out in passing that it is not a good sign when the authoritative notes to the monumental critical edition of a poet have to be written in the tone of a polemical article. A third group of commentators, theologians and philologists, maintains that the king of the feast can only be Christ himself. This "battle about the peace," as this controversy has come to be known, is inconclusive: the three main readings (Napoleon, the German spirit, or Christ) all lead to a coherent interpretation and can be defended. A decision can only be reached by reference to Hölderlin's general statement, as it emerges from the development of his entire work.

The fact that at least three groups of perfectly competent and honest interpreters are not only unable to agree on the identity of a central symbol, but offer interpretations that lead to altogether incompatible conclusions, indicates that the fundamental significance of Hölderlin is not yet understood. It is perfectly normal that there would be divergencies of interpretation, but in the case of other writers, such as Goethe or Schiller or Racine or Shakespeare, there exists a common basis of agreement, an indisputable image which is shared by all interpreters, whatever differences of method or opinion may otherwise separate them. No such common basis exists as yet for Hölderlin; the controversy over "Friedensfeier" revealed this very clearly.

We should ask ourselves why this is the case. Is it because Hölderlin has been the monopoly of a certain critical school which has approached him with its particular prejudices and limitations? This can hardly be said. A recent Italian study by Allessandro Pellegrini gives a comprehensive history of Hölderlin criticism up to 1955; almost inevitably the book becomes a complete survey of critical methodology in Europe from 1920 to the present. The widest variety of approaches have been used in Hölderlin studies: purely objective and formal analysis

of style; the more subtle stylistic criticism of the school of
Staiger; the erudite and conservative philology of Beissner; the
mythological and Jungian criticism of Kerényi; the Marxist criticism of Lukács; the history of ideas of a Hegelian type—as in
Korff—as well as of a neo-Kantian and idealist type—as in
Cassirer or Jaspers; the ontological poetics of Heidegger; the
existential analysis of Rehm, Kommerell, or, in France, of
Maurice Blanchot. The list could be continued, but it should
suffice to indicate the considerable eclecticism of Hölderlin
criticism. If the work remains problematic, it is not because of a
lack of variety or, for that matter, of talent among its critics.

Would the difficulty not rather stem from Hölderlin's
relationship to the tradition within which he is assumed to
belong? However varied they may be, contemporary critical
methods all originated within a poetic tradition which is that of
romanticism—using the term in a sense wide enough to encompass Novalis as well as Rilke, Blake as well as Yeats, Nerval
as well as Valéry. It is natural that critical theory should evolve
in conjunction with the dominant poetic trends of a period,
even when the authors claim to be opposing those trends. We
are well used to such ironies of history as, for instance, T. S.
Eliot attacking romanticism in the name of the concept of "dissociation of sensibility," a concept which is itself one of the
most characteristic inventions of romanticism. Nor should the
apparent objectivity of stylistic criticism blind us to the fact that
it deliberately (and often consciously) takes for its object the
formal attributes of romantic and postromantic poetry: our
interest in metaphor, for instance, cannot be separated from
the predominantly metaphorical structure of romantic poetry.
(It is because of our romantic heritage that we are able to gain
insight into the nature of metaphorical language in baroque
and Renaissance literature.) It is unavoidable, therefore, that
present-day critical methods, whether they be stylistic, historical, or philosophical, are best equipped to deal with the kind
of literature that becomes predominant from the second part of
the eighteenth century on. Our question in relation to Hölderlin becomes then whether something in his poetry puts him
outside of this tradition. If this were the case, it would not be so
surprising that present-day methods of literary interpretation

fail to gain the fundamental insight which they can achieve for his contemporaries. The irreducible difficulty of Hölderlin would then be that his poetry contains something essentially different from what we have come to take for granted in poetry, and we could only penetrate into this world by understanding the nature of the difference.

But does not Hölderlin appear to be the most romantic of all poets? Is it not his hyperromanticism which Goethe was attacking when he reproached him for being "absolut und unter allen Umständen so subjektivisch, so überspannt, so einseitig" (absolute and in all circumstances so subjective, excessive and lopsided)."[6] If this image were correct, would then not modern criticism, derived as it is from romanticism and refined by its proximity to such late romantic developments as symbolism (surrealism or expressionism), be particularly well suited to interpret Hölderlin? The answer can only be found by examining Hölderlin's attitude toward the dominant romantic themes. This is a complex inquiry, but I would like to make some suggestions as to the direction which such an inquiry could take.

Most of the mythological figures that appear by name in Hölderlin's later elegies and hymns are of a divine nature. Dionysos, Heracles, and Christ are the most frequently mentioned. Among the others, the most revealing for our purpose and the only literary name ever to appear is Jean-Jacques Rousseau. He was to be the subject of an unfinished ode which bears his name, and he appears in the center of the poem that we will use for our text tonight, "Der Rhein."

The presence of Rousseau among Hölderlin's myths, given semidivine status, would certainly tend to confirm his romantic allegiance. We think of Rousseau as the very source of the romantic sensibility; he is the human being totally alienated from his present reality, who finds in the suffering resulting from this alienation the imaginative power to conceive an ideal image of unity and reconciliation. This image, moreover, is pantheistic in intent: the essence of unity resides in the natural object, and it is from the remembered experience of unity with nature as it exists in youth or in earlier civilizations that we gain a premonition of the state of permanent unity toward which we strive. The combination of those related characteristics— separation, pantheism, and a temporal structure that moves from a remembered past to an ideal and fictional future— defines for us Rousseau and the tradition that originates from Rousseau. The rebellious and revolutionary nature of romanticism results from the original alienation, regardless of whether this alienation is from the self, from society, or even from nature itself. The temporal structure that moves from past to future accounts for the particular combination of tones which is found in poets so distant in time and place as Wordsworth and Rilke: the constant modulation from the elegiac, the regretful evocation of past unity and innocence, to the praise (*Rühmen*) of the hymn or, what amounts to the same, to the prophetic announcement of the returning praiseworthy. The ideal of the future unity accounts for the totally inward or mythological language in which it must be expressed, since it can have nothing in common with what is presently real. And the pantheistic element appears in the very structure of the romantic image or metaphor, which is always a tension (and not a mere analogy or imitation) between a consciousness and a natural object, in which consciousness tries to achieve the status of being of the natural object without losing its status as a consciousness. The romantic image is always pastoral, in that its ideal resides in a state of nature, but it is always image, because it can only conceive of nature as of what is not in its present possession. It is a longing of the language toward nature, not an identity with nature; therefore it contains a constitutive element of tragic failure, because it is born from a conflict between two irreconcilable ways of being.

We associate, perhaps all too easily, such characteristics with Rousseau, and it is particularly the last, pantheistic element that is generally emphasized. We should not forget that they survive in fact in later authors. The following passage from Yeats, written in 1902, is a typical example of the memorable texts possessing the characteristics that have been mentioned: Yeats is contrasting our time with that of Spenser,

a time when men in every land found poetry and imagination in one another's company and in the day's labour. Those stately

goddesses . . . belong to Shelley's thought, and to the religion of
the wilderness—the only religion possible to poetry today. Certainly Colin Clout, the companionable shepherd, and Calidore,
the courtly man-at-arms, are gone, and Alastor is wandering from
lonely river to river finding happiness in nothing but in that Star
where Spenser too had imagined the fountain of perfect things.
This new beauty, in losing so much, has indeed found a new
loftiness, a something of religious exaltation that the old had not.
It may be that those goddesses, moving with a majesty like a
procession of the stars, mean something to the soul of man that
those kindly women of the old poets did not mean. . . . Has not
the wilderness been at all times a place of prophecy?[7]

It is all there: the separation and barrenness of the wilderness,
the desert wasteland; the nostalgia for a time when the imagination was natural; the pantheistic nature symbolism of stars
and rivers; the exaltation of a prophetic tone. Yeats was probably premature in referring to himself as the *last* romantic, for
there is little in the poetry of our century that cannot be included within this broadly considered framework of the romantic tradition. The themes have become so thoroughly familiar that we tend to identify them with the very essence of
poetry.

It is perhaps for this reason that we fail to notice how Hölderlin as well as Rousseau—or, at any rate, Hölderlin's conception of Rousseau—differ from this pattern. The poem you have
in front of you, "Der Rhein," is highly revealing in this respect.
Like "Friedensfeier," it contains the promise of a reconciliation
in the form of a feast or celebration:

> Dann feiern das Brautfest Menschen und Götter,
> Es feiern die Lebenden all,
> Und ausgeglichen
> Ist eine Weile das Schiksaal.[8]
>
> [Then gods and mortals celebrate their nuptials,
> All the living celebrate,
> And Fate for a while
> Is levelled out, suspended.[9]]

The reconciliation follows immediately upon the appearance of Rousseau; it will again be possible when men will have
become like Rousseau. The key to the poem then becomes:

Hölderlin's understanding of Rousseau. The literary allusion is clear enough. Not even the most casual of editors would miss it: it is to the fifth of the *Rêveries du promeneur solitaire* and to book 12 of the *Confessions*, famous passages where Rousseau describes the happy and peaceful respite he found for a while on an island located in the lake of Bienne; Hölderlin mentions it in stanza 11. But if the source of the passage is clear, the interpretation is difficult, especially in the eleventh stanza. To understand what Rousseau signifies for Hölderlin, we first have to relate the passage to the poem as a whole.

From the first stanza on, a double movement is apparent. The original situation which the poet assigns himself and which, as always in the late Hölderlin, is to be taken altogether literally as well as symbolically, is itself a double situation: the golden noon of the sun is at its most present as a giver of life, but on the other hand the poet has sought shelter in the darkest shade: "dunkeln Epheu" balances with "goldene Mittag," and this antithetical balance is itself the burden and the mystery of the poem. This static opposition very soon becomes a movement in two contrasted directions: the poet's soul drifts, he says, "towards Italy and far to Morea's shores," Hölderlin's paraphrase for the Roman and hellenic world, but, in the emphatic "Jetzt" of the second stanza, this movement is checked at once by another entity which does not belong to the hellenic world at all but is part of the poet's own, national landscape: the German river Rhine. We are at the point of extreme tension between those two forces, the one moving to the East in the direction of the world of antiquity, the other to the West to the German cities of the Rhineland. This point is called the source (geographically the source of the stream), and the line, which is also the actual course of the river, graphically represents the destiny, the particular *moira* (*Schiksaal*), of man in Hölderlin's time and place.

The Rhine, we are told, is the noblest of rivers; it is born free and distinguishes itself from its two brothers (the Rhône and the Tessin) in being royal (*königlich*) and in aspiring to different, higher hopes. These qualities mark its destiny in a very specific way: the Rhine, and this is an actual fact of geography, begins its course by flowing, not to the West but to the East; it is "driven impatiently towards Asia," in a movement parallel to the attraction of the poet's mind toward Greece. At this point, the poem pauses and the description is interrupted by a meditative passage, "Doch unverständig ist / Das Wünschen . . . ," exactly as the Sophoclean tragedy pauses at the moment of highest tragic intensity and interrupts the action with a reflective chorus. This is the unmistakable sign that we have reached a moment in the development that requires pause and reflection. What is meant by the Rhine's impatient impulse toward the East?

The analogy with the poet's longing for Greece in the first stanza suggests an answer. Greece is, of course, a dominant theme throughout Hölderlin's work. As always in German neohellenism, it is the elegiac theme *par excellence*; it is prominent in the earlier *Hyperion* novel as well as in the great elegies of the middle period: "Archipelagus," "Brod und Wein," and others. The line from Goethe's *Iphigenie*, "Das Land der Griechen mit der Seele suchend [With the soul seeking the land of the Greeks]," certainly applies to a large fraction of Hölderlin's work—as it does to so many of his contemporaries. But for Hölderlin, the myth of Greece had acquired a more specific and conscious significance; his contact with Greek poetry was much closer than Goethe's or Schiller's,[10] and his translations of Pindar and Sophocles are a high moment in the poetic dialogue between the Greek and the modern Western world. Hölderlin has a conscious knowledge of the hellenic mind as it is, and therefore Greece is not for him a purely ideal realm; his relationship to Greece[11] is not purely elegiac or imitative but dialectical, in the sense that the modern attraction toward the specific virtue of the Greeks is counterbalanced by a Greek attraction toward the specific virtue of the West. Greece and the West are opposed and distinct in their essence; the attraction of Greece for Western man is not that of something intrinsically superior and desirable but of something essentially other, possessing a virtue which he does not possess, but lacking the one he has in his power. Naturally, we long for what we do not have and scorn what is already in our possession; it is in the essence of the dialectic to give ideal status to the negation of the self until sufficient consciousness is reached to [see] both the self and the other within their proper distinction.

In one of his latest texts, the commentaries on the translation of the *Antigone*, Hölderlin defines the specific Greek virtue very clearly: the Greek poetic language is aimed toward an actual, natural object, and it is capable of hitting its mark—he uses the expression *etwas treffen*; it reaches the object that it names with the same accuracy with which the Greek athlete reaches his aim or the warrior's spear its enemy; in a tragic context, it can literally kill the body at which it is aimed, as Creon's word kills Antigone. The word is immediately present to the signified natural object, and the logos captures nature and holds it in its immediate possession. The pantheistic longing of the moderns, lamenting their separation from nature, is inconceivable to them as a poetic theme (Hölderlin is referring to Homer, not to the later Greece of Theocritus). On the other hand, however, they lack the self-reflective power which enables modern man to know his own consciousness, and their nostalgia, corresponding to our elegiac treatment of nature, is most apparent in the repeated choral question of the early tragedians lamenting their ignorance of the nature of man's existence: the chorus at the beginning of act [2] of the *Antigone*—of which Hölderlin's translation is particularly beautiful—would be a striking instance:

> [Ungeheuer ist viel. Doch nichts
> Ungeheuerer, als der Mensch. . . .]
> [Much is monstrous. But nothing
>
> More monstrous than man. . . .[12]]

We must imagine, to use Schiller's vocabulary, within the naive Greek a sentimental longing for consciousness of self as strong as the modern "sentimental" longing for nature.[13]

With this in mind, we can interpret the movement of the Rhine near its source as it first flows eastwards and then turns back to move toward the West. If the movement toward Asia is like the neohellenic nostalgia for Greece, it is equivalent to the pantheistic ideal that longs for the immediate possession of its object, a possession the Greek poetic language can achieve without effort. This is a traditional romantic theme; the difference, however, resides in the place assigned to this theme in the total development. The traditional river symbol for this unity is the ocean, where all rivers mingle in the common All; Hölderlin uses this sea image in earlier works. As the sea symbol indicates, pantheistic unity, for the romantic mind, is the final consummation of all individual destinies, the end point of the quest. In the Rhine poem, however, the sea is not even mentioned, and the last glimpse we are given of the river is as it flows through the cities and by the towers of civilized Europe. The pantheistic urge does not appear at the end, as the culmination of the Rhine's destiny, but happens at the source: it is the initial moment in a movement that will later reverse its direction. Pantheism is only the first stage in the history of the Western mind.

With great affirmative strength Hölderlin asserts that the presence of this stage reveals the superiority of the Rhine over the other rivers: those who have not felt this urge do not have the same claim to freedom and nobility. The entire subsequent movement is in the other direction, away from Greece, but if it had not been for the initial attraction toward the hellenic form of virtue, the Rhine's power to create a nonhellenic, national world would never have existed. However, if the movement toward Greece had continued, it would have grown from mere rebellion into pure *hubris*. It is violent and destructive, as the stream near its source is savage, undaunted. In its desperate desire to possess a nature which it can never reach, it tears and destroys (much as the technology of our day tears and destroys):

> wie der Bliz, muß er
> Die Erde spalten, und wie Bezauberte fliehn
> Die Wälder ihm nach und zusammensinkend die Berge.

> [like lightning he
> Must rend the earth and like things enchanted
> The forests join his flight and, collapsing, the mountains.
>
> (Hamburger, 413)]

Moreover, it is not really within the power of the Rhine

itself, as the entity dominated by the particular destiny of the Western world, to reverse this original direction. It takes the intervention of a higher divine power which controls the demigod Rhine much as the Greek destiny or *moira* dominates divine and human power in the *Iliad*. The intervention of this power, merely designated as a God (*ein Gott*), bends the Rhine back in the other direction and forces him away from his desire to escape from what he is (the spirit of the West) back into his actual destiny and his own being. To the Rhine himself, this merciful intervention must appear intolerable, a tragic death and defeat, the most difficult sacrifice of all; renouncing one's drive to[14]

8

Heaven and Earth in Wordsworth and Hölderlin

RECENT INTERPRETATION of Wordsworth and Hölderlin has taken us well beyond the point at which their religious experience could still be defined as pantheistic. The movement away from the pantheistic interpretation has taken several divergent roads. On the one hand, as in H. W. Piper's study of romantic pantheism entitled *The Active Universe*, the concept of nature has been secularized to such a degree that nature becomes a purely material entity; in that case, when the imagination achieves "full response to, and implication with, the living qualities of natural objects,"[1] this occurs without involving any transcendental elements whatsoever. On the other hand, one can stress the visionary power of the poetic faculty and see the imagination acting apocalyptically, moved by "an inner necessity to cast out nature, to extirpate everything apparently external to salvation, everything that might stand between the naked self and God, whatever risk in this to the self."[2] I have quoted from Geoffrey Hartman's recent book on Wordsworth, though I hasten to add that this quotation does not represent his view of Wordsworth; his talent for phrasing positions he does not necessarily espouse exposes him to the risk of being quoted misleadingly out of context. Between the position of total immanence and that of total transcendence, various forms of reconciliation or of dialectical mediation have been attempted. As a matter of fact, the notion of reconciliation looms up large in many recent statements on romanticism: in René Wellek's description of romanticism as "the concern for the reconciliation of subject and object, man and nature, consciousness and unconsciousness";[3] in Meyer Abrams's recent insistence on the positive humanism of romanticism as compared to the nihilistic destructiveness of later nineteenth-century aestheticism;[4] in Geoffrey Hartman's definition of Wordsworth's imagination renewing, after a long periplus or excursion, "the connection between the waters above and the waters below, between heaven and earth" in the guise of a "marriage of heaven and earth [towards which—PdM] the poet proceeds despite apocalypse" (69). The mediating entity that allows the marriage to take place is for all these authors, in the last analysis, nature, albeit in such a refined form that it has lost all traces of the original pantheism. Hence Wordsworth's religious feeling can be called a "highly qualified form of natural religion" (Hartman, 33).

It is the avowedly somewhat sinister purpose of this paper to put into question whether this "connection" (Hartman's and, for that matter, Wordsworth's term) can indeed be called a "marriage" and whether the mediating entity is indeed nature. Since, from the perspective of this argument, both the critical tradition and the actual poetic vocabulary will offer the greatest resistance in the case of Wordsworth, I will merely use Hölderlin to throw light on Wordsworth and not vice versa. As for the religious and theological implications of my statement, due to the confines of the eighteen minutes allotted to me they will have to remain implicit. It should be clear, however, from my interpretation that it would be very difficult to refer to Wordsworth's or Hölderlin's religion as "natural," though it would be even less accurate to call it "supernatural." The question indeed arises whether the term "religion," with any of its usual connotations, can still in any way be applied to them.

In the early Hölderlin, one is able to find many examples of a nature experience that could be called pantheistic. Among several others, the following passage from an early version of the novel *Hyperion* comes to mind; it is stated by an elderly sage whose word is supposed to be true wisdom: "We cannot deny . . . that something in us expects and hopes for as-

sistance from nature, even when we are fighting against it.
And why shouldn't we? Does our Spirit not encounter a kindred Spirit in all that exists? Doesn't a benign Master hide
behind the shield even when he turns his weapons against us?
Call him by whatever name you please, he is always the
same!" (*Werke*, 3:200).[5] This kindred Spirit suggests the con-
ciliatory mood, the mutual attraction founded on affinity that
is to be the basis of a true marriage—"selbst im Kampfe (even
when we are fighting against it)." And it may seem indeed that
this Spirit is powerful enough to bring us into contact with
what Hölderlin calls, in the paragraph immediately following
the one just quoted, the Archetype of all Unity ("das hohe
Urbild aller Einigkeit"), or God.

Yet the same text, or other fragments closely related to it
and from the same period, puts this possibility radically into
question; the movement toward unity has to be counterbalanced by the repeated assertion that it can never succeed:
"The blessed Unity, Being in the unique sense of the word [*die
selige Einigkeit, das Sein, im einzigen Sinne des Worts*], is lost for
us. And we must lose it if we are to strive, to struggle for it. We
tear ourselves away from the peaceful En kai Pan of the world
in order to reconstruct it with our own means. We are fallen,
with nature, and what one may believe to have once been
united is now torn by division, with master and slave changing
over from side to side" (*Werke* 3:236). One would be mistaken
in reading these passages as emphasizing that the possibility
of "uniting ourselves with Nature in one infinite totality"
could exist for us as an actual, unmediated experience. Hölderlin's statements are remarkable for the stress they put on the
prevalence of the division, which lasts for the entire duration
of our conscious existence, and not on the unity, which is
relegated to a remote and fictional past or to an unreachable
future: "Aber weder unser Wissen noch unser Handeln
gelangt in irgend einer Periode des Daseyns dahin, wo aller
Widerstreit aufhört, wo Alles Eins ist; die bestimmte Linie ver-
einiget sich mit der unbestimmten nur in unendlicher An-
näherung. [Neither in knowledge, nor in action do we ever
reach, in any period of our existence, the point where all op-

position ends and where all is one; the definite line unites with the indefinite one only in infinity by drawing forever nearer and nearer]" (*Werke*, 3:237).

Unity is present to us only in a mediated form called Beauty, but this Beauty is not to be equated with unmediated Being. Yet we would also be misunderstanding Hölderlin entirely if we thought of Beauty[6] as the discovery of an affinity or correspondence between mind and nature, an affinity that would allow us to ascend gradually, as in a Neoplatonic processive scheme, to Schelling's ultimate Identity, by ways of a series of increasingly transcendentalized marriages. The analogy between nature and consciousness is not for Hölderlin a part of the actual order of things. It is a creation of the human mind, an illusion invented by us to hide the fact that we are forever fallen away from Being. Shortly after the quoted affirmation of pantheistic unity, a crucial statement is made to this effect. Having discovered in his pupil Hyperion a more advanced state of maturity, his master can now reveal to him a higher truth:

> I know that only an inner shortcoming [*Bedürfnis*] forces us to give nature an affinity with whatever immortal element we carry within ourselves and makes us believe that a spirit inhabits matter. . . . I know that, when the beautiful forms of nature seem to announce the very presence of the divine, it is we ourselves who inspire the world with our own soul [*wir selbst beseelen die Welt mit unserer Seele*]. Is there anything in the world that does not receive its attributes from us? [*Was ist dann, das nicht durch uns so wäre wie es ist?*] (*Werke*, 3:192)

The key concept here is *Bedürfnis*, a word that makes its reappearance in Hölderlin at central moments, such as the oft-quoted "dürftige Zeit" from *Brod und Wein*. Our earthly condition is one of barrenness, of *dénuement*, because we are forever separated from divine origin. We try to cope with this by inventing an affinity with nature, which in fact does not exist, thus giving ourselves the illusion of an eternity which we do not possess. This form of analogical thought is, however, a flight into inauthenticity. The true way is the way of love, Eros (the son of poverty and wealth), which sustains the knowledge of the discrepancy between divine origin and earthly predicament. This knowledge is the very essence of all consciousness and is linked with the full awareness of our temporal finitude: "Also da, als die schöne Welt für uns anfieng, da wir zum Bewusstsein kamen, da wurden wir endlich. [At the moment when the beauty of the world began for us, we gained consciousness and became finite]" (*Werke* 3:192). Without leaving the same group of texts, we have moved from the naive statement of pantheistic unity to a statement of the (ontological) priority of consciousness over nature, dismissing the analogy between mind and nature as illusory and inauthentic.

The concept of analogy, as is well known, figures prominently in Wordsworth's poetry as well as in his theoretical writing. The first preface to the *Lyrical Ballads* speaks of the poet as he who "considers man and nature as essentially adapted to each other, and the mind of man as naturally the mirror of the fairest and most interesting properties of nature";[7] and although we may find in the same preface several statements that upset this reassuring picture, analogy certainly plays an important part in Wordsworth's poetry. I deliberately say "plays a part" for it appears there in a dramatic context, in conflict at times with other conceptions of poetic language that may well supersede it.

As the above quotation suggests, images of reflection such as mirrors or echoes will be frequently associated, in Wordsworth, with his evocation of analogy. And no richer "echo" is to be found in his poetry than that caused by the boy of Winander when he stood alone,

> Beneath the trees, or by the glimmering Lake,
> And there, with fingers interwoven, both hands
> Press'd closely, palm to palm, and to his mouth
> Uplifted, he, as through an instrument,
> Blew mimic hootings to the silent owls
>
> (*Prelude*, 5:394–98)[8]

and heard in reply ". . . echoes loud / Redoubled and redoubled; concourse wild / Of mirth and jocund din!" The reassuring response is that of a stable world in which man and nature are indeed "interwoven." Why is it then that, in the same poem, when the owls suddenly remain silent and are replaced by the "voice / Of mountain torrents," this reassurance disappears, to be replaced by the precarious adjective "uncertain" that qualifies Heaven?

> . . . the visible scene
> Would enter unawares into his mind
> With all its solemn imagery, its rocks,
> Its woods, and that uncertain Heaven, receiv'd
> Into the bosom of the steady Lake.
>
> (*Prelude*, 5:409–13)

This note of uncertainty has in fact entered the poem before, when we were shocked into "mild surprize" by the use of the word "hung" at a place where we would have expected "stood":

> Then sometimes, in that silence, while he hung
> Listening, a gentle shock of mild surprize
>
> (*Prelude*, 5:406–7)

It is as if, at the very moment that the analogical echo fails us, the stable ground of an interwoven world were taken away from under our feet and we were left suspended between heaven and earth. But the word *hung* in "hung / Listening" is interesting for other reasons still. Wordsworth singled out the very word *hung* in the 1815 Preface to the *Lyrical Ballads*, in examples taken from Virgil and Milton, to designate the precise moment where fancy, dependent on kinship between mind and nature, is superseded by imagination, a faculty defined by its power *not* to remain analogically or mimetically faithful to sensory perception but able to create appearances "for the gratification of the mind in contemplating the image itself."[9] The passage from perception to imagination involves a higher pitch of audacity in the language which, by contrast, makes the "jocund din" of the "mimic hootings" seem trivial but also introduces a note of danger and uncertainty.

We understand this uncertainty better when we become aware that the word *hung* appears in the second section of the poem also and furnishes us with the thematic link uniting the two apparently disjointed parts. When we have been told, blandly and abruptly, that the boy has died, and we would expect the quiet lament of an elegy or the serene detachment of an epitaph, we hear instead the song of a Wordsworthian ode to a particular place, its earnestness contrasting sharply with the exuberance of the former echo:

> —Fair are the woods, and beauteous is the spot,
> The Vale where he was born; the Churchyard *hangs*
> Upon a Slope above the Village School
>
> (*Prelude*, 5:416–18)

Now it is clear from where the uncertainty stems. A firm link is established between, on the one hand, the loss of the sense of analogy and, on the other hand, the experience of mortality. The scene of the boy surprised by the sudden silence is in fact a prefiguration of his death, the growth of a consciousness from the assumed safety of an analogical world to the precarious world in which consciousness sees itself suspended ephemerally upon an earth in whose stability it does not share, hung from a heaven that has cast it out. The best it can hope for is that, by fully understanding the contingency of its condition, the fall into death will be as gentle as that of the "uncertain heaven, received / Into the bosom of the steady Lake." The poetic language capable of stating, in the ode that honors the very place of our contingency, the frailty of our condition is the true language of the imagination; this language is opposed to the sensory and mimetic language of organistic analogy. The Preface of 1815 can only be understood in its real difference from Coleridge by realizing that Wordsworth is moving, not back to a mechanical concept of association, but well beyond the concept of analogy.

The significance of this insight grows when one realizes that this thematic sequence—from analogical echo to imagination, by way of a consciousness of mortality—is a recurrent figure in Wordsworth, gaining in complexity from the various contexts in which it appears. One single illustration is all I have time for, but there are many others. In book 2 of *The Prelude*, in a passage probably written later than "There was a Boy," a very similar scene associated with the same geographical region occurs. There, in a gaudy and somewhat pretentious inn that has replaced a humble hut "more worthy of a poet's love," Wordsworth and his friends play noisy games, making "all the mountains ring" with their shouts. As in "There was a Boy" the jocund echoing noise disappears, to be replaced this time by the song of a solitary flute:

> Alone upon the rock; Oh! then the calm
> And dead still water lay upon my mind
> Even with a weight of pleasure, and the sky
> Never before so beautiful, sank down
> Into my heart, and held me like a dream.
>
> (*Prelude*, 2:176–80)

The passage evokes the tenuous mixture of terror and acquiescence before mortality even more subtly than the end of "The Winander Boy." But the texts that frame this particular passage allow us to add to the description of Wordsworth's feeling of existence. The contrast between the splendid inn and the original hut it has replaced prepares the contrast between the loudly echoing shouts and the "dead still water" at the end; the same contrasting effect has occurred somewhat earlier, near the beginning of book 2, when we are told how an ancient rock, named after an old woman who is herself as gray, barren, and patient as this rock, has been "split, and gone to build / A smart Assembly-room that perk'd and flar'd / With wash and rough-cast elbowing the ground / Which had been ours" (*Prelude*, 2:39–41). Rather than a contrast between past and present, the sequence is that of the genuine usurped by the fake, a movement from authenticity to inauthenticity. This dialectic is exactly symmetrical to the ensuing opposition between the imaginative and the analogical. It indicates that for Wordsworth also, as for Hölderlin, the analogy between mind and nature is an inauthentic covering up of the barrenness of our condition. His poetry records this barrenness even more convincingly than Hölderlin's; the demolished poetic hut and the stonelike human being humbled into patience by poverty are typical examples of this mood.[10]

The same section in book 2 is followed at once, without apparent transition, by a curious passage in which Wordsworth speaks of his love for the sun. We are told that, as a boy, he loved the sun in a different way than he has loved it since. Now, it is for him merely "a pledge / And surety of our earthly life" (*Prelude*, 2:185–86). The boy's love for the sun did not seek such reassurance. He loved the sun:

> . . . for this cause, that I had seen him lay
> His beauty on the morning hills, had seen
> The western mountains touch his setting orb,
> In many a thoughtless hour, when, from excess
> Of happiness, my blood appeared to flow
> With its own pleasure, and I breath'd with joy.
>
> (*Prelude*, 2:188–93)

The very contact between heaven and earth that we mentioned as our starting point is taking place here. The contact is only possible, first of all, when the illusion of eternity founded on a similarity with nature has been cast out; the contact we have here is not a mirrorlike reflection or an "exquisite fitting" of mind to nature. Heaven touches the earth for a passing moment only and within the orbit of a purely temporal movement, in the transience of the morning and the evening hour, not in the out-of-time stasis of noon or midnight. When the poetic language is authentic, it becomes essentially temporal; it loves the light, not as a pledge of duration, but because it comes to it in the fluid form of time itself. We have moved from the eternalistic world of analogical thought into the temporal world of the imagination. The contact between heaven and earth occurs literally as a spot *of time*, authentic time disrupting for an instant the false texture of everyday existence. The marriage metaphor does not express this encounter at all, all the less since, as the 1815 Preface and many passages in the poetry make clear, the contact occurs as an act of consciousness and not as a natural sensation. When memory dispels the false image of time as mere succession—an illusion of physical continuity borrowed from the geometrical world of space—the poetic imagination can come into play. This is not a reconciliation between mind and nature, but a passing alliance between the self and time. The mind asserts its priority over nature while at the same time asserting its unbreachable separation from Being. That Wordsworth would still have to use the same word, *Nature*, to designate what he moves beyond as well as what he can never reach indicates the hold that an analogical ontology has over our minds and vocabulary. The entire *Prelude* strives toward establishing the distinction between Nature and Being.

In mythology, the offspring of the contact between the Titans Heaven and Earth, Urania and Gaea, is called Mnemosyne—memory, or time as it appears to consciousness. *Mnemosyne* is also the title of one of Hölderlin's last hymns. This hymn asserts the necessity for man to pursue his historical existence while resisting the temptation to escape from temporality into eschatological or apocalyptic schemes. Memory is always a memory of death; in Hölderlin's poem, it is a memory of the death of the heroes whose actions engendered history. The temptation arises then, out of sorrow, to forget memory itself, blotting out consciousness by a leap into transcendence which is in fact a leap into death. Being a truly dialectical mind, Hölderlin escaped the tendency toward analogical thought easily, but the apocalyptic always remained a strong temptation for him. Wordsworth's truly Kantian rationality, on the other hand, shelters him from the apocalyptic mood that is certainly present in other English romantics, but he had to disengage himself gradually from the trappings of analogical thought. Yet, in the long run, both Wordsworth and Hölderlin are equally poets of the earthly soul, of consciousness, and of historical time—and not poets of nature, of eternity, or of transcendental vision. As such they make of romanticism a crucial articulation in the history of human consciousness. With Rousseau, they stand at the threshold of a posthellenic, post-Christian, new dispensation.

9

The Double Aspect of Symbolism

W HEN HISTORIANS of literature refer to such general concepts as classicism or romanticism, they have a reasonably accurate notion of what they mean. They are thinking of a more or less specific set of characteristics, some thematic, some formal, and some historical, which distinguish these movements from the literary norms of other periods. Of course, even such established terms are not altogether stable; from time to time someone points out that they cover a group of characteristics too diverse to be grouped under one heading, however comprehensive it may be. Such a crisis occurred, for instance, when the American philosopher and literary historian Arthur O. Lovejoy, founder of the very prominent school of literary theory known as the history of ideas, claimed in 1924 that the term *romanticism* had become so vague and meaningless that it had better be abandoned.[1] A polemic ensued during which more orthodox historians such as René Wellek tried, on the whole successfully, to defend the usefulness of the term.[2] Until further notice, one is allowed to speak, with reasonable objectivity, of a romantic movement as of a definite and distinctive event in the history of Western literature. Such questions are not purely academic; for it is in such variations of interpretation that the deeper tensions of history are reflected.[3]

If romanticism proved to be a problematic term, what then shall we say of the more recent addition to the literary vocabulary of *symbolism*? It would be difficult to point to an instance in which a word has wandered further from its original meaning and moved from a narrow and local use to an extraordinarily broad and comprehensive meaning. The occasion on which the word was first applied to a specific literary group is now almost forgotten, and rightly so; it was in a manifesto published in 1885 by a group of minor French poets headed by Moréas. They were disciples of Stéphane Mallarmé who wished to distinguish themselves from another group, followers of Verlaine, who called themselves *décadents*. Technically, this is still the correct meaning of the term *symbolistes* as it appears in French literary history: a minor and short-lived school of poets at the end of the nineteenth century, at a moment when French poetry is going through a rather barren period stretching from the productive years of Mallarmé, Rimbaud, and Verlaine in the 1870s and 1880s to the publication of Apollinaire's *Alcools* in 1913 or of Valéry's *La Jeune Parque* in 1917, which marks the beginning of better times. If this were the full meaning of the term *symbolism*, it would hardly still concern us today.

At the other extreme, as referring to the metaphorical use of poetic language, symbolism has such a broad meaning that it would be hard to point to any poetry which would not be symbolist poetry. Nowadays, we often meet the term in this all-encompassing sense. In a recent book on Rimbaud, (or rather, on the myth that grew up around the person of Rimbaud), Etiemble points out the inability of critics to state clearly why they consider the famous poem "Le Bateau ivre" as *the* symbolist poem par excellence (which, indeed, it is not).[4] As further instances of the inability to give a specific meaning to the word, he quotes the statements of the Parnassian poet Heredia: "But why the devil do they call themselves symbolists? . . . All poets are symbolists!" (72) and of Verlaine: "[Symbolism] is a pure pleonasm, since the symbol is the essence of poetry" (70). As the term *romanticism* had become useless to Lovejoy, it is clear that the term *symbolism* seems useless to Etiemble.

In between the all-too narrow historical definition and the all-too wide equation with all metaphorical poetry, symbolism has come to mean a certain tradition in nineteenth-century

French poetry which is summarized in the excellent title of an otherwise rather shallow book: Marcel Raymond's *De Baudelaire au surréalisme*.[5] It is felt that a common conception of the use of poetic language, for the first time openly apparent in Baudelaire, unites such otherwise diverse poets as Baudelaire, Mallarmé, Verlaine, Rimbaud, Valéry, and Breton—or, to be more precise (and less historical), it is felt that all of those poets raised certain questions about the nature of poetic language which are the very same questions with which we are concerned today. Symbolism, in other words, is an *a posteriori*, retrospective historical scheme we have superimposed upon the poetry of the last century, isolating more or less arbitrarily certain elements in this poetry that are close to our own problems—regardless of whether we favor or object to the raising of those questions. Whether such questions were asked with the same urgency and lucidity by all of these poets, and asked fundamentally in the same manner, could only be determined by a detailed comparative study of their works—a study that is not available, since no measure of common agreement has been reached on the exegesis, let alone on the interpretation, of these poets. But we can state with certainty, as a matter of historical fact, that the tendency has existed in the recent past, and still exists today, to link them together as if they were a single group—and this phenomenon is interesting enough in itself to warrant our concern with a literary movement that is perhaps a somewhat mythical projection of our own uncertainties.

It may well be true that all literature is symbolic, but it is not sure that all literature has been explicitly aware of it, and it is still less obvious that all literature has felt the symbolical nature of its language to be a problem that made its own possibility of existence highly problematic but also of exceptional importance and value for human consciousness in general. When we look at symbolist literature—and I will now take the term to mean the postromantic tradition that started in France with Baudelaire and influenced the whole of European literature at the end of the nineteenth century—we find it haunted by two apparently contradictory concerns: first the very negative one contained in the question that keeps arising in a variety of forms: how can literature continue to exist? Mallarmé: *Comment la littérature est-elle possible? . . . A savoir s'il y a lieu d'écrire.*[6] Simultaneously with this profound skepticism a very positive attitude appears: the extraordinary claim that poetry is man's only way of salvation out of an inner division that threatens his very being. On the one hand, the poet questions with growing anxiety the necessity to continue a task that becomes increasingly difficult; on the other, he does not hesitate to take over obligations and duties that, up to then, had been the exclusive concern of the religious life. To combine in this manner Satanic doubt with the promise and the burden of a Salvation is typical of what we call a "symbolist" poet—although it is certainly already present, potentially and sometimes explicitly, in the greatest among the earlier romantics.

To set oneself up as a Savior, to speak in tones of prophetic hope or apocalyptic destruction, implies that there is something in the nature of the existing reality that makes it unbearable and requires radical change. This urge may be expressed in the violently destructive rebellion of Rimbaud, or in the subtle self-alienation of Mallarmé when he speaks of the "duty to recreate everything by means of memories in order to establish that we are indeed there where we ought to be (something of which we are not altogether certain)" (481). The symbolist poet starts from the acute awareness of an essential separation between his own being and the being of whatever is not himself: the world of natural objects, of other human beings, society, or God. He lives in a world that has been split and in which his consciousness is pitted, as it were, against its object in an attempt to seize something that it is unable to reach. In terms of poetic language—which as an agent of consciousness is on the side of the subject (or poet)—this means that he is no longer close enough to things to name them as they are, that the light and the grass and the skies that appear in his poems remain essentially other than actual light or grass or sky. The word, the logos, no longer coincides with the universe but merely reaches out for it in a language that is unable to *be* what it *names*—a language that, in other words, is *merely* a symbol.

We could question incessantly and vainly why, how, and even when this separation came about. One is tempted to look for specific facts, historical events, or sociological determinations that caused it, as a certain virus causes a disease. But when we try to think in such a mechanistically historical way, the problem becomes more and more elusive and vanishes in a series of endless circular reasonings in which it becomes impossible to distinguish cause from effect. Much rather than falling prey to the all-too-simplistic historicism one finds most prominently displayed by writers who claim to be against or above history—and of which T. S. Eliot's attempt at "dating" what he calls dissociation of sensibilities is a striking example— we should ask ourselves how this particular group of writers approached a problem that may well be at the root of all human consciousness.[7] What matters then is not why the symbolists happened to be concerned with the separation between the realm of consciousness and the realm of objective being, but in what specific manner they experienced this eternal question.[8]

If the poet finds himself in this state of separation and solitude, his consciousness cut off from the unity of the natural world, his first and natural impulse will be to use poetical language as a means to restore the lost unity. He can then look on the symbol as on a key to reenter the world of unity from which he has been exiled. Something in the structure of the symbol allows for this, since it states the identity between two entities that are normally experienced as being different. When Baudelaire writes a line like the following: "Et mes chers souvenirs sont plus lourds que des rocs [And my precious memories are heavier than stones],"[9] he is conferring upon a purely mental consciousness, by means of a mere act of symbolic language, the very quality one feels to be the essence of matter: weight and opacity, eternal stability, whatever contrasts most with the fleeting transparency of a subjective awareness such as "memories." In such a metaphorical statement, the infinite distance that separates object from consciousness is crossed at lightning speed, and unity is restored not merely among the diversity of natural objects but also between the spiritual and material world.

In the case of Baudelaire, we know that this use of the symbol was deliberate and founded upon a belief in the fundamental unity of all being; this unity is not immediately accessible to us and is not to be found in the direct apprehension of the real world as we meet it in our ordinary perceptions. But it is accessible by means of an act of the imagination, as the imagination discovers the hidden roads that lead (assisted by a very old and almost imperceptible memory) to a world of re-covered oneness. The symbols are these roads. In the sonnet on correspondences, Baudelaire speaks about the dark and mysterious unity, "une ténébreuse et profonde unité," to which man is led through the "forest of symbols." Elsewhere, in his prose, he has stated several times the same belief that "God has made the world as a complex but divided totality." And in an article on Hugo, he says:

> Everything, form, movement, number, color, smell, in the *spiritual* as well as in the *material* world, is significant, reciprocal, converse, *correspondent.* . . . We know that symbols are obscure only relatively, that is to say, according to the purity, the responsiveness or the inborn clarity of vision of each individual soul. And what is a poet . . . but a translator, a decipherer? Among outstanding poets, all metaphors, comparisons or epithets are mathematically precise and fit the particular circumstance, because those metaphors, comparisons and epithets are taken from the inexhaustible fund of the *universal analogy*, and could not have been found elsewhere. (2:133)

More than thirty years later, another symbolist poet, W. B. Yeats, who at that time hardly knew Baudelaire and had never read "Correspondances," wrote:

> All sounds, all colours, all forms, either because of their preor-dained energies or because of long association evoke indefinable and yet precise emotions, or, as I prefer to think, call down among us certain disembodied powers whose footsteps over our hearts we call emotions; and when sound, and colour, and form are in a musical relation, a beautiful relation to one another, they become as it were one sound, one colour, one form and evoke an emotion that is made out of their distinct evocations and yet is one emotion.[10]

We find this same concept of the symbol stated at the beginning and at the end of the movement by what are probably its two greatest poets. No wonder then that symbolism has often been described by this broad definition: the use of language as a means to rediscover the unity of all being that exists in the realm of the imagination and of the spirit. One of the great advantages of this definition is that it resituates symbolism among familiar and established aspects of the Western tradition. It is indeed no mere coincidence that Baudelaire and Yeats would have made such closely similar statements about the nature of the symbol. In the sentence that precedes the one just quoted, Baudelaire mentions Swedenborg as his master, and when the young Yeats is writing his essay, "Symbolism in Poetry," he is under the direct influence of William Blake, whose works he has been editing and who is, of course, also a disciple of Swedenborg. And beyond Swedenborg, Baudelaire as well as Yeats were interested and to some extent initiated in occult wisdom. During the nineteenth century, a period of strong scientific and positivistic leanings, the hermetic tradition appears both disreputable and philosophically suspect, but one does not have to go further back than to the Renaissance to find it in the much more reputable guise of Neoplatonism. And even in the nineteenth century, although it had by then fallen into ill repute, no other intellectual influence, including orthodox Christianity, had such profound effect on a large number of writers. Blake, Balzac, Gérard de Nerval, Baudelaire, Villiers de l'Isle Adam, and, closer to us, Yeats, Rilke, Stefan George, and the French surrealists are only some instances among many. In all of them we find the Neoplatonic vision of a full, ordered universe, one that is a unified totality but can only be reached by the practice of a specific discipline that, for poets, is the discipline of literary form and symbolical invention. And they are all indebted to the representatives of this doctrine, from Plato himself to the obscure Cabalists pursuing their shady business in the Paris of the eighties. Remaining within Baudelaire's definition of the symbol, one could well argue that symbolism is the public aspect by means of which the occult, Neoplatonic tradition asserts and maintains itself in the nineteenth century.

Although it is historically convenient and brings out one important aspect of symbolism, this definition still does not cover the entirety of a literary phenomenon that, in some of its aspects, moves in an altogether different direction. To begin with, in the work of the very authors who seem to be closest to this concept of the symbol, there are inner tensions and hesitations that put in question their adherence to what can rightly be called a creed. A first complication arises from the necessity to name the unity to which they aspire, to describe this state as if it were a region that one naturally would inhabit. They are committed to this because, for them, unity of being is not merely an intent, a future state toward which one moves without knowing it, but an actuality of which, in certain privileged moments, language can state and hold the true experience. Since the symbol achieves identity of all things, the poet in fact never names anything but the universal One of which the "minute particulars" are only immediately accessible emanations—or, as Yeats put it: "All things hang like a drop of dew / Upon a blade of grass."[11]

But, as readers of Plato's dialogue *Parmenides* well know, it is a particularly vexing problem to develop the apparently simple statement that the One *is*. The ontological status of the One is ambiguous, and it is impossible to state unity of being except in terms of not-being. This metaphysical problem has a direct equivalence in the thematic evolution of all poets of the Baudelairean type: inevitably, they come to express unity in terms of death. The only human experience that offers a symbolical correspondence with unity is that of death, and we should not be surprised to find Baudelaire invoking death as the pilot on his voyage toward recovered unity:

> O Mort, vieux capitaine, il est temps! levons l'ancre!
> Ce pays nous ennuie, ô Mort! Appareillons!
> Si le ciel et la mer sonts noirs comme de l'encre,
> Nos coeurs que tu connais sont remplis de rayons!

> (*Oeuvres* 1:134)

> [O Death, old captain, it is time! Let us get underway! This land wearies us, o Death, let us make ready to leave. If the sky and the sea are as black as ink, you know our hearts are filled with light!]

We find many similar prayers in the earlier poetry of Yeats, for instance:

I would that the Boar without bristles had come from the West
And had rooted the sun and moon and stars out of the sky
And lay in the darkness, grunting, and turning to his rest.

> ("He Mourns for the Change That Has
> Come Upon Him and His Beloved,
> and Longs for the End of the World," 59)

In a very helpful note, Yeats tells us that this "boar without bristles" is "the darkness which will at last destroy the gods and the world."

That the most powerful of all human desires, the desire for unity, should have to be stated in terms deriving from the most dreaded of all experiences, that of death, is a supreme paradox that is bound to introduce an almost unbearable tension in a poetry that set out to be all quietness and appeasement. It becomes impossible for these poets to maintain an attitude of positive assertion toward unity: instead, they have to resort to devices that are, all of them, to a point, methods of deceit. They try to elude the problem by means of a substituted language that covers up the original desire as under a mask. We recognize this strategy in the unsettling irony with which Baudelaire celebrates the most repulsive aspects of death in a language of natural and joyful sensation, or in his deliberate use of necrophilic imagery (the source, by the way, of the symbolist admiration for Poe) that allows him to state desire in terms of death, hiding, as it were, the very inevitability of this association behind a pretense of the bizarre and the abnormal. Baudelaire's mask is this series of poses by means of which he releases his language from the burden of telling the truth; Yeats's mask is the highly complicated machinery of antithetical themes he sets up to hide his very persistent longing for annihilation. In his early work he allowed this idea to come freely to the surface, but later he suppresses it, letting instead his language act out antithetical conflicts that, actually, have no reality for him. Such poets are at their greatest when, at rare moments, they drop the mask—as in the extraordinary poem in which Baudelaire perceives that the promise of unity contained in death is itself a theatrical fiction, a game of the imagination that does not end with the real torture of the eternal waiting for a reconciliation of opposites that will never occur:

> —J'allais mourir. C'était dans mon âme amoureuse,
> Désir mêlé d'horreur, un mal particulier;
>
> .   .   .   .
> J'étais comme l'enfant avide du spectacle,
> Haïssant le rideau comme on hait un obstacle . . .
> Enfin la vérité froide se révéla:
>
> J'étais mort sans surprise, et la terrible aurore
> M'enveloppait.—Eh quoi! n'est-ce donc que cela?
> La toile était levée et j'attendais encore.
>
> ("Le rêve d'un curieux," *Oeuvres* 1:128–29)

[—I was dying, and in my amorous soul it was a desire mixed with horror, a peculiar illness . . . I was like a child waiting for the performance, hating the curtain's obstacle . . . And finally the cold truth was revealed: death had come without surprise, and the terrible dawn enveloped me.—What! Is this all there was? The sheet had been lifted and I was still waiting.]

The same thing happens in some of Yeats's last poems, where he uses the promise of a highly problematic and nonexistent future as a trick to reintroduce into his poetry the ecstasy of annihilation he had carefully left unmentioned for well over thirty years. It permits him to name again this "rich, dark nothing" that reappears in such passages as:

> . . . Those that Rocky Face holds dear,
> Lovers of horses and of women, shall,
> From marble of a broken sepulchre,
> Or dark betwixt the polecat and the owl,
> Or any rich, dark nothing disinter
> The workman, noble and saint . . .
>
> ("The Gyres," 291)

or:

> We Irish, born into that ancient sect
> But thrown upon this filthy modern tide
> And by its formless spawning fury wrecked,
> Climb to our proper dark, that we may trace
> The lineaments of a plummet-measured face.
>
> ("The Statues," 323)

By then, we have moved a long way from the Neoplatonic promise of unity; the voice we recognize is very similar to that of Nietzsche, and we are in the familiar world of modern nihilism. From symbolic language as the restorer of unity we have come to symbolic language as the agent of cosmic destruction, although those poets would never openly relinquish their original commitment to the ideal of unity.

One might well ask, at this point, whether there appears, in the symbolist tradition, an alternate road—starting from the same awareness of human separation but using poetic language with a different purpose. The work of Stéphane Mallarmé suggests what is perhaps a different pathway, a different conception, which has been given much less attention and emphasis in general studies of symbolism. It is impossible to account for the general development of Mallarmé's work if one confines oneself to the definition of symbolism derived from Baudelaire. Another dimension, a different aspect of symbolism appears here.

It is clear, for instance, that after a brief initial period during which Mallarmé remains close to Baudelaire, a radical change of themes occurs. At first, we see Mallarmé accepting the image of a divided world in which man is a prisoner of reality and aspires with all his strength to an ideal condition "anywhere out of this world." The symbol of this ideal state is *l'azur*, the blue sky of the natural universe. In his earliest poems Mallarmé prays for union with *l'azur*, exactly as Baudelaire had prayed for his harmonious paradise. But very soon, *l'azur* changes from an altogether positive into a highly ambiguous symbol that still haunts the poet but from which he now tries, with even greater effort, to escape. And as the poetry develops we see that the union with natural being, Baudelaire's highest hope, becomes for Mallarmé man's greatest—and unavoidable—misfortune and that, instead, his entire poetic effort goes to avoid direct identification between consciousness and the natural object. In a well-known later poem, for instance, the poet is symbolized in the figure of a swan caught in a frozen lake and cruelly separated from the warmth and freedom to which its entire nature aspires. But we are told that the only possible chance the swan may ever have had to free itself was not by finding in its own desire the necessary strength but, to the contrary, by contemptuously scorning this need:

> Un cygne d'autrefois se souvient que c'est lui
> Magnifique mais qui sans espoir se délivre
> Pour n'avoir pas chanté la région où vivre
> Quand du stérile hiver a resplendi l'ennui.

("Le vierge, le vivace et le bel aujourd'hui," 68)

[A swan of bygone times remembers that it is he, magnificent but who without hope delivers himself by not having sung where to live when in the sterile winter the ennui sparkled.]

Baudelaire's entire work is driven by a desire for direct, unmediated contact with Being, which for Mallarmé is precisely what the poet should reject. He has an acute awareness that the kind of unity to which Baudelaire aspired is in fact the annihilation of a consciousness absorbed, as it were, by the power of being in which it searches to drown itself. This kind of unity does not tempt Mallarmé, because it lies beyond the realm of language. Annihilation of consciousness is primarily the annihilation of language, and since the poet's only but irrevocable commitment is to language, he can never accept unity on those terms. He has to be, by his essential choice, on the side of consciousness and *against* natural being. The poetic act, then, is for him an act by means of which natural being is made accessible to consciousness. Consciousness attempts to think through the essential otherness of the object, to transform this otherness into a cognitive knowledge stated in language. Poetry is not an identification with the object but a reflection on the object, in which consciousness moves out toward the object, attempts to penetrate it and then, like a reflected ray of light, returns to the mind, enriched by its knowledge of the outside world. And it is by means of this process of thinking the other that the mind learns to know itself.

The Mallarmean symbol, then, is not an identification between two entities that were originally separated. It is, much rather, a mediation between the subject on the one side and nature on the other in which both keep their separate identities but in which a third entity, language, contains within itself their latent opposition. If we look at a Baudelairean symbol, we always find it to be a statement of identity; he tells us that one thing is exactly like some other thing: "La Nature est un temple," for instance, or the innumerable comparisons introduced by the conjunction *comme*, the word that establishes identity between distinct entities and which is probably the key word of Baudelaire's poetry. In the mature poetry of Mallarmé, we find something altogether different. The common structure of Mallarmé's symbol is always that of some object in the process of metamorphosis into another object or, more frequently still, in the process of dissolving into nothing: the sea becoming a boat, a cloud becoming a wing, a finger becoming a candle, the sun sinking behind the horizon, a boat sinking into the ocean, a curtain vanishing like foam on the water. Mallarmé's things act out, as it were, the movement of the human mind as it grows in consciousness of its own self. The symbolic object that we can observe in its strange transformations represents the motion of the mind as it goes back and forth between the natural world and its own realm. It partakes, up to a point, in the nature of things (since they are always described as objects), but they are things completely emptied of their material substance, become transparent as the mind takes possession of them. The language reflects this ambiguity of being: it is handled very much as if it were an object, with considerable attention given to its objective qualities of sound, visual appearance, and form; but on the other hand it is altogether determined by the necessities of cognitive consciousness, which means, for instance, that the choice of each word and its place in the sentence is determined by the demands of truth and precision. At the limit, if language were able to be a perfect mediation and to contain within itself the essence of natural being as well as that of the subjective consciousness, it would succeed in establishing a true unity, not the kind of unity one had in Baudelaire, where consciousness is sacrificed, but the balanced unity in which, in Hegel's words, "the concept expresses the object and the object the concept."

We must state at once that, in Mallarmé, language does not succeed in this task and that the poet knows it. The intrinsic superiority of natural being over consciousness is such that all attempts to master it are doomed at the outset. Following a coherent development it would take too much time to retrace, we see in Mallarmé's work how consciousness progresses by means of a succession of failures. The general structure of these failures is always the same: the poet acquires a certain knowledge of himself in relation to the natural world, which he hopes to be the foundation on which to build his poetic language. He thinks to have discovered a strategy that will allow him to accomplish the kind of ideal mediation described above. But it always turns out that, when he thought to have reduced the totality of being to a status that makes it fit to be expressed in language, he had been deceived by a part of it that he did not reach and that reappears to destroy the certainty he had achieved. For instance, at an early moment in his development, Mallarmé hopes to have founded his work on the central attitude we mentioned earlier: the description of the refusal to be reunited directly with the world of nature, the preference of a deliberately artificial and self-created, formal universe over the world of natural desires. It is in the scene from *Hérodiade* that this purely formalist, Parnassian poetry finds its fullest expression. But it becomes clear to him soon enough that this solution is deceitful: the stoic resignation of his heroine, her refusal to yield to any temptation of spontaneous happiness, instead of leading to the heroic greatness she expects, is merely a cause of ruin and death. The rejection of nature in favor of form turns out to be merely a choice for death, a death that means not only the death of the fictional Hérodiade, but also the death of the work in which she was to appear, the failure of the poetic conception on which this was to be founded.

Mallarmé's development appears then as a succession of such failures. But although they are totally destructive failures, in which one passes from the death of the heroine (in *Hérodiade*) to the death of the poet himself (in *Igitur*) and finally to cosmic death (in *Un Coup de dés*), they are not altogether meaningless. The growth of spirit is a tragic growth, which implies ever-increasing pain and destruction, but it nevertheless is a movement of becoming that marks a kind of progression. The failures are not just an alignment of identical absurdities; each one is enriched by the knowledge of the one that precedes it, and spirit grows by reflecting upon its successive aberrations. At the limit, the total accomplishment of spirit will also be a total annihilation, but this event, of which *Un Coup de dés* tries to be a symbolical evocation, remains in the future as long as there remains a language able to express it. This language is the poetic work, and we see how Mallarmé's entire enterprise is centered, not on unity like Baudelaire's, but on the incessant movement of becoming by means of which language grows to new dimensions of precision, universality, and clarity.

If Baudelaire's poetry can be called a poetry of being, Mallarmé's can be called a poetry of becoming, and in this contrast is summarized the double aspect of symbolism. For Mallarmé, the only enterprise that mattered was the incessant pursuit of the supreme Book, the project that was always ahead of him and that was, in the most literal sense possible, his only concern. We know that when he died, he had progressed well beyond his latest published poem (*Un Coup de dés*) in the elaboration of this supreme work, of which the remaining outlines have recently been published and which was to be a strange and altogether unsettling combination of a theatrical performance with a highly abstract mathematical puzzle and which, by some secret known only to Mallarmé, was going to be a kind of universal best-seller, like the Bible.

Symbolism leaves us with these alternatives: Mallarmé's barren and ascetic concentration of a consciousness that has to learn to face the irrevocable division of being, and to find in this knowledge the power for its own growth—or Baudelaire's dangerous promise that unity can be restored, in spite of the growing realization that this unity would merely be a form of immediate death. In spite of this warning, it is a very natural impulse to prefer the second choice, partly because it requires less patience and partly too because it contains a form of hope, the hope that if being ever were to return in the form of a direct revelation that would not be deadly, the poet would have prepared its return by his prayer and would be the only man ready to receive it on earth. Most poetic developments that have followed symbolism have preferred this latter choice, and the

modern poet has often become like one of the magi, underway
toward a new epiphany. In order to see the choice in its true
light, however, it is necessary to extend the perspective a little
beyond symbolism and to refer briefly and in conclusion to the
poet who has stated and lived this choice with more intensity
than any other: the German poet of the romantic era Hölderlin,
whose work has of late become more and more associated with
this vocation of the poet as a kind of magus. In one of his most
admired poems, "Bread and Wine," Hölderlin takes up one of
his frequent themes and contrasts the greatness of Greece,
when the gods lived like actual presences among men, with
the barrenness of the modern world, in which man has been
abandoned by the gods. And he asks the question which the
symbolists will in their turn ask so insistently:

> . . . Indessen dünket mir öfters
> Besser zu schlafen, wie so ohne Genossen zu seyn,
> So zu harren, und was zu tun und zu sagen
> Weiss ich nicht, und wozu Dichter in dürftiger Zeit.

> [. . . But meantime too often I think it's better to sleep than to be
> without companions, alone, always waiting, and what to do or to
> say I don't know, and what are poets for in a time of need?][12]

In the part of the elegy that follows, Hölderlin considers the
possible answer: the poet can be one of the magi preparing for
the return of the gods; he can be like the priests of Dionysus
who traveled from land to land:

> Aber sie sind, sagst du, wie Weingotts heilige Priester
> Welche von Lande zu Land zu zogen in heiliger Nacht.

> [But they are, you say, like the holy priests of the wine god who in
> the holy night traveled from land to land.]

Hölderlin does not present this as his own attitude, however,
but as the opinion of the friend to whom the poem is dedicated
and who was a boundless admirer, in the romantic manner, of
the hellenic world. Hölderlin is more hesitant, but nevertheless, in the first version of this poem, he seems to agree with
his friend. Later, however, he changed the end of the poem to

five lines that are very difficult to interpret but that gain in clarity if one considers them together with prose texts of Hölderlin dating from the same period. Our period of barrenness, says Hölderlin, has already ended, and the new and specifically Western (not hellenic) form of divine presence has already occurred, not in the form of a closer proximity to the world of nature but as an increased consciousness of the self. But it is in the nature of men to prefer to state their desire for that which they do not have rather than dare to be what they really can be. We envy the physical proximity of the object which was natural to the Greeks, while the task in which we can excel, increased consciousness, appears to us as the most repellent and barren of roads. The late Hölderlin expects from us the difficult act Mallarmé also demanded: to sacrifice our desire for what is not ourselves, to increase clarity and insight within our mind. Always according to Hölderlin, Western poetry has not yet dared to take this most difficult of all roads; it has not found itself yet, and its greatest period still lies ahead in the future. We see then that, however eccentric and unattractive Mallarmé's outlook may be, he is not the only one to have preferred a poetry of becoming to a poetry of prayer and salvation.

The fact that, for an increasing number of minds, the later poetry of Hölderlin and of Mallarmé has become the starting point of fundamental questioning may be a sign that their road, however barren it may seem, is for us the road of truth.

10

Roland Barthes and the Limits of Structuralism

DESPITE THE refinements of modern means of international communication, the relationship between Anglo-American and continental—especially French—literary criticism remains a star-crossed story, plagued by a variety of time lags and cultural gaps. The French have only just gotten around to translating an essay by Empson,[1] and by the time American works of literary theory or literary criticism appear in Paris, they often have lost much of their youthful freshness. There is more good will and more curiosity in the other direction, yet here too a mixture of misguided enthusiasm and misplaced suspicion blurs the issues. Even some of the most enlightened among English and American critics keep considering their French counterparts with the same suspicion with which English-speaking tourists might approach the *café au lait* they are served for breakfast in a French provincial hotel: they know they don't like it but aren't entirely certain whether, for lack of some ritualistic initiation, they are not perhaps missing out on a good thing. Others are willing to swallow French culture whole, from breakfast coffee to Mont Saint Michel and Chartres, but since intellectual fashions change faster than culinary tastes, they may find themselves wearing a beret and drinking Pernod when the French avant-garde has long since switched to cashmere sweaters and a diet of cold milk. The essays[2] by Roland Barthes that have just become available in excellent English translations date from 1953 to 1963; *Mythologies*, which appears in a regrettably shortened version, goes back to 1957.[3] I cannot help worrying about all the things that could go wrong in the reception of texts that now combine a nostalgic with a genuine but out-of-phase revolutionary quality. Perhaps the most useful function for an American-based view of Roland Barthes may be to try to anticipate unwarranted dismissal for the wrong reasons as well as excessive enthusiasm for parts of the work with which Barthes himself might no longer be so pleased. *Writing Degree Zero*, the first of Barthes's essays to be translated into English, appeared with an introduction by Susan Sontag that raises very high expectations which, at first sight, may not seem to be fulfilled by these two later volumes.[4]

For despite the considerable emphasis on structure, code, sign, text, reading, intratextual relationships, etc., and despite the proliferation of a technical vocabulary primarily derived from structural linguistics, the actual innovations introduced by Roland Barthes in the analytical study of literary texts are relatively slight. Even in his more technical works such as *S/Z*, the study of a story by Balzac,[5] and the various articles on semiology and on narrative techniques published mostly in the review *Communications*,[6] the contribution to practical criticism is not as extensive as the methodological apparatus would lead one to expect. The work of "pure" structuralists such as the linguist Greimas and his group or of some among Barthes's most prominent associates, such as Gérard Genette or Tzvetan Todorov, is more rigorous and more exhaustive than Barthes's—though it is only fair to point out its avowed indebtedness to him. Hence the risk of disappointment or overhasty dismissal.

Barthes is primarily a critic of literary ideology, and as such, his work is more essayistic and reflective than it is technical, perhaps most of all when the claim to methodological precision is most emphatically stated. The close integration of methodology ·with ideology is an attractive characteristic of European intellectual life ever since structuralism became a public issue in the sixties—and, for better or worse, French writers on literature are still much closer to being public figures, committed to articulate positions, than their American equivalents. Barthes played a very prominent part in the recent "Battles of the Books," and his work bears the traces of his involvements. It has to be read and understood as an intellectual adventure rather than as the scientifically motivated development of a method. He is at least as interested in the reasons for advocating certain technical devices as in their actual application. Hence the polemical tone of many of the essays, the many interviews, pamphlets, position papers, etc. Barthes should be read within the context of the particular situation to which he reacts, which is that of the ideological tensions underlying the practice of literary criticism in France. This situation is idiosyncratically French and cannot be transposed *tel quel* to the American scene. It does not follow however that the story of Barthes's intellectual journey is without direct interest for American readers. American criticism is notoriously rich in technical instruments but frustrated in its attempts to relate particular findings to the larger historical, semantic, and epistemological issues that have made these findings possible. That such difficulties exist is by no means a sign of weakness; it only becomes one if the broader inferences of a method are misconstrued. Barthes's enterprise is of wide enough significance to have paradigmatic value for all students of literature willing to put the premises of their craft into question.

A somewhat euphoric, mildly manic tone runs through Barthes's writings, tempered by considerable irony and discretion, but unmistakeably braced by the feeling of being on the threshhold of major discoveries: "A new anthropology, with unsuspected watersheds of meaning is perhaps being born: the map of human *praxis* is being redrawn, and the form of this enormous modification (but not, of course, its content) cannot fail to remind us of the Renaissance."[7] This statement dates from 1966, but one still finds similar trumpet blasts, only slightly muted, in recent utterances. It is the tone of a man liberated from a constraining past, who has "the earth . . . all before (him)" and who looks about "with a heart / Joyous, not scared at its own liberty."[8] The exact nature of this liberation can best be stated in linguistic terms, in a formula partly borrowed from Barthes himself: it is the liberation of the signifier from the constraints of referential meaning.

In all the traditional polarities used throughout the ages to describe the inherent tension that shapes literary language— polarities such as content/form, *logos* (what is being said) and *lexis* (the way of saying it), meaning/sign, message/code, *langue/parole*, *signifié/signifiant*, voice/writing, etc.—the implicit valorization has always privileged the first term and considered the second as an auxiliary, an adjunct or supplement in the service of the other. Language itself, as the sign of a presumably nonlinguistic content or "reality," is therefore devalorized as the vehicle or carrier of a meaning to which it refers and that lies outside it; in the polarity man/language, it seems commonsensical enough to privilege the first term over the second and to rate experience above utterance. Literature is said to "represent" or "express" or, at most, to transform an extralinguistic entity which it is the interpreter's task to reach as a specific unit of meaning. Whatever shadings are used in describing the relationship (and they are infinite), it remains best expressed by the metaphor of a dependence of language on something in the service of which it operates. Language acquires dignity only to the extent that it can be said to resemble or to partake of the entity to which it refers. The Copernican revolution heralded by Barthes consists not in simply turning this model around (and thus in claiming that, instead of being the slave of meaning, language would now become its master) but in asserting the relative autonomy of what the linguist Saussure called the signifier, that is, the objective properties of the sign independently of their semantic function as code, such as, for example, the redness of a traffic light considered as an optical, or the sound of a word considered as an acoustic, event. The possibility for the signifier to enter into systems of relationship with other signifiers despite the constraint of the underlying[9] meaning proves that the relationship between sign and meaning is not simply one of dependence. It suggests that the metaphorical language of hierarchies and power structures fails to do justice to the delicate complexity of these relationships. The science that sets out to describe the functions and interrelations of signifiers (of which reference is one among others) is called semiology or semiotics, the study of signs independently of their meanings, in contrast to semantics, which operates on the level of meaning. Barthes is one of the leading representatives of this science, not so much as its initiator—he is the first to acknowledge his debt to Saussure, Jakobson, Hjelmslev, and others—but as one of its most effective advocates.

One may well wonder why ideas about language leading up to the science of semiology acquired such polemical vigor in the hands of Roland Barthes. They had been around for quite a while, not only in the field of linguistics, but in various philosophies of language and in the formalist schools of literary criticism that dominated the scene in many countries, with the notable exception of France. It is true that the French have a way of taking hold, often belatedly, of other people's ideas and suddenly rediscovering them with so much original energy that they are positively reborn; this happened, in recent years, with Hegel, Heidegger, Freud, and Marx, and it is about to happen with Nietzsche. In Barthes's case, however, there is more to it than mere Gallic energy. His deliberate excursion into the realm of ideology is typical of the development that made the catchall phrase *structuralism* part of intellectual popular culture. And of all his books, the early *Mythologies* is perhaps best suited to illustrate the process I am trying to describe.

Barthes is a born semiologist, endowed with an innate sense of the formal play of linguistic connotation, the kind of eye and mind that notices at once how an advertisement for a brand of spaghetti seduces the onlooker by combining, in the picture of the *red* tomatoes, the *white* spaghetti, and the *green* peppers, the three colors of the house of Savoia and of the national Italian flag, thus allowing the consumer to taste all that makes Italy Italian in one single bite of canned pasta.[10] He has used this gifted eye to scrutinize not only literature, but social and cultural facts as well, treating them in the same manner as a formalistically oriented literary critic would treat a literary text. *Mythologies*, a book that remains remarkably fresh although the facts it evokes belong to the bygone era of pre-

Gaullist France in the early fifties, undertakes precisely this kind of semiocritical sociology. Walter Benjamin and Theodor Adorno are among the undisputed masters of the genre, but I doubt that Barthes, although he was an early exponent of the work of Brecht in France, knew their work well at the time of writing the *Mythologies*. The common ancestry is nevertheless apparent from the reference, in the important concluding essay on history and myth, to Marx's *German Ideology*, the model text for all ideological demystifications.

Almost any of the *Mythologies* can be used to illustrate Barthes's main insight. Take, for instance, the opening essay on catch-as-catch-can wrestling as an example of the contrast between a referential, thematic reading and the free play of signifiers. The point is not that, in the world of catch as catch can, all the fights are rigged; this would not make the event less referential but merely displace the referent from the theme, "competition," to that of "deceit." What fascinates Barthes is that actors as well as spectators fully acquiesce to the deceit and that all pretense at open contest has been abandoned, thus voiding the event of all content and all meaning. There only remains a series of gestures that can be highly skillful at mimicking competition (the triumph of winning, the abjection of defeat, or the drama of reversal or peripeteia) but that only exist formally, independently of an outcome that is no longer part of the game. Catch is not a game but a simulacrum, a fiction: Barthes calls it a "myth."

Myths of this kind abound in the fabric of any society. Their attraction is not due to their actual content but to the glitter of their surface, and this glitter, in turn, owes its brilliance to the gratuity, the lack of semantic responsibility, of the fictional sign. This play is far from innocent. It is in the nature of fictions to be more persuasive than facts and especially persuasive in seeming more real than nature itself. Their order, their symmetry is possible because they are accountable only to themselves, yet these are precisely the qualities wishfully associated with the world of nature and necessity. As a result, the most superfluous of gestures also become the hardest to do without. Their very artificiality endows them with a maximum of natural appeal. Fictions or myths are addictive because they substitute for natural needs by seeming to be more natural than the nature they displace. The particular shade of bad conscience associated with fiction stems from the complicity involved in the partial awareness of this ambivalence, coupled with an even stronger desire to avoid the revelation, public or private, of this knowledge. It follows that fictions are the most marketable commodity manufactured by man, an adman's dream of perfect coincidence between description and promotion. Disinterested in themselves, they are the defenseless prey of any interest that wishes to use them. When they are thus being enlisted in the service of collective patterns of interest, including interests of the highest moral or metaphysical order, fictions become ideologies. One can see why any ideology would always have a vested interest in theories of language advocating correspondence between sign and meaning, since they depend on the illusion of this correspondence for their effectiveness. On the other hand, theories of language that put into question the subservience, resemblance, or potential identity between sign and meaning are always subversive, even if they remain strictly confined to linguistic phenomena.

Barthes's *Mythologies* are fully aware of this; they bring the subversiveness into the open by exposing the structure of the social myths as well as their manipulation. The political implications are clearly visible as the *Mythologies* move from the relatively harmless mystifications of catch as catch can or the Tour de France to consumer goods such as the Citroën DS, *steak pommes frites*, or the singing style of the baritone Gérard Souzay, to reach finally the domain of the printed word and image as they appear in *Paris-Match* or in the movies. After having been the target of a heavy-handed and vicious attack by Raymond Picard, a Sorbonne professor of French literature whose main field of specialization is the life of Racine, Barthes wrote perhaps his best "mythology" in the first part of the counterattacking pamphlet entitled *Critique et vérité* (1966), in which the ideological infrastructure of the French academic literary establishment is revealed with masterful economy and without an ounce of personal spite.

The demystifying power of semiology is both a source of

strength and a danger. It is impossible to be so consistently right at the expense of others without some danger to oneself. Barthes's social criticism and the means used in accomplishing its highly laudable aim engender their own mystification, this time at the level of method rather than of substance. The very power of the instrument creates an assurance that generates its own set of counterquestions. In this case, the questions have to do with the claim of having grounded the study of literature on foundations epistemologically strong enough to be called scientific. The heady tone alluded to earlier appears whenever this claim is being made. Putting it, in its turn, into question nowise means a desire to turn the clock back, a foolish wish at best, for there can be no return from the demystifying power of semiological analysis. No literary study can avoid going through a severe semiocritical process, and there is much to be said for going through these fires with as urbane, surefooted, and entertaining a guide as Roland Barthes. What happens on the far side of this crossing remains an open question. At stake here is the future of structuralism as an intellectual movement but also as a methodological blueprint for scientific research that, like Rousseau's state of nature, "no longer exists, has perhaps never existed and will probably never come into being"[11] but which we nevertheless cannot do without.

As in Barthes's social myths, the referential, representational effectiveness of literary language is greater than in actual communication because, like his wrestlers, it is so utterly devoid of message. As we say of bombs that they overkill, we can say of literature that it overmeans. This referential suggestiveness, which accounts for the fact that one responds with much stronger emotion to a fictional narrative than to an actual event, is of course illusionary and something for which a science of literature (whether we call it stylistics or semiology) should account without being taken in by it. The classical way of dealing with the question is to bypass it, as when Roman Jakobson rightfully asserts that, in literature, language is autotelic, i.e., "focused on the message for its own sake,"[12] rather than on its meaning. By getting rid of all the mess and muddle of signification, the formula opens up a heretofore undiscovered world of scientific discourse covering the entire field of literary syntax, grammar, phonology, prosody, and rhetoric. With the inevitable result, however, that the privileged ade- quation of sign and meaning that governs the world of literary fictions is taken as the ideal model toward which all semantic systems are assumed to tend. This model then begins to func- tion as a regulatory norm by means of which all deviations and transformations of a given system are measured. Literature becomes, to borrow a phrase from the title of Barthes's first book, a degree zero of semantic aberration. We know that it owes this privileged position to the bracketing of its referential function, which is dismissed as contingency or ideology and not taken seriously as a semantic interference within the semi- ological structure.

The seduction of the literary model has undoubtedly worked on Barthes, as it is bound to work on all writers en- dowed with a high degree of literary sensitivity. Up through *Mythologies*, it takes at times a rather naive form, as when, in the concluding essay of that book, literature, in opposition to ideology, is held up as a "transformation of the sign into mean- ing: its ideal would be . . . to reach, not the meaning of words, but the meaning of things in themselves" (*Mythologies*, 241). In the manifesto *Critique et vérité*, in which the vocabulary is more transformational than structural, closer to Chomsky than to Jakobson, the position is more complex but not essentially dif- ferent. It now takes the form of a three-pronged, hierarchized scheme of approach to literature, in which a distinction is made among literary science, literary criticism, and literary readings. The controlling authority of the first discipline, the only one to be free from the error of semantization and to lay claim to truth, is beyond question:

> If one is willing to admit the textual nature of the literary work (and draw the proper conclusions from this knowledge), then a *certain type* of literary science becomes possible. . . . Its model will undoubtedly be linguistic. . . . The object of literary science will have for its aim not to explain why a certain meaning has to be accepted, not even why it has been accepted (this being the task of historians), but why it is acceptable not in terms of the philological rules of literary meaning but in terms of the linguistic rules of symbolic connotation. (*Critique et vérité*, 57–58; de Man's transla- tion)

By emphatically drawing attention to its own methodological apparatus, *S/Z*, Barthes's most systematic piece of literary analysis to date, allows itself to be taken as a first exemplary move in the elaboration of such a science. The impact of this example on literary studies deserves to be extensive and long lasting, although it will be resisted in many ways, including the most insidious way of all: the use of praise in order to protect oneself against the consequences of insight. It will not do, for example, to dismiss the methodological claims as a device used by a writer of more traditional literary virtues. We cannot reassure ourselves by stressing the elegance, the sensitivity, the strongly personal, even confessional, element that is part of Barthes's tone and that makes him one of the "best" writers at work today in any genre, in the most traditional sense of this qualitative epithet. Nor can we merely classify and dismiss him as one more example of a "modern" alienated consciousness. The theoretical challenge is genuine, all the more so since the particular quality of Barthes's writing is due to his desire to believe in its theoretical foundations and to repress doubts about their solidity.

The unresolved question remains whether the semantic, reference-oriented function of literature can be considered as contingent or whether it is a constitutive element of all literary language. The autotelic, self-referential aspect of literature stressed by Jakobson cannot seriously be contested; why then is it always and systematically overlooked, as if it were a threat that had to be repressed? The just-quoted passage from *Critique et vérité* laying down the directives for the literary science of the future is a good example: Barthes can be seen fluttering around the question like a moth around a live flame, fascinated but backing away in self-defense. All theoretical findings about literature confirm that it can never be reduced to a specific meaning or set of meanings, yet it is always reductively interpreted as if it were a statement or message. Barthes grants the existence of this pattern of error but denies that literary science has to account for it; this is said to be the task of historians, thus implying that the reasons for the recurrent aberration are not linguistic but ideological. The further implication is that the negative labor of ideological demystification will eventually be able to prevent the distortion that superimposes upon litera-

ture a positive, assertive meaning foreign to its actual possibilities. Barthes has never renounced this hope; in a recent
interview, despite many nuances and reservations, he still
speaks of "the ultimate transparency of social relationships"[13]
as the goal of the critical enterprise. Yet, in the meantime, his
methodological postulates have begun to erode under the impact of the question which he hoped to delegate to other, more
pragmatic disciplines.

That literature can be ideologically manipulated is obvious
but does not suffice to prove that this distortion is not a particular aspect of a larger pattern of error. Sooner or later, any
literary study must face the problem of the truth value of its
own interpretations, no longer with the naive conviction of a
priority of content over form, but as a consequence of the much
more unsettling experience of being unable to cleanse its own
discourse of aberrantly referential implications. The traditional concept of reading used by Barthes and based on the model
of an encoding/decoding process is inoperative if the master
code remains out of reach of the operator, who then becomes
unable to understand his own discourse. A science unable to
read itself can no longer be called a science. The possibility of a
scientific semiology is challenged by a problem that can no
longer be accounted for in purely semiological terms.

This challenge reached Barthes from the somewhat unex-
pected quarter of philosophy, a discipline that earlier structuralists had discarded in favor of the so-called sciences of
man: psychology, anthropology, and linguistics. The dismissal
proved to be premature, based as it was on an inadequate
evaluation of the specifically philosophical ability to put the
foundations of its own discipline into question in a self-
destructive manner that no science could ever dare to emulate.
The work of Michel Foucault and especially of Jacques Derrida
(whose determining influence on literary theory is confirmed
by the recently published book *La Dissémination*) treats the
problem of linguistic delusion in a manner which semiological
critics of Barthes's persuasion cannot afford to ignore.[14]

Barthes's intellectual integrity is apparent in his reaction to
this philosophical challenge. For the time being, it has taken
the form of a retreat from the methodological optimism that

still inspired *S/Z*. More recent theoretical papers—though not more recent books such as *L'Empire des signes*, inspired by a trip to Japan, or *Sade, Fourier, Loyola*, in which the semiological euphoria is allowed to reign undisturbed—sketch out a much less ambitious program that sounds like a return to a pragmatic collecting of literary data. One of these papers, available in English translation and sharply aware of the inability of semiology to account for the stylistic tension between written and spoken language, invites us to embark on

> the search for models or patterns: sentence structures, syntagmatic clichés, divisions and *clausulae* of sentences; and what would inspire such work is the conviction that style is essentially a citational process, a body of formulae, a memory (almost in the cybernetic sense of the word), a cultural and not an expressive inheritance. . . . These models are only the depositories of culture (even if they seem very old). They are repetitions, not essential elements; citations, not expressions; stereotypes, not archetypes."[15]

Traces of many readings, from Propp to Gilles Deleuze, are noticeable in these sentences, and American readers will rightly think of Northrop Frye's *Anatomy* as a related enterprise. But the attitude cannot represent a definitive position. The mind cannot remain at rest in a mere repertorization of its own recurrent aberrations; it is bound to systematize its own negative self-insights into categories that have at least the appearance of passion and difference.

There is every reason to suppose that Barthes's future work will participate in this development, as he participated decisively in the development that led up to it. The avant-garde review *Tel Quel*, whose attitude toward orthodox structuralism has always been healthily uncomplacent, recently devoted an entire issue to Roland Barthes,[16] thus creating, probably unintentionally, the impression that it was trying to make a monument out of a man who is about as monumental as a Cheshire cat. Whoever assumes this to be possible would seriously misjudge the resilience of one of the most agile minds in the field of literary and linguistic studies.

As far as American criticism is concerned, its reaction to

Barthes is still unclear. The recent translations are a useful but still inadequate first step in introducing his work to English readers. The *Critical Essays* stem from the period that precedes the development of semiology—roughly 1963—and are mostly interesting in that they map out the domain of Barthes's discontent with the prevailing methods of literary criticism in France during the fifties and his delight at discovering the new perspectives opened by his readings in linguistics. They create the somewhat misleading impression that his main interests are confined to the theater of Brecht and to the novels of Robbe-Grillet, and they should certainly not be taken as a comprehensive sample of his accomplishments.[17] There is more semiological finesse to be gathered from the *Mythologies*. How the availability of his more important theoretical writings (*Critique et vérité*, *S/Z*, various theoretical papers) might influence American criticism can begin to be inferred from the reaction of some specialists who are already familiar with this work. It is fair to assume that it will meet with considerable resistance. Even as informed a scholar as the American practitioner of stylistics, Seymour Chatman, who has done a great deal to bring continental and American literary theory closer together, takes Barthes to task for putting the referential function of literary language into question. In a recent essay entitled "On Defining Form," he writes: "It is difficult to understand why one should deny that there are, ultimately, contents or *signifiés* referred to. . . . The content of a literary work is not the language but what the language stands for, its reference. . . . The language is a mediating form between the *literary* form (structure-texture) and the ultimate content."[18] The main point to be learned from Barthes is not that literature has no referential function but that no "ultimate" referent can ever be reached and that therefore the rationality of the critical metalanguage is constantly threatened and problematic. I have suggested that Barthes may have been all too hopeful in having believed, for a time, that the threat could be ignored or delegated to historians. The self-assurance he thus gained was productive and has a negative validity, as far as it goes; now that it seems to know its horizons, it remains a necessary part of any critical education. To return to an unproblematic notion of signification is to take a step backwards into a pseudoscience too remote from its object to be demystified by it. As long as the "libération du signifiant" is being resisted for the wrong reasons, the full impact of Barthes's work cannot become manifest.

Part III

RESPONSES

11

Murray Krieger: A Commentary

*T*HERE IS obviously a great deal of material and strategy in Murray Krieger's paper with which I wholeheartedly agree. I am bound to approve, for instance, of his choice of dialectical opponents since it includes my own name and thus invites me to give in to the fondest desire of all literary critics and theoreticians, a desire which grows stronger and stronger in direct ratio to their apparent detachment and abstractness, namely the desire to talk about themselves. I will of course do nothing of the sort and will talk about nightingales instead.

I am also grateful to Murray Krieger for having continued in Hayden White's direction and having introduced genuine textual entities, such as Keats's odes, into a controversy about critical controversies. It not only provides a convenient device to dodge the question of my own aberrations but also allows one to return from general considerations to the actual business of reading. I welcome Krieger's allegiance to the most valuable and technical premises of the New Criticism, namely the obligation to *read* the text one *quotes* in support of an argument, regardless of whether this helps or invalidates the argument in question. I know it is fashionable nowadays to consider any overt or covert affiliation with the New Criticism, any suspicion of coming "after the New Criticism," as tantamount to a recognition of weakness and personal alienation. But for me it has always been a filiation I have no difficulty construing as a compliment rather than a denunciation—and the way things are nowadays, one has to be grateful for whatever denunciation that can be thus construed.

What I have always found admirable in the work of the New Critics is that they let the efficacy of their technical procedures, as they developed in close contact with the points of resistance they encountered in the understanding of texts, reach beyond and even turn against the limits of their own ideologies. The more remote or even hostile one feels with regard to these ideologies, the more impressed one should be with techniques of reading which force the believers in these ideologies to be, by their own textual work, the most effective undoers of their own beliefs. Murray Krieger is a true continuator of this tradition when he selects Keats's "Ode to a Nightingale" in support of a symbolist aesthetic. This is infinitely preferable to the bizarre, though certainly consistent, demand of so many contemporary censors who ask us to stop reading altogether. They declare that the trouble with contemporary theoretical discourse stems from the need to read a text with some attention before enlisting it in the service of one's wishes, desires, or resentments. Very few critics of what is being misconstrued under the unread name of "deconstructive" criticism, instead of speculating about the motives that may prompt such a misguided procedure, would ever allow for the possibility that these readings have power to the precise extent that the technique accounts for the occurrence of the desire rather than the other way around—and that, consequently, the readings can only be refuted by a more refined technique of reading rather than by wanting not to listen to what one doesn't wish to hear. Murray Krieger has put the question exactly where it belongs: in a discussion of the function of linguistic, rhetorical devices in texts complicated by a substantial and inconclusive exegetic tradition.

It is all the more noteworthy that Krieger feels compelled to couch his own argument in terms of preferential value judgments for one linguistic structure, in this case a trope, over another, following in this a pattern we tend to take for granted at least since Coleridge. As his title ["A Waking Dream: The Symbolic Alternative to Allegory"] indicates, he wants to protect what he calls symbol from what he calls allegory, to prefer and defend one trope over and against another. Classical rhetoricians in the Aristotelian tradition would have a lot to say about the proper *use* of specific tropes within a particular convention or situation, but they would not agonistically pit one trope against another. Tropes are resources inherent in any language, semantic tools, as it were, and we have no jurisdiction over their existence; to want to do away with one of them in favor of another is like doing away with hands because they don't help much in walking, or with feet because they don't allow one to grasp: pitting metaphor against metonymy, for instance, is like pitting hands against feet. But we all feel that something different is at stake when we pit symbol against allegory, because symbol, which Krieger also calls metaphor, and allegory are not *mere* tropes. The prevalence of symbol over allegory is indeed something more than merely rhetorical: it is the prevalence, in Krieger's concluding formulation, of the *aesthetic* over the *thematic*. Allegory is equated with a thematic assertion of finitude, defeat, and mortality of which symbol is the aesthetic sublimation and redemption. The symbol is the negation of a cognitive negation concretely carried out in the labor of composition or, as it is also called here, in the act of fiction-making. The pattern is as familiar as it is convincing. It is not a dialectical but a synechdochical pattern in which allegory simply becomes the negation of metaphor, cognition the negation of an aesthetic intuition maintained in all its originary primacy and thus allowing for the assimilation of metaphor to the totalizing symbol. The scheme allows Murray Krieger to equate allegory with Rosalie Colie's "un-metaphor"[1] or with his own counter- or antimetaphor. He thus recovers the fragmentation of time and of the self in the beautiful song of the severed head, reconciles the clear-eyed scepticism of knowledge with the fervor of vision, the language of fusion with that of separation, the gesture of conceding with that of asserting or countering. The only point that should concern us here is whether Keats's "Ode to a Nightingale" can indeed be invoked in support of such a synthesis.

Krieger's reading, and the exemplarity of his title, hinges on the symmetry of the two concluding lines of the ode:

> Was it a vision; or a waking dream?
> Fled is that music:—Do I wake or sleep?

Guided by the apparent symmetry of the two *or* constructions (a vision *or* a waking dream; wake *or* sleep), Krieger can suspend the uncertainty of the wake/sleep opposition and make it into a stable cognition by stressing the symbolic complementarity of "a vision" with "a waking dream"—in which the "second alternative" is indeed not "wholly a denial of the first" [288]; it is a cliché, but not an unreasonable one, to call a waking dream a vision. But this symmetry is in fact a device to subsume or suspend the asymmetry that also occurs between the two lines: the first, which refers to the perception, to the experience of the nightingale's song, is in the past, the second in a present which, as the cognitive questioning of the performative "*I do*" in "Do I?" can only be that of the writing of the poem, the only "now" to be actually present to the poet Keats, who writes the ode to a no-longer-present nightingale as a letter *addressed to* him in the apostrophic mode of the ode. To assimilate this past "was" to the present of "do I" is to preserve the phenomenality of the pre- or subtext (the song) in the inscription of the text, to make the text into the representation of the phenomenon, and thus to bridge the temporal gap between them without any fundamental disruption. The negation that intervenes between the two events, and which Krieger accurately calls the "uncertainty of the present," is thus entirely benign from the point of view of the category that is at stake in this symmetrical substitution between past and present. This category is that of the aesthetic as such, which therefore, not unexpectedly, has to surface as the metaphysical "cloud of glory" that allows for the reconciliation of play or fiction with what is called a "provisional" immortality—an oxymoron only in appearance more unintelligible than a "waking dream" [Krieger 285].

The past of recollection and the present of writing (or thinking) can be brought together because sleeping relates to waking as vision relates to waking dream, that is to say, in the mode of the symbol. "Vision" and "waking dream" must both partake of waking *and* of sleeping. There is no problem with "vision," a cliché coded to evoke precisely this union and therefore a mere tautology. But since "dream," in "waking dream," refers to a material, physiological (Nietzsche) symptom (dreams),[2] it actually says something that can be analyzed, namely, that "to sleep" and "to dream" are coextensive, that to sleep includes and envelops, so to speak, to dream, as the imaginary might be hoped to include and envelop the real in an aesthetic sublimation.[3] But we don't even have to invoke Freud to point out that the relationship between sleeping and dreaming is not so simple; Descartes will suffice, and as we all know, *he* at least is philosophically and academically respectable. For it is Descartes who, in the first two *Meditations*, opened up a Pandora's box when he pointed out that the possibility of phenomenal (and consequently aesthetic) cognition is denied us from the start because when we dream (that is to say, have visions, that is to say, perceive) we always dream that we are awake. We never dream that we sleep for the simple reason, pointed out later by Freud, that sleep, a physiological drive, is the desire of the dream and thus always foreclosed. If we ever dreamed we were sleeping, we would at once wake up for good or, in other words, die. The passage in Descartes has never ceased to haunt rigorous epistemologists, from Pascal, who made it the starting point of one of his furthest reaching *pensées* on the impossibility of a humanist definition of man, to contemporary analytical philosophers. Unlike reverie or daydream, dream and wake (or sleep) are mutually exclusive, not symbolically complementary. If this is indeed the case, then it follows on the basis of Keats's ode as read by Murray Krieger, that past and present, recollection and thought, history and action (doing), the aesthetic and the actual, allegory and symbol are also mutually exclusive.

Lest it might appear that I have strayed from Keats's text to Descartes's, Freud's, or whatever, let me conclude by pointing out how the articulation between waking and sleeping actually occurs in the poem. Krieger paraphrases the passage as follows: "When, in the final stanza, he returns from his all-unifying fancy to his 'sole self' he looks back upon his momentary trance as mere deception. . . . From his perspective as 'forlorn' individual . . . there can no longer be an entertaining of his fancy's visionary reality" [287]. He wakes up, in other words, from his sleep or trance, as Baudelaire claims to be brought back to reality at the end of "Rêve parisien" by a knock at the door, here the tolling of a bell, an alarm clock. The experience epitomizes the very banality of the quotidian. This, however, is not what happens in Keats's poem, and the paraphrase (as paraphrases always do, and the better they are the better they do it, and Murray's is a very good one) elides the decisive segment. What awakens Keats and tolls him back from the nightingale to his "sole self" is the assonance in the "very word" *forlorn*, which is, he says, like a bell: ["Forlorn! The very word is like a bell / To toll me back from Thee to my sole self"].

It is curious that such a thematically powerful and pathos-laden poem would suddenly interrupt, in an inopportune parabasis, the flow of its own pathos to point out a meaningless "play" (as we say) of the signifier, the trivial fact that, in English (and only in English) forlorn can be said to sound (more or less) like a death knell or *glas*—though, frankly, to me it sounds more like a foghorn, something I mistakenly attributed for years to the fact that I spend my summers on a foggy island in the state of Maine until I discovered the obvious fact that the word *forlorn* looks very much like the word *foghorn*. (You see that I finally managed to speak about myself after all.) But it is more curious still that this trivial observation has to serve as the thematically most important articulation or dramatic transition in a lyric poem, when it would have been so easy to have a fictional bell ring instead of the material, "very" word. Finally, and most important of all, this moment in the text, and this moment alone, occurs as an actual present in the only material present of the ode, the actual moment of its inscription when Keats writes the word "forlorn" and interrupts himself to reflect on its arbitrary sound. At that precise moment, is it possible to say whether Keats, in the present of that moment, is awake or asleep? Thematically speaking, it is the very moment at which the subject in the text states that it awakens; textually speaking, however, it is also the moment at which this same subject starts to dream—for as we also all know since Freud, such plays of the letter are also the work of the dream, accessible to us only within a system in which the difference between waking and dreaming cannot be decided and can, henceforth, not be assimilated to a symbolic reconciliation of opposites.[4] The actual inclusion, in the texture of the lyric, of an alien piece of metalanguage makes the "Ode to a Nightingale" one of the very poems, the very allegory, of the nonsymbolic, nonaesthetic character of poetic language.[5]

12

Blocking the Road:
A Response to Frank Kermode

F RANK KERMODE'S attractive title, like all metaphors, can mean at least two incompatible things. "Keeping the road open" is the sound procedure of trailblazing by which as large as possible a number of travelers can hope to reach the summit at which all roads cease to be. It also means as much as "clearing the way," the removal—in this case by the gentlest and most civilized of means—of squatters who obstruct the flow of traffic. As one who cannot fail to hear that he is asked to "get moving," I hope you will not consider me unduly paranoid if I focus on the second reading of Kermode's title; I trust, indeed, that you would be disappointed if I didn't.

I want to start out from two sentences in Kermode's fine talk. My reference to the first of these sentences occurs only in a spirit of warning to those among you who might be tempted to become theoretical roadblockers, and who may want to do so for the wrong reasons. Kermode states at one point that "membership in the formerly small and specialized group [of literary theorists—PdM] offers many satisfactions—not only those of power and some celebrity." Lest you misunderstand this to mean that, in doing theory, you are going, as another critic puts it, to participate in an "immense and lucrative fuss," I feel it my duty to warn you against cruel disappointment. The last check I received from a publisher—and I hasten to add that it was neither Oxford nor Yale Press—was returned by the bank marked "no account," one step worse than "lack of funds." Things are not all that much better with Oxford; my last royalty statement first states that, instead of the $6.14 I owed them last September (as the consequence of something called "returns"), I now owe them only $3.46 as the result of two sales "overseas." So much for lucre. As for "power" and "some celebrity," what is the use, I ask you, of notoriety without cash, and in New Haven at that? No, if it is the entrepreneurial spirit that moves you, it is clear that you should join the growing ranks of institutionalized antitheorists, a little subgenre that is doing very well these days and which Frank Kermode has done a lot, tonight, to raise to a higher level of literate distinction.

The second sentence from the talk says that "the *fashion* for theory endangers the stability of the institution and interferes with its proper and primary work." I trust we'll come to the institution in later discussion but I want to stay, for the moment, with *fashion*. I know it is fashionable to deride theory as fashionable, but I don't think the point at all well taken. For surely the claim to be fashionable does not come from the theorists but from their denouncers. It is coupled with the somewhat contradictory complaint that they are also unreadably technical, as well as with Kermode's more original complaint that they, and especially their so-called disciples, are too "enthusiastic." I don't know about Hillis Miller, but as far as I am concerned, overenthusiasm is not what my readers have chastised me for most energetically. A very short book of mine, only 185 pages long, was said by another reviewer to be "the most boring book he had ever read in any language." Whatever enthusiasm I have does not seem to have communicated itself very well to my readers. Neither do I feel in the least entitled to complain about not being read—which, as we all know, is not the same as not being reviewed. I am grateful to Frank for having been an exception to the rule since his talk contains judiciously quoted evidence that he got at least as far as the first paragraph of the preface.[1] He suggests there that I enthusiastically believe, at least in principle, in a new, noncanonical rhetoric of reading. He must have run out of steam very quickly, for the next sentence rather says the opposite. All this is fine with me. I feel less tolerant, however, about the dismissal of all theoretical articles and first (that is, untenured) books as "very wretched . . . a sort of dessicated rant." Is Frank Kermode certain that he has read all these unreadable articles and books and that he has given them, as the saying goes, a fair shake? Is he certain he has not overlooked some half-hidden grain among all this chaff that "dismays" and "repels" him? At other moments he can be quite solicitous about the fate of the young, as when he asserts, "I do not believe that theory as such should be taught to undergraduates." Parental guidance, it is clear, should keep the young sheltered from the hard porn of theory. Really, Frank, how avuncular can one get?

But feel reassured that I will not use up my fifteen minutes in self-centered self-indulgence. I will try to suggest to you a theoretically considered explanation—though hardly a rebuttal—for the manifest irritation that people of Kermode's and Abrams's high caliber, people whose work I greatly admire and read with considerable profit and satisfaction, feel with some contemporary theoretical discourses—an irritation for which there is no *prima facie* evidence that it is not shared, to some degree, by the practitioners of this discourse. The key term around which this entire issue turns is perfectly highlighted, or foregrounded (or whatever trite metaphor one chooses to use), in Kermode's talk when I hear him say, with genuine defensive anguish, such things as, "It must be obvious that the formation of rival *canons*, however transient, is very dangerous," or, "The continuance of the academic institution depends wholly upon our ability to maintain the *canon* and to replace ourselves, to induce sufficient numbers of younger people to think as we do," or, "All that can last, if we properly exercise our authority, is the *canon* and the power somehow to teach it. The canon is the metal of the road that has to be kept open." The key term, obviously, is "canon," a term of religious connotation. What is at stake, in these recent debates, is not personalities or fashions but a very genuine and important issue: whether or not the teaching of literature, in the university, should be a substitution for or a complement to the teaching of religion or, a little less pragmatically put, whether we can say that the language of poetry and of literature have an affinity with the language of religion. This has, of course, nothing to do with the intrinsic quality of religious belief or with the philosophical value of theology. Nor is the question settled by historical perspectives that see literature as a secularization of religious experience; the concept of secularity is itself a deeply religious concept that could never reach critical insight into the complex relationship between poetic and religious discourse.

From the moment, and only at the moment, that theory touches the cherished notion of an affinity between art and religion, as it stands inscribed in the masterpieces, literary and otherwise, of the Western cultural tradition, it provokes a flow of irrationally hostile response. A certain kind of theoretical inquiry does this when it dares to touch upon such notions as intent, aesthetic judgment, the authority of the subject, genetic history, the referential reliability of linguistic signs, and so on. All these issues have been debated, for centuries and centuries, among philosophers, grammarians, and practical politicians, but always with particular passion, bordering on violence, when literature gets involved. For it is possible that, of all human activities, literature is the one least compatible, in the final analysis, with religious experience—though it is also the activity that is easiest to confuse with this experience. Despite its irresistible tendency toward canon formation, literature is noncanonical, the critique or, if you wish, the deconstruction of canonical models.

You can certainly not expect me to develop or establish this by no means simple assertion in a few sentences. But let me at least mention one instance of a canonical anticanonical theoretical text to give you some sense of what is involved. The text, as it happens, is written, not by a nihilist, but by someone of exceptionally deep religious sensitivity who was also a scrupulous and inspired interpreter of Marx. In a brief essay entitled "The Task of the Translator,"[2] Walter Benjamin sets up what amounts to a sharp division between the experience of sacred and that of poetic language. Poetic language comes into its own, not by a process of reception, not by the communication of meaning "in the author's expectation," as Abrams puts it, "that the expert reader's interpretation . . . will approximate his own," but in what Benjamin calls, somewhat cryptically, its "translation." Literary texts are capable of historical survival only if they prove worthy of such a translation, which turns out to be something very close to what used to be called criticism but which now can better be called literary theory. It is by such a process that literary texts make apparent what Benjamin calls pure language, *"die reine Sprache."* Pure language, however, is as remote as can be from what Valéry called pure poetry, *la poésie pure*. Benjamin's pure language is the language of the sacred to the precise extent that it is *not* the language of poetry, that it is unlike it. What "translation," in Benjamin's sense, reveals is precisely the fragmentary, impure, transient, uncanonical nature of literature. And it does so by making us aware, not of what literature says—for literature, says Benjamin, "says very little to him who understands it" (69)—but of certain linguistic discrepancies by which poetic language is structured, articulated, and undone. Benjamin identifies these discrepancies with a considerable degree of precision as: (1) the discrepancy between the meaning of the text and the manner in which it produces meaning, (2) the discrepancy between the word (or the letter) and the proposition (*Wort und Satz*), and (3) the discrepancy between the symbolic function and what it symbolizes—the very problems with which contemporary rhetorical analysis is most extensively concerned. These discrepancies prevent poetry from ever coming within sight of the canonical, of being anything resembling the "interlinear version of Holy Scripture" which Benjamin calls the ideal of all translation or theory (89). This does not mean that theory comes any closer than literature or poetry to a canonical status or even that it "keeps the road open" to our access to it. The only virtue of theory is that it resists the unwarranted condensation of what comes together only in the negative mode of the dialectic. The reasons why this resistance is resisted are clear: "The procedures of theory," says Benjamin, "are analogous to the arguments by which a critical epistemology [the allusion is to Kant—PdM] has to demonstrate the impossibility of a theory of knowledge as resemblance, copy, or imitation" (73). Theory, in other words, which tries to respond, in the literary work, to what it is and does, is not only noncanonical, nonpastoral and nontheological, but it is also nonaesthetic. It goes against the grain of pleasure and writes all those wretched and boring books.

In saying all this, Benjamin stands by no means alone and is not, in Abrams terms, an "off-center exception." There are plenty of canonical names among his ancestors, be it Nietzsche, Kierkegaard, Marx, Hegel, Friedrich Schlegel, Hamann, and many others. I say this to acknowledge Kermode's genuine theoretical point that nothing is so easy to canonize as an anticanonical stance. This is true enough and most worthy of further discussion. Such discussions, however, will never even get under way if the negative thrust of the anticanonical arguments is censored or repressed. All the names I have mentioned are exemplary in never giving in to this urge. The only discourse any of them would have suspected of being totalitarian is their own.

If art and poetry do not resemble religion in any way, if they are thoroughly noncanonical, what then do they resemble? Or, to put it with some more rigor, if the relationship between theory and the work is not like the relationship between the sacred and the secular, what then is it like? Perhaps like the relationship between a dream and its interpretation in analysis; or between a joke and its understanding in ordinary language; or between canonical (or constitutional) law and jurisprudence; or between political power and political justice; between political ideology, political economy, and political action; or between historical narrative and historical actuality. Literature is like psychoanalysis, like ordinary language philosophy in its better days, like materialist theories of politics and of history, rather than like religion. The reasons for this are neither psychological nor epistemological nor ideological nor strictly speaking historical but purely linguistic—and that is the hardest thing to admit of all, the Pandora's box to which literary theory, deliberately or not, holds the key. The fact that we are so universally accused of blocking the road must indicate that, knowingly or not, we are doing something right.

Notes

Editors' Preface

1. De Man's table of contents for *The Unimaginable Touch of Time* reads as follows:

2. Paul de Man, *Allegories of Reading* (New Haven: Yale University Press, 1979), ix.

Chapter 1. *The Contemporary Criticism of Romanticism*

This is the first of the Gauss lectures. It was announced under the title, "Romanticism and Demystification," and delivered at Princeton on Thursday, April 6, 1967. All notes supplied by the editors.

1. The reference is to Marcel Raymond, *De Baudelaire au surréalisme* (Paris: Corti, 1940).

2. Irving Babbitt, *Rousseau and Romanticism* (Boston: Houghton Mifflin, 1930).

3. René Girard, *Mensonge romantique et vérité romanesque* (Paris:

Bernard Grasset, 1961). Further references appear in the text; English translations of Girard in this lecture are de Man's.

4. Crossed out in manuscript: "of Dasein."

5. The reference is to Edward Everett Bostetter's *Romantic Ventriloquists* (Seattle: University of Washington Press, 1963).

6. The following comments on Lévi-Strauss and structuralism appear in slightly modified form as pp. 9–15 of "Criticism and Crisis," in *Blindness and Insight* (Minneapolis: University of Minnesota Press, 1983).

7. Claude Lévi-Strauss, *Mythologiques: Le cru et le cuit* (Paris: Plon, 1964), 13; translations of Lévi-Strauss in this lecture are de Man's.

8. Gustave Flaubert, *Madame Bovary*, ed. and trans. Paul de Man (New York: W. W. Norton), 26.

9. Crossed out in manuscript:

> The classical Aristotelian rhetorical figures of plot are in fact nothing but such double-oriented patterns of temporality (anagnorisis, for instance, being the retrospective understanding of an event as a prefigurative signal). The duration of the fiction becomes articulated in these temporal reversals which give the two-dimensional world of fiction an illusory dimension of pastness. A system of meaningful relationships appears and can be understood; but this understanding depends on the actual movement that travels from the present moment of origin to the future moment of conclusion, and then returns upon itself to invent a fictional past (since the movement is now from the point of arrival to the source) with understandable meaning.

10. On the back of this manuscript page the following note appears:

> Ceci est faux. L'origine comme pré-savoir, doit se mettre en question en tant qu'origine (cf. Poulet). Elle est fictive, et conduit à une regression infinie. C'est la structure du roman de Proust mais la conclusion est encore bien moins que l'origine, qui n'est rien. La fin est moins que *rien*. [This is false. The origin as foreknowledge must put itself into question insofar as it is an origin (cf. Poulet). It is fictitious and leads to an infinite regress. This is the structure of Proust's novel, but the conclusion is even less than the origin, which is nothing. The end is less than *nothing*.]

11. René Girard, "Expérience romanesque et mythe oedipien," *Critique* 21 (November 1965): 919; de Man's translation.

CHAPTER 2. *Rousseau and the Transcendance of the Self*

This is the second of the Gauss lectures. It was announced under its present title and delivered at Princeton on Thursday, April 13,

1967. The lecture, an early version of "Self (*Pygmalion*)" in *Allegories of Reading: Figural Language in Rousseau, Nietzsche, Rilke, and Proust* (New Haven: Yale University Press, 1979), presents significant differences from the later piece. All notes supplied by the editors.

1. Meyer Abrams, *The Mirror and the Lamp: Romantic Theory and the Critical Tradition* (New York: W. W. Norton, 1953).

2. Germaine de Staël-Holstein, *Lettres sur les écrits et le caractère de J. J. Rousseau*, in *Oeuvres complètes* (Paris: Treuttel & Würtz, 1820), 1:89.

3. Germaine de Staël-Holstein, *De la littérature*, in *Oeuvres complètes* (Paris: Treuttel & Würtz, 1820), 2:346.

4. William Hazlitt, "On the Character of Rousseau," *The Round Table*, in *The Complete Works*, ed. P. P. Howe (London: J. M. Dent & Sons, 1930), 4:92. Further references appear in the text.

5. J. J. Rousseau, *Les Confessions*, in *Oeuvres complètes*, 4 vols., ed. M. Raymond and B. Gagnebin (Paris: Gallimard, 1959–69), 1:122. Cited in Hazlitt's "Rousseau" 91. Further references appear in the text.

6. Jean Starobinski, *Jean-Jacques Rousseau: La Transparence et l'obstacle* (Paris: Gallimard, 1971). The essay referred to is "Jean-Jacques Rousseau et le péril de la réflexion" in *L'Oeil vivant* (Paris: Gallimard, 1961). Further references appear in the text. Translations of Starobinski's essay are by de Man.

7. Stéphane Mallarmé, "Tombeau d'Edgar Poe," in *Oeuvres complètes*, ed. H. Mondor (Paris: Gallimard, 1945), 70.

8. William Wordsworth, Preface to the *Lyrical Ballads*, in *The Poetical Works of William Wordsworth*, ed. E. de Selincourt (London: Oxford University Press, 1952), 2:400.

9. Ovid, *Metamorphoses*, Loeb Classical Library (Cambridge: Harvard University Press, 1916), 156. Quotation supplied by the editors.

10. Translations of *Pygmalion* are by Patricia de Man. They come from an anthology of Rousseau's works projected by Paul de Man for Viking Press.

CHAPTER 3. *Patterns of Temporality in Hölderstein's "Wie wenn am Feiertage . . ."*

This is the third of the Gauss lectures. It was announced under the title, "The Problem of Aesthetic Totality in Hölderlin," and delivered at Princeton on Thursday, April 20, 1967. All notes supplied by the editors.

1. Jean-Jacques Rousseau, *Julie, ou la nouvelle Heloïse*, in *Oeuvres Complètes*, ed. B. Gagnebin and M. Raymond, (Paris: Gallimard, 1964), 2:693.

2. Crossed out in manuscript: "Yeats would be another, more devious, example."

3. Crossed out in manuscript: "and the subsequent reinterpretation of romantic nature imagery as a subject-object relationship in which the form appears as the organic fusion of both derives from such an objectification."

4. Alessandro Pellegrini, *Friedrich Hölderlin; sein Bild in der Forschung* (Berlin: Walter de Gruyter, 1965).

5. Friedrich Hölderlin, *Friedensfeier*, ed. Friedrich Beissner (Stuttgart: Kohlhammer, 1954).

6. Crossed out in manuscript:

> But this hardly seems like the proper occasion to try to add to the mass of Hölderlin studies, or even to the often acrimonious critical debates that surround this very active area of German studies. We want to use a relatively untechnical issue in Hölderlin criticism, illustrated in a not too complicated and still rather early poem, to show how the principle of totalization—or more precisely the relationship between origin and totalization—operates in Hölderlin's language. It could be shown (though it is not my intention to do so) that this issue naturally underlies many of the much more highly technical aspects of Hölderlin criticism today.

7. Martin Heidegger, *Erläuterungen zu Hölderlins Dichtung* (Frankfurt am Main: Klostermann, 1951). Further references appear in the text. The translations are de Man's.

8. Friedrich Hölderlin, *Sämtliche Werke*, Grosse Stuttgarter Ausgabe, ed. Friedrich Beissner (Stuttgart: Cotta, 1943–85), 2(1):120. Further references appear in the text.

9. Michael Hamburger's translation in: Friedrich Hölderlin, *Poems and Fragments* (Cambridge: Cambridge University Press, 1966), 377. Further references appear in the text.

10. De Man did not copy out the stanza in his manuscript but wrote only a notation to himself: "Read it."

11. See Hölderlin 2(2):667–70.

12. Stefan George and Karl Wolfskehl, eds., *Deutsche Dichtung 3: Das Jahrhundert Goethes* (Berlin: Blätter für die Kunst, 1900–1902), 48–50. George and Wolfskehl title the poem "Hymne."

13. See Peter Szondi, "Der andere Pfeil: Zur Entstehungsgeschichte des hymnischen Spätstils," in *Hölderlin-Studien* (Frankfurt am Main: Insel, 1967), 37–61. Further references appear in the text. Translations are de Man's.

14. Crossed out in manuscript: "In this poem, at least three entities are named, in the first four stanzas, as thus disclosed: nature, in the ordinary, limited sense in stanza 1, history in the form of particu-

larly meaningful and heroic events in stanza 3, and the gods, as the most general form of."

15. Crossed out in manuscript: "(parousia)."

16. In German, the passage reads: "Es ist dieses Moment persönlichen Leids, das aus dem hymnischen Raum, der den Dichter nur als *Dienenden* kennt, verbannt ist. Dass Hölderlin, als er die Feiertagshymne zu schreiben unternahm, sich davon noch nicht ganz befreit hatte, geht daraus hervor, dass es dem hymnischen Ich am Ende ins Wort fällt und sein Recht verlangt. Daran scheiterte die Vollendung der Hymne."

17. See Paul de Man, "Wordsworth and Hölderlin" and "The Image of Rousseau in the Poetry of Hölderlin," now in *The Rhetoric of Romanticism* (New York: Columbia University Press, 1984). De Man's later "The Riddle of Hölderlin," which originally appeared in the *New York Review of Books* in 1972, is also suggestive in this context. It is reprinted in his *Critical Writings 1953–1978*, ed. Lindsay Waters (Minneapolis: University of Minnesota Press, 1988).

18. Theodor W. Adorno, "Parataxis: zur späten Lyrik Hölderlins," in *Noten zur Literatur 3* (Frankfurt am Main: Suhrkamp, 1965). De Man's translation. Further references appear in the text.

19. Erich Auerbach, *Mimesis: The Representation of Reality in Western Literature*, trans. Willard Trask (Princeton: Princeton University Press, 1968), 71.

CHAPTER 4. *Time and History in Wordsworth*

This is the fourth of the six Gauss lectures. It was announced under the title, "Nature and History in Wordsworth," and delivered at Princeton on Thursday, April 27, 1967. All notes supplied by the editors except where otherwise indicated. When de Man gave this lecture again (in 1971 or 1972), he wrote several additional passages and interpolated them in the lecture of 1967. These passages appear in notes number 2, 8, 11, 13, and 14.

1. References to Hartman's text throughout this essay follow the pagination of *Wordsworth's Poetry 1787–1814* (New Haven: Yale University Press, 1964).

2. The opening paragraphs seem to have been left out when de Man gave this lecture again (around 1971 or 1972). The new lecture began with some more informal remarks about what it means to *read* based on a version of the following notes:

reading

> not declaim it—pure dramatic, vocal presence
>
> not analyze it structurally—as in Ruwet
>
>> semantic, thematic element remains present in Jakobson/ Riffaterre

but *read*, which means that the thematic element remains taken into consideration

we look for the delicate area where the thematic, semantic field and the rhetorical structures begin to interfere with each other, begin to engage each other

they are not necessarily congruent, and it may be (it is, as a matter of fact, it *is* the case) that the thematic and the rhetorical structures are in conflict and that, in apparent complicity, they hide each other from sight

in truth, there are no poems that are not, at the limit, about this paradoxical and deceptive interplay between theme and figure; the thematization is always the thematization of an act of rhetorical deceit by which what seems to be a theme, a statement, a truth-referent, has substituted itself for a figure

I can't begin to prove this, but want to hint at what I mean by reading two Wordsworth poems

Wordsworth, because he is the antirhetorical, *natural* poet (i.e. thematic) par excellence, not only because he explicitly attacked the use of figure as *ornatus*, but also because the thematic seduction is particularly powerful, in its transparency and clarity—one gets very far very quickly by meditative participation

no one has reached the point where this question of Wordsworth's rhetoricity can begin to be asked, except Hartman.

3. *Wordsworth. Poetry and Prose*, selected by W. M. Merchant (Cambridge, Mass.: Harvard University Press [The Reynard Library], 1955), 352–53. *1805 Prelude*, book 5, lines 389ff. Merchant prints only the 1805 version of *The Prelude*. All quotations from Wordsworth and page references, unless otherwise noted, are from this edition (which de Man used).

4. Preface [1800], in Wordsworth and Coleridge, *Lyrical Ballads 1798*, ed. W.J.B. Owen (London: Oxford University Press, 1967), 150–79 at 167. De Man quotes from a section Wordsworth added for the 1802 edition.

5. Quoted in M. H. Abrams, gen. ed., *The Norton Anthology of English Literature*, (New York: W. W. Norton, 1962), 2:152, n. 5.

6. The earliest version of "The Boy of Winander" can be found in the Norton critical edition of *The Prelude* edited by Jonathan Words-

worth, M. H. Abrams, and Stephen Gill (New York: W. W. Norton, 1979), 492. A carefully edited critical version (along with a facsimile of the manuscript page) can be found in Stephen Parrish's edition of the 1798–99 *Prelude* (Ithaca: Cornell University Press, 1977), 86–87.

7. De Man's manuscript reads "Death men." If words crossed out in the manuscript are restored, the sentence fragment reads: "Death men, as we all know from Western movies, tell no tales, but the same is not true of Western romantic poetry, which knows that the only interesting tale is to be told by a man who."

8. In the second version of the lecture, the final sentences of this paragraph seem to have been replaced by the following passage:

It is always possible to anticipate one's own epitaph, even to give it the size of the entire *Prelude*, but never possible to be both the one who wrote it and the one who reads it in the proper setting, that is, confronting one's grave as an event of the past. The proleptic vision is based, as we saw in the poem, on a metaphorical substitution of a first-person subject by a third-person subject, "the boy" for "I." In fact, this substitution is, of all substitutions, the one that is, thematically speaking, a radical impossibility: between the living and the dead self, no analogical resemblance or memory allows for any substitution whatever. The movement is only made possible by a linguistic sleight-of-hand in which the order of time is reversed, rotated around a pole called self (the grammatical subject [first and third persons] of the poem). The posterior events that are to occur to the first person, I, (usually death) are made into anterior events that have occurred to a third person, the boy. A pseudometaphorical and thematically inconceivable substitution of persons leads to a temporal reversal in which anteriority and posterity are inverted. The structural mechanics of metaphor (for, I repeat, the substitution of the dead *he* for the living *I* is thematically, literally, "unimaginable" and the metaphor is not a metaphor since it has no proper meaning, no *sens propre*, but only a metaphorical structure within the sign and devoid of meaning)—the structural mechanics of metaphor lead to the metonymic reversal of past and present that rhetoricians call metalepsis. The prolepsis of the Winander boy, a thematic concept—for we all know that we can proleptically anticipate empirical events, but not our death, which is not for us an empirical event—is in fact metalepsis, a leap outside thematic reality into the rhetorical fiction of the sign. This leap cannot be represented, nor can it be reflected upon from within the inwardness of a subject. The reassurance expressed in the poem when the "uncertain" heaven is received in the lake or when the meditative surmise seems to promise the reflective time of the meditation is based on the rhetorical and not on thematic resources of language. It has no value as truth, only as figure. The poem does not reflect on death but on the rhetorical power of language that can make it seem as if we could anticipate the unimaginable.

This would also be the point at which we are beginning to "read" the poem, or to "read" Wordsworth according to the definition I gave at the start, namely to reach the point where the thematic turns rhetorical and the rhetorical turns thematic, while revealing that their apparent complicity is in fact hiding rather than revealing meaning.

9. A crossed-out clause here reads: "and with the understanding that what is here called immortality stands in fact for the anticipated experience of death."

10. A sentence crossed out here reads: "Being the father of man, the child stands closer to death than we do."

11. In reworking this passage for the second version of the lecture, de Man wrote the word *rhetorical* above the word *temporal* here (without crossing out *temporal*) and then rewrote the opening sentence of the following paragraph as: "Another brief poem of Wordsworth's will give us another version of his rhetorical movement" in place of "Another brief poem of Wordsworth's will allow us to take one further step in an understanding of his temporality." But ultimately de Man seems to have replaced this passage (from "Stripped of whatever remnants . . .") by interpolating the following transitional passage:

> The metaphor of the voyage, with its vast stellar and heliotropic movements of rising and setting suns and stars here makes the link between life and death, origin and end and carries the burden of the promise. But this is precisely the metaphor that was "deconstructed" in the Winander boy, in which this kind of analogism is lost from the start and never recovered; as is often, but not always, the case, a poetic text like the Boy of Winander takes us closer to an actual "reading" of the poet than discursive statements of philosophical convictions and opinions, especially when these statements are themselves heavily dependent on metaphor.
>
> Another brief poem by Wordsworth may make the movement we are trying to describe less abstract

12. All quotations of the 1850 version of *The Prelude* are from the Norton critical edition.

13. In the second version, the final sentences of this paragraph (beginning with "We see it therefore . . .") seem to have been replaced by the following passage:

> Middle and end have been reversed by means of another metonymic figure in which history, *contained* within a larger dimension of time, becomes, in the poem, the *container* of a temporal movement that it claims to envelop, since it is present at the end of the text. But, again, as in the boy of Winander, this metonymy of a content becoming a container, of an *enveloppé* becoming an *enveloppant*, is a rhetorical device that does not correspond to a thematic, literal reality. When Wordsworth chooses to name

mutability for what it is, in one of his most suggestive poems, the "Mutability" sonnet from the Ecclesiastical Sonnets, no historical triumphs are mentioned but only decay. It would take us a great deal more time and effort than we have available tonight to reveal the de-constructive rhetoricity of the "Mutability" poem, though it could be done. It would take us closer to an actual reading of Wordsworth, for which these remarks are only introductory exercises.

My entire exposition could be seen as a gloss on a sentence in Hartman's admirable book on Wordsworth in which he speaks of the need, for Wordsworth, to "respect the natural (which includes the temporal) order" if his poetry is to continue as narrative. The narrative (which is itself metonymic) depends indeed on making the natural, thematic order appear as the container, the *enveloppant*, of time rather than as its content; the narrative is metonymic not because it is narrative but because it depends on metonymic substitution from the start. I can therefore totally subscribe to Hartman's reading of Wordsworth's strategy. The only thing I might

Note that in this interpolated passage de Man seems to be rereading his own metaphor of "enveloping" above (the more authentic temporality "envelops the other" in the fourth sentence of the paragraph), that is, is reading his own text rhetorically.

14. In the second version, the following passage was inserted after the words "no longer" to replace the rest of the sentence:

a natural metaphor but a veiled metonymy. Wordsworth's most daring paradox, the claim to have named the most unnamable of experiences, "the unimaginable touch of time," is still based on a metonymic figure that, skillfully and effectively, appears in the disguise of a natural metaphor. In this least rhetorical of poets in which time itself comes so close to being a theme, the theme or meaning turns out to be more than ever dependent on rhetoric.

Chapter 5. *Fragment of the Fifth Gauss Lecture*

The fifth of the Gauss lectures was announced under the title, "Nature Imagery and Figural Diction," and delivered at Princeton on Thursday, May 4, 1967. It exists now only in fragmented form. All notes supplied by the editors. It is more than likely that, between the introductory and concluding pages printed here, de Man read a version of what was eventually to become the first part of "The Rhetoric of Temporality," called "Allegory and Symbol," and now published in the second edition of *Blindness and Insight* (Minneapolis: University of Minnesota Press, 1983).

1. This conclusion resembles closely, in both substance and formulation, the end of the first part of "The Rhetoric of Temporality," in *Blindness and Insight*, 206–8.
2. William Wimsatt, "The Structure of Romantic Nature Poetry," in *The Verbal Icon* (Lexington: University of Kentucky Press, 1954). Further references appear in the text.
3. M. H. Abrams, "Structure and Style in the Greater Romantic Lyric," in *The Correspondent Breeze: Essays on English Romanticism* (New York: W. W. Norton, 1984), 107.
4. William Wordsworth, "Essays upon Epitaphs," *Wordsworth's Literary Criticism*, ed. W. J. B. Owen (London: Routledge & Kagan Paul, 1974), 123.

CHAPTER 6. *Allegory and Irony in Baudelaire*

This is the sixth of the Gauss lectures. It was announced under the title, "The Romantic Heritage: Allegory and Irony in Baudelaire," and delivered at Princeton on Thursday, May 11, 1967. All notes supplied by the editors.

1. Georg Lukács, "Die Subjekt-Objekt Beziehung in der Ästhetik," *Logos* 7 (1917–18): 35; de Man's translation.
2. Crossed out in manuscript:

> The assertion of the autonomy of the self is as far as an idealist conception can take us. But Rousseau, Wordsworth, Hölderlin, and, at times, other romantic writers have gone beyond it. They are indeed speaking of an infinite process of literary activity, but of the process that takes place after the leap of radical renunciation. Romanticism can rise, indeed by the leap of a radical renunciation, beyond the subject/object dichotomy, but it cannot leap beyond temporality.

3. De Man refers to Martin Turnell's translation of Sartre's *Baudelaire* (New York: New Directions, 1950, 1967). Further references appear in the text.
4. Jean-Pierre Richard, *Poésie et Profondeur* (Paris: Seuil, 1955), 161.
5. Walter Benjamin, *Zentralpark*; de Man's translation. De Man was undoubtedly using the 1955 edition of *Schriften*, ed. Th. W. Adorno and Gretel Adorno (Frankfurt: Suhrkamp, 1955), 1:482, 481. The corresponding passages can be found, though in slightly different formulations, in *Gesammelte Schriften*, ed. R. Tiedemann and H. Schweppenhäuser (Frankfurt: Suhrkamp, 1972), 1(2): 671, 673, 670.
6. Charles Baudelaire, *Oeuvres complètes* (Paris: Gallimard, Bibliothèque de la Pléiade, 1976), 2:627, de Man's translation. Further references appear in the text.

7. See Antoine Adam's edition of *Les Fleurs du mal* (Paris: Garnier Frères, 1959), 275.

8. This sentence, as well as several of the sentences that follow, can also be found in a somewhat modified form in the essay, "Ludwig Binswanger and the Sublimation of the Self," in *Blindness and Insight*, 45–46.

9. For another discussion of this essay, see Paul de Man, "The Rhetoric of Temporality," in *Blindness and Insight*.

10. For another discussion of this poem, see Paul de Man, "Anthropomorphism and Trope in the Lyric," in *The Rhetoric of Romanticism*.

11. William Wordsworth, *The Prelude: 1805*, ed. Ernest de Selincourt, and rev. Helen Darbishire (London: Oxford University Press, 1959), 121–22. The manuscript only indicates the passage with the words "How often. . . ." We quote the entire blind beggar passage, 7:592–622. The lines from Milton to which de Man refers, and which are quoted by Wordsworth near the end of the 1815 Preface to *Lyrical Ballads*, are: "Sky lowered, and, muttering thunder, some sad drops / Wept at completion of the mortal sin" (*Paradise Lost*, 9:1000–1002).

CHAPTER 7. *Hölderlin and the Romantic Tradition*

Internal evidence suggests that this essay was written around 1958. The manuscript is particularly rough and required more extensive editing than the other essays in this volume. All notes supplied by editors except where otherwise indicated.

1. De Man had written "1920?" but clearly was referring to the Hellingrath/Seebaß/Pigenot edition in six volumes.

2. De Man notes that the recent book by Alessandro Pellegrini, *Hölderlin: Storia della critica* (Firenze: Sansoni, 1956), gives a comprehensive overview of Hölderlin scholarship, grouped by critical methodology. The book is also available in an expanded German translation, *Friedrich Hölderlin, Sein Bild in der Forschung* (Berlin: Walter de Gruyter, 1965).

3. Benedetto Croce, "Intorno allo Hölderlin e ai suoi critici," *La Critica* 39, no. 4 (1941): 201–14.

4. Crossed out in manuscript:

provided only that it is read in the original and nothing more has to be said about this aspect of the problem. To encounter and to discuss Hölderlin's work gives one a shock that transfers into a realm where there is no room for problems of personal or political expediency aside from those of pure poetic expression, and Croce, of all critics, if he had known the work, would have been aware that this is one of the poets in whose work, as in that of Goethe and a few other obvious names, personal experience (*Erlebnis*), poetic form, and time-bound reactions have been entirely transcended.

5. Wilhelm Böhm, *Studien zu Hölderlins Empedokles* (Weimar, 1902).

6. De Man's quotation is not from Goethe but rather from Schiller's letter to Goethe (August 17, 1797). This passage of the letter is quoted in Pellegrini, *Hölderlin*, 15.

7. William Butler Yeats, "Edmund Spenser," in *Essays and Introductions* (New York: Macmillan, 1961), 377–78.

8. De Man quotes "Der Rhein" from Friedrich Beissner's big Stuttgart edition: Friedrich Hölderlin, *Sämtliche Werke* (Stuttgart: Cotta, 1943–85), 2(1):149–56. Further references appear in the text.

9. The translation is by Michael Hamburger from: Friedrich Hölderlin, *Poems and Fragments* (Cambridge: Cambridge University Press, 1966), 419. Further references appear in the text.

10. Crossed out in manuscript: "One should never forget that translation from the Greek was for him a supreme poetic genre of the highest rank."

11. Crossed out in manuscript: "again unlike most of his contemporaries with the possible exception of Hegel."

12. Cf. Martin Heidegger's retranslation of these opening lines of the choral ode as "Vielfältig das Unheimliche, nichts doch / über den Menschen hinaus Unheimlicheres ragend sich regt" in his *Einführung in die Metaphysik* (Tübingen: Max Niemeyer, 1953), 112. Ralph Manheim in turn renders these lines as "There is much that is strange, but nothing that surpasses man in strangeness" in Martin Heidegger, *An Introduction to Metaphysics* (Garden City, N.Y.: Doubleday, 1961), 123. See also Heidegger's justification for his not using Hölderlin's own translation of the choral ode in the attempt to understand Hölderlin's own understanding of the Greek (and the Greeks) in Martin Heidegger, *Hölderlins Hymne "Der Ister"* (Frankfurt am Main: Vittorio Klostermann, 1984), 70; and the reading of the difference between Heidegger's and Hölderlin's (and, perhaps, de Man's) "translation" of the Greeks in Andrzej Warminski, "Monstrous History: Heidegger Reading Hölderlin," *Yale French Studies* 77 (1990), 193–209.

13. Crossed out in manuscript: "The definition is reminiscent of Schiller's *Über naive und sentimentalische Dichtung*, with the important difference that, while in Schiller, Greece and the West are opposed as nature is opposed to consciousness, in Hölderlin there is a dialectical reversal: our experience of nature is like the Greek's experience of consciousness and vice versa. What is naive to them is self-conscious to us (art)."

14. The manuscript breaks off here at the bottom of a manuscript

page in midsentence. After the word "to," de Man wrote "transcend," crossed it out, and then above it "abandon," which he also crossed out.

CHAPTER 8. *Heaven and Earth in Wordsworth and Hölderlin*

This paper was delivered as part of a 1965 MLA panel chaired by Geoffrey Hartman and entitled "Romanticism and Religion." All notes supplied by the editors except where otherwise indicated.

1. H. W. Piper, *The Active Universe: Pantheism and the Concept of Imagination in the English Romantic Poets* (London: Athlone Press, 1962), 2.

2. Geoffrey H. Hartman, *Wordsworth's Poetry: 1787–1814* (New Haven and London: Yale University Press, 1964), 49. Further references appear in the text.

3. René Wellek, "Romanticism Re-examined," in *Concepts of Criticism* (New Haven: Yale University Press, 1963), 218.

4. De Man may have M. H. Abrams's essay "Coleridge, Baudelaire, and Modernist Poetics" in mind. The essay was originally a colloquium paper delivered at Cologne in 1964 and first printed in *Immanente Ästhetik, ästhetische Reflexion: Lyrik als Paradigma der Moderne*, ed. Wolfgang Iser (Munich: Wilhelm Fink, 1966), 113–38. It is now reprinted in: M. H. Abrams, *The Correspondent Breeze* (New York: W. W. Norton, 1984), 109–44.

5. Friedrich Hölderlin, *Sämtliche Werke*, ed. Friedrich Beissner (Stuttgart: Cotta, 1943–85), vol. 3. Other references to this volume given in text. Translations are de Man's.

6. Crossed out in manuscript: "(akin, in the figure of Diotima, to Love)."

7. *The Poetical Works of William Wordsworth*, ed. E. de Selincourt (Oxford: Oxford University Press, 1952), 2:396. Further references appear in the text.

8. De Man quotes the 1805 version (book 5) of Wordsworth's *Prelude*, ed. Ernest de Selincourt, rev. Helen Darbishire (Oxford: Clarendon, 1959).

9. *Poetical Works*, 2:437.

10. For another discussion (often identical) of "The Boy of Winander" and passages from book 2 of *The Prelude*, see Paul de Man, "Wordsworth and Hölderlin," in *The Rhetoric of Romanticism* (New York: Columbia University Press, 1984). For de Man's most extended reading of "The Boy of Winander," see "Time and History in Wordsworth" (which dates from 1967) in this volume.

CHAPTER 9. *The Double Aspect of Symbolism*

The occasion and date of this manuscript are unknown, but judging from its concerns, tone, and choice of textual examples, it seems to have been written at Harvard between 1954 and 1956. All notes supplied by the editors. For more on de Man's thinking at that time about the relation between Baudelaire, Mallarmé, and Hölderlin, see, "Process and Poetry," in *Critical Writings* (Minneapolis: University of Minnesota Press, 1989).

1. Arthur O. Lovejoy, "On the Discrimination of Romanticisms," *PMLA* 29 (1924): 229–53; and "The Meaning of Romanticism for the Historian of Ideas," *Journal of the History of Ideas* 2 (1941), 261.

2. René Wellek, "The Concept of Romanticism in Literary History," *Comparative Literature* 1 (1949): 1–23, 147–72.

3. Crossed out in manuscript:

> It is undoubtedly much more rewarding for a critic to state what a certain movement means to us at present, and to adopt a purely subjective point of view, ignoring or distorting what is not of immediate relevance within the present situation of literary invention. But the historian is even more fascinated by the discrepancies between what a movement actually means to the authors who made it and what it means to a later period: these discrepancies are the real content of history, and in order to perceive them one needs to know not only the later, subjective vision but also the original, objective phenomenon. The establishment of general categories such as classicism, romanticism, etc., is one means among others to describe this original fact.

4. Etiemble, *Le Mythe de Rimbaud. Vol. 2: Structure du mythe* (Paris: Gallimard, 1952). De Man's translation; further references appear in the text.

5. Marcel Raymond, *De Baudelaire au surréalisme* (Paris: José Corti, 1940).

6. Stéphane Mallarmé, "La Musique et les lettres," in *Oeuvres*, ed. Henri Mondor and G. Jean-Aubrey (Paris: Bibliothèque de la Pléiade, 1945), 645. De Man's translation; further references to the *Oeuvres* appear in the text.

7. Crossed out in manuscript: "Even a dating of the event becomes impossible; we are often told that this kind of 'dissociation of sensibility' occurred around 1800 with the advent of romanticism, but one can argue just as convincingly with the German philosopher Heidegger that it is the essential experience from which stems the whole of Western poetry and thought or, more radically still, claim with Hegel that separation is the beginning of all human consciousness."

8. Crossed out in manuscript:

A description, however schematic, of their attitude is not simple—as should be all too clear to whoever is familiar with the abundant literature devoted to the subject and which always leaves one with an impression of incompleteness and confusion about the movement as a whole as well as about particular works. A certain pattern has emerged from the majority of studies on French symbolism which, though it is certainly partly correct, seems to be in need of some amplification. Following a precedent set by Marcel Raymond, it is customary to take the famous poem by Baudelaire, "Correspondances," as the fundamental statement of the symbolist aesthetic, a statement with which the majority of the later experimentations and themes are merely a further development.

9. See, "Le Cygne," *Oeuvres*, ed. Claude Pichois (Paris: Bibliothèque de la Pléiade, 1975), 1:86. Further references to the *Oeuvres* appear in the text.

10. William Butler Yeats, "The Symbolism of Poetry," in *Ideas of Good and Evil* (London: Bullen, 1903), 243.

11. William Butler Yeats, "Gratitude to the Unknown Instructors," in *The Collected Poems* (New York: Macmillan, 1974), 249. Further references to the collection appear in the text.

12. Friedrich Hölderlin, *Sämtliche Werke*, ed. Friedrich Beissner (Stuttgart: Kohlhammer, 1951), 2:94. Translation, somewhat modified, from *Poems and Fragments*, trans. Michael Hamburger (Cambridge: Cambridge University Press, 1980), 251.

CHAPTER 10. *Roland Barthes and the Limits of Structuralism*

This essay appears to date from 1972. It was commissioned by the *New York Review of Books* as a review of extant translations of Barthes's work into English but was never printed. Correspondence indicates that the editors found the essay too technical for a general readership. The essay differs from the previously published version appearing in *Yale French Studies*, 77 (1990). It is based on a typescript that came to light after the *YFS* publication and that incorporates de Man's revisions. The notes accompanying this essay are de Man's. The editors have supplied additional bibliographical information where necessary (i.e., to bring the apparatus into conformity with current practices or to provide missing references).

1. William Empson, "Assertions dans les mots," *Poétique* 6 (1971): 239–70. It must be added, however, that the same review has also published very recent American work of younger authors, in some cases before they appeared in this country.

2. Roland Barthes, *Essais Critiques* (Paris: Seuil, 1964), trans. Richard Howard as *Critical Essays* (Evanston: Northwestern University Press, 1972).

3. The book consists of a series of brief texts on miscellaneous topics. The texts are complete in themselves, but several have been left out, probably on the wrong assumption that their local setting would make them unintelligible for English readers. Roland Barthes, *Mythologies* (Paris: Seuil, 1957), trans. Annette Lavers as *Mythologies* (New York: Hill & Wang, 1972). Further references appear in the text.

4. *Writing Degree Zero*, ed. Susan Sontag (New York: Hill & Wang, 1968).

5. The enigmatic title *S/Z* is deliberately and playfully ambiguous. It takes off from an anomaly in Balzac's spelling of his hero's name: the sculptor Sarrasine, who falls in love with the castrato singer Zambinella and whose name would normally be spelled Sarrazine. Beyond this fact, the title has many allusive connotations. The most obvious points to the work of the French psychoanalyst Jacques Lacan, author of an influential article on the revelatory power of letter substitutions. The formulaic figure S/Z mimics the notation S/s, also used by Jacques Lacan to represent the relationship between signifier and signified (*signifiant* and *signifié*) in which the slash, /, can be read as the symbolic sign of the repression or castration represented as a thematic event in Balzac's fiction. *S/Z* (Paris: Seuil, 1970), trans. Richard Howard as *S/Z* (New York: Hill & Wang, 1974).

6. Some of the essays first published in *Communications* have been reprinted in Roland Barthes, *L'Aventure sémiologique* (Paris: Seuil, 1985) and in English in Roland Barthes, *The Semiotic Challenge*, trans. Richard Howard, (New York: Hill & Wang, 1988).

7. Roland Barthes, *Critique et vérité* (Paris: Seuil, 1966), 48. Further references appear in the text.

8. See the opening of Wordsworth's *Prelude: 1805*, ed. E. de Selincourt, rev. Helen Darbishire (London: Oxford University Press, 1959), bk. 1, ll. 15–16.

9. One could just as well say, with equal metaphorical authority, overstanding (or transcendental) as underlying.

10. The example is taken from an article published in the journal *Communications* 8 (1964) and entitled "Rhétorique de l'image," trans. Stephen Heath as "Rhetoric of the Image," in Roland Barthes, *Image-Music-Text* (New York: Hill & Wang, 1977).

11. Jean-Jacques Rousseau, *Discours sur l'origine et les fondements de l'inégalité parmi les hommes*, in *Oeuvres complètes*, ed. B. Gagnebin and M. Raymond (Paris: Gallimard, 1964), 123. De Man translates.

12. Roman Jakobson, "Closing Statement: Linguistics and Poetics," in *Selected Writings*, ed. Stephen Rudy (The Hague: Mouton, 1981), 3:25.

13. See Roland Barthes, "Réponses," *Tel Quel* 47 (Autumn 1971), special issue on Roland Barthes, 107.

14. Jacques Derrida, *La Dissémination* (Paris: Seuil, 1972). In English as *Dissemination*, trans. Barbara Johnson (Chicago: University of Chicago Press, 1981).

15. Roland Barthes, "Style and Its Image," in Seymour Chatman, ed., *Literary Style: A Symposium* (London: Oxford University Press, 1971), 9–10.

16. *Tel Quel* 47 (Autumn 1971).

17. The important group of essays *On Racine* was published in English translation in 1964 but, possibly because of the specialized French subject matter, has not received the attention it deserves. The book raises the question of Barthes's complex relationship to psychoanalytical methods of interpretation, a topic perhaps best approached from the perspective of the later *S/Z*. See Roland Barthes, *On Racine* (New York: Hill & Wang, 1964).

18. In *New Literary History* 2 (1971): 219–28.

CHAPTER 11. *Murray Krieger: A Commentary*

The occasion of this response was a conference held in the spring of 1981 at Northwestern University to mark the transfer of the School of Criticism and Theory from the University of California at Irvine to Northwestern. The paper by Murray Krieger to which it responds was called, "A Waking Dream: The Symbolic Alternative to Allegory," now published in a revised form in *Words about Words about Words: Theory, Criticism, and the Literary Text* (Baltimore: Johns Hopkins University Press, 1988). Further references appear in the text. Some of the points made by de Man about Keats's ode—for example, the undecidability of the waking/dreaming distinction and the materiality of the word—can also be followed in the roughly contemporaneous essays collected in *The Resistance to Theory* (Minneapolis: University of Minnesota Press, 1986), especially, "Hypogram and Inscription." All notes supplied by editors.

1. See Rosalie L. Colie, *"My Echoing Song": Andrew Marvell's Poetry of Criticism* (Princeton: Princeton University Press, 1970).

2. De Man was undoubtedly thinking here of the opening of *The*

Birth of Tragedy, where Nietzsche considers the problematic status of dreaming at length.

3. De Man refers here, in a crossed out phrase, to the possibility of eliding the "perchance" in Hamlet's soliloquy: "to sleep, perchance to dream."

4. On the back of the page de Man has noted: "Repetition for-lorn/Forlorn is not like repetition fade/fades read so well by Krieger. It is Kierkegaardian, not symbolic."

5. On the back of the page de Man has noted: "Allegory is not *dualistic* but passage from grammatical to experiential 'subject'— . . . temporality is not early/late (alarm clocks) but *horizon* (phenom-enal dialectics)."

CHAPTER 12. *Blocking the Road: A Response to Frank Kermode*

The occasion of this response was the Trilling seminar at Colum-bia University held in February of 1981. A paper by Frank Kermode entitled "To Keep the Road Open," was followed by responses by M. H. Abrams and Paul de Man. Some of the points de Man makes here in reference to literary theory, canonicity, and translation receive fuller treatment in essays now collected in *The Resistance to Theory*, especially "Conclusions: Walter Benjamin's 'The Task of the Transla-tor.'" All notes supplied by editors.

1. De Man's earlier reference to "a very short book" is to *Blindness and Insight*, whereas the "preface" in question here is to *Allegories of Reading*, which begins by tracing the emergence of a "theory of read-ing" back to a "historical reflection on Romanticism." The two sen-tences to which de Man will allude state unequivocally that, in his own case at least, a "rhetoric of reading reaching beyond the canoni-cal principles of literary history . . . remains dependent on the initial position of these very principles" (ix).

2. For the Benjamin essay, see *Illuminations*, trans. Harry Zohn (New York: Schocken Books, 1969). Page references appear in the text.

DATE DUE